The Abacus and the Rainbow

Studies in the Humanities
Literature—Politics—Society

Guy Mermier
General Editor

Vol. 50

PETER LANG
New York • Washington, D.C./Baltimore • Boston • Bern
Frankfurt am Main • Berlin • Brussels • Vienna • Canterbury

Donald R. Maxwell

The Abacus and the Rainbow

Bergson, Proust, and the Digital-Analogic Opposition

PETER LANG
New York • Washington, D.C./Baltimore • Boston • Bern
Frankfurt am Main • Berlin • Brussels • Vienna • Canterbury

LIBRARY OF CONGRESS CATALOGING-IN-PUBLICATION DATA

Maxwell, Donald R.
The abacus and the rainbow: Bergson, Proust, and the digital-analogic
opposition / Donald R. Maxwell.
p. cm. — (Studies in the humanities; vol. 50)
Includes bibliographical references and index.
1. Bergson, Henri, 1859–1941—Influence. 2. Proust, Marcel, 1871–1922.
À la recherche du temps perdu. 3. Philosophy in literature—History—
20th century. I. Title. II. Series: Studies in the humanities
(New York, N.Y.); vol. 50.
B2430.B43M39   194—dc21   98-46160
ISBN 0-8204-4435-9
ISSN 0742-6712

DIE DEUTSCHE BIBLIOTHEK-CIP-EINHEITSAUFNAHME

Maxwell, Donald R.:
The abacus and the rainbow: Bergson, Proust, and the
digital-analogic opposition / Donald R. Maxwell.
–New York; Washington, D.C./Baltimore; Boston; Bern;
Frankfurt am Main; Berlin; Brussels; Vienna; Canterbury: Lang.
(Studies in the humanities; Vol. 50)
ISBN 0-8204-4435-9

The paper in this book meets the guidelines for permanence and durability
of the Committee on Production Guidelines for Book Longevity
of the Council of Library Resources.

Printed in the United States of America

For Catherine,

and

Monica, Nicholas, Christopher, Caroline, Denis, Dominic,

Marie-Claire and Philip

and their children

Madeleine, Luke, Timothy, Hannah, Rebecca, and . . .

Table of Contents

Acknowledgements

This book is a revised and slightly enlarged version of a dissertation submitted in partial fulfillment of the requirements for the degree of Doctor of Philosophy in Romance Languages: French, in the University of Michigan, and as such its writing has incurred many debts. Primarily I am grateful to, Floyd Gray, Marcel Muller and William Paulson, members of my Doctoral Committee, for sharing with me not only their professional expertise, but also their skill, patience and unstinting help throughout the writing of the dissertation. Their advice and critical comments immeasurably improved both its content and style. I also thank Guy Mermier, Editor of this Series, for his corrections and comments on this final text.

In addition to their advice and help with the original and the revised text, I owe these scholars and teachers a special debt of gratitude for their outstanding graduate seminars. These helped me make the journey from the world and language of science, to the equally wonderful, yet so different culture, of literature. In innumerable ways, these seminars were *Sesame* to me, for they opened a door of perception into the enchanted world of literature and were the seed, the inspiration and incentive for present study.

This book necessarily contains comprehensive citations from the works of both Henri Bergson and of Marcel Proust. The quotations from Bergson come from his works published by Les Presses Universitaires de France. All the quotations from *À la recherche du temps perdu* are reproduced from the Gallimard Pléiade (1987–89) edition in four volumes prepared under the direction of Jean-Yves Tadié, and the citations from Proust's correspondence are taken from *Choix de lettres*, edited by Philip Kolb and published by Éditions

Plon. I am grateful to these publishers for permission to reproduce these extensive quotations.

D.R.M.
Ann Arbor, Michigan
October, 1998

Chapter 1

Introduction

Montaigne's emblem of a pair of scales may be interpreted[1] as metaphor for the oscillations between his texts-past and his texts-to-come, as well as the weighing of the two sides of an argument and the perpetually provisional nature of his conclusions. Perhaps, *The Abacus and the Rainbow* may be seen as an emblem and metaphor, not only for the differences between the styles of Bergson and Proust, as well as of the movement between the two texts that takes place in this book, but more importantly of the duality inherent in the questions addressed by Bergson, who, in the preface to his first major work, stated that the principal errors in the deterministic philosophy of his period arose from the confusion between the concepts of space and time, between succession and simultaneity, and between quantity and quality. The abacus, containing a row of identical and separate elements, is clearly representative of the quantitative, logical and digital. The rainbow is, however, very different, for it contains a multiplicity of qualitative images with no demarcation or separation, one color flowing imperceptibly into another, in an interpermeating and coherent continuity, in the same manner as one non-verbal thought flows imperceptibly into another, and as one moment of time is intimately affiliated with, and drifts indiscernibly into the next. Although Newtonian physics gives an excellent description and analysis of the colors and the shape of the rainbow, such a quantitative analysis fails to reproduce or explain the qualitative feelings and impressions evoked by it's sight. The rainbow is thus metaphor, not only for poetry and art, but also for the analogic manner of perceiving the qualitative, continuous, possibly unrational aspects of reality. Perhaps the two opposing manners of viewing reality that are revealed and described to us both by Henri Bergson and Marcel Proust may be represented metaphorically and figuratively by *the Abacus and the Rainbow*.

* * *

Objectives of this Study

I somewhat accidentally stumbled on Bergson's *Essai sur les données immédiates de la conscience*[2] at a time when I was reading Proust's *Combray*, and was struck both by the poetic style of Bergson's prose and the interesting content of his writing. On reading some of the passages discussed in Chapter 6, I remarked to myself that they reminded me of portions of *Combray*, and this lead to a more detailed comparison and juxtaposition of passages by the two authors and subsequently to the subject matter of this book. It was only later that I became aware of the previous long "Bergson and Proust" history. My purpose in recounting this is to illustrate that the similarity in the styles and content of the two authors may become apparent to even the most naïve reader, and that it is perhaps not surprising that the affinities between the philosopher and novelist should have become evident to critics ever since the publication of the first volumes of *À la recherche du temps perdu*.[3]

Indeed, since the publication in November 1913 of *Du côté de chez Swann*, the first of the novels that comprise Proust's *À la recherche*, a number of authors and critics have commented on the affinities and resemblance between some key notions in Proust's great novel and the philosophy of Henri Bergson, which attained great popularity and fashionability in the Paris of the same period.

The purpose of this study is *not* to prove or disprove whether Proust consciously incorporated some of Bergson's notions into his novel, but rather to compare and review in detail some of the key elements and features, enumerated below, and then discuss some possible reasons for this convergence of thought and the commonality of the key themes. Thus, one function of this study is to compare and contrast the notions of time, memory, self and thought, as well as the doubling of self in memory as expounded in Bergson's philosophy with the same or similar elements in Proust's great novel. The first four of these key Bergsonian concepts exist as binaries, each enantiomer[4] of which may be coded either digital or analogic, and hence another purpose of the book is to explore this digital to analogic opposition in Proust's writing. A third aim of this study is to compare the use of language by Bergson and Proust, to contrast them with the poles of 'scientific' and 'literary' language, as well as to compare their notions of esthetics and artistic creation. The reason or reasons for the com-

monality between Bergson's and Proust's work has not been satisfac-
torily explained and some new insight into this is presented in the
final chapter after these common elements have been compared.

The 'Bergson–Proust' question has a history and Joyce Megay[5]
points out that the presence of a similarity in some of the concepts in
Proust's novel in Bergson's philosophy was noticed as early as 1914
by reviewers of his book. For example in January 1914 Jean de
Pierrefeu published a long and not entirely complementary review of
Du côté de chez Swann, in which he states: "M. Proust disciple intégral
de Bergson, applique, comme on le voit, les théories artistiques que
le philosophe de *Matière et Mémoire* a exprimées, çà et là, au cours
de son oeuvre et particulièrement dans *Le Rire*."[6] Later the same
year, Gaston Rageot published a twenty-two page review of recent
books, in which he devotes all of thirteen lines to Proust's *Du côté de
chez Swann* including the comment: "Puisqu'il se recommande de la
pensée bergsonienne, que n'emprunte-t-il d'abord au philosophe qu'il
veut honorer un peu de la lumière et de la sobriété qui ont fait rayonner
la doctrine mystérieuse?"[7] In yet another contemporary review of the
book, Louis Latourrette says: "M. Bergson doit estimer défaillante
l'application de ses théories essayée dans le roman de M. Marcel
Proust."[8] Thus, at a time when Bergson and his philosophy were in
vogue, these reviewers found the affiliation between Proust's novel
and Bergson's writings so obvious that they did not consider it necessary to expand on the point. Detailed early studies include those of
the English critic Gladys Turquet-Milnes[9] in 1926, the 1927 MA dissertation of Beatrice Watson[10] at the University of Chicago, and a
book by the German critic Ernst-Robert Curtius[11] published in 1928.
All of these works pointed to the similarity, in some degree, between
some basic ideas of the novelist and the philosopher. Of the more
recent Bergson–Proust studies are those of Pilkington[12] and of
Demoncel.[13] The latter relates both to the writings Bergson and Proust
as well as the philosophy of Gilles Deleuze. This introductory chapter
will review four major studies comparing the work of Henri Bergson
and Marcel Proust and then outline and discuss the origins of
Bergsonian philosophy.

The Shoulders of Influence

Although it is not the prime purpose of this book to prove or disprove
any conscious interpretation or incorporation of Bergson's philoso-

phy by Proust, it is not irrelevant to consider briefly the nature of literary or poetic influence and how this might be recognized. In *The Anxiety of Influence*, Harold Bloom puts forth his central vision of the relationships between precursors and individual writers when he says:

> Poetic Influence—when it involves two strong, authentic poets, always proceeds by a misreading of the prior poet, an act of creative correction that is actually and necessarily a misinterpretation. The history of fruitful poetic influence, which is to say, the main tradition of Western poetry since the Renaissance, is a history of anxiety and self-saving caricature, of distortion, of perverse, willful revisionism. . . .[14]

This interpretation of 'influence' could possibly lead to the conclusion that there indeed was 'influence' of Bergson's work on Proust, for there certainly was active denial by Proust of any direct influence, and clearly if Proust did read Bergson, his novel is a misreading of that philosophy. The etymology of 'influence' is interesting and relevant in this context. In the middle ages it meant:[15] "The supposed flowing or streaming from the stars or heavens of an ethereal fluid acting upon the actions or destiny of men."

Later this evolved into *influence* meaning: "The exercise of personal power by humans figured as something similar to astral influence." This image of influence as something, possibly an ethereal fluid, streaming or emanating from the stars, is not as strange as it perhaps seems, for it is interestingly reminiscent of the image one still has of gravitational force, of the gravitational influence of one body on another by virtue of an unseen and, as yet, unknown emanation that somehow radiates undetected from one mass and influences another.

The relevance of this notion of 'influence' to the present discussion is that it evokes the idea of the inflow of knowledge or information without precisely knowing its origins or the means of transmission. The notion of a rather vague inflow of ideas from the general sea of current concepts and knowledge may be relevant to the convergence of Bergson's and Proust's thought, for as we shall discuss in the final chapter, it would seem that Proust was, to some extent, tapping into a flow of information and ideas that were prevalent in the Paris of the time and that it is not possible (or perhaps relevant) to determine a precise origin of those ideas. Following this meaning of influence, one might say that 'influence' may be both conscious and more importantly the unconscious incorporation of ideas and notions that are prevalent in the society of the time and that are part of the intellectual inheritance of the writer. Harold Bloom commences his arguments by referring to Shelley's speculation that poets of all ages contributed to one Great Poem perpetually in progress. This statement and Bloom's definition of 'poetic influence' are interestingly similar to the notion of scientific (as distinct from poetic) influence and progress described by Pascal, who in his *Préface sur le traité du vide* states:

> De là vient que, par une prérogative particulière, non seulement chacun des hommes s'avance de jour en jour dans les sciences, mais que tous les hommes ensemble y font un continuel progrès à mesure que l'univers vieillit, parce que la même chose arrive dans la succession des hommes que dans les âges différents d'un particulier. De sorte que toute la suite des hommes, pendant le cours de tous les siècles, doit être considérée comme un même homme qui subsiste toujours et qui apprend continuellement:[16]

Thus consciously, unconsciously, or sub-consciously we all stand on the shoulders[17] of our predecessors and although we may see the universe differently from our various vantage points and although we may deny any direct influence, we nevertheless see and describe reality diversely because of those giants, poets or scientists, who have preceded us. Interestingly, Proust himself evokes an image of influence not dissimilar to Pascal's when he states:

> Et j'arrivais à me demander s'il y avait quelque vérité en cette distinction que nous faisions toujours entre l'art, qui n'est pas plus avancé qu'au temps d'Homère, et la science aux progrès continus. Peut-être l'art ressemblait-il au contraire en cela à la science: chaque nouvel écrivain original me semblait en progrès sur celui qui l'avait précédé; (II 624)[18]

In that sense, the highly original work of Proust may be seen as an advancement and progression from that of his predecessor, Henri Bergson, and implies the sort of indirect and subtle influence mentioned above.

This study will attempt to show that although there was not any direct influence of Bergson's work on Proust's novel in the sense implied by Megay's study; (namely that Proust deliberately studied Bergsonian philosophy or that by direct contact with the philosopher he acquired a knowledge of its tenets and consciously incorporated these notions into his novel), but rather that Bergson most certainly did have an indirect influence on Proust's literary creation in the sense referred to by Bloom, Pascal and perhaps more than suggested by

André Gide. In the last chapter I will suggest that, although the concepts and philosophy of Bergson, the precursor in time of Proust,
were the crystallization and enunciation in digital terms of themes and
notions that were prevalent in the society of the time, this was not the
whole extent of Bergson's influence on Proust. For in addition to the
parallel yet possibly independent convergence of Proust's philosophy
with that of Bergson's, the latter's lectures and philosophy became so
popular and fashionable, even to the the non-academic members of
Parisian society frequented by Proust, that although Proust may never
have attended Bergson's lectures or read many of his books, he nevertheless acquired, as the narrator possibly indicates in À la recherche,
considerable, albeit not entirely correct, knowledge of it from the social conversations of others.

Previous Studies Comparing Bergson with Proust

The inter-weaving of the careers of Henri Bergson and Marcel Proust
is quite striking (see Addendum to Chapter 8). Proust entered the lycée
Condorcet in 1882 five years after Bergson had left. Bergson's first
major philosophical work, the Essai, was published in 1889, and in
1890 Proust entered L'École des Sciences Politiques and the Faculté
de Droit of the University of Paris, and was thus working in the same
geographical area as Bergson who was then teaching at the lycée
Henri-IV.

In January 1892 when Proust was 21 years old, he was garçon
d'honneur at the marriage of his cousin Louise Neuburger[19] to Henri
Bergson, who thus became Proust's cousin-in-law. The next well documented interaction between Bergson and Proust was in May 1904
when Bergson presented to L'Académie des Sciences Morales et
Politiques, (ML 629)[20] with his own flattering introduction, Proust's
translation of Ruskin's The Bible of Amiens. The interaction between
the philosopher and the writer then becomes more difficult to trace
but is outlined by Megay and summarized in my brief review of her
study. I will concentrate this survey of previous studies on four works
selected because they are both comprehensive and reasonably contemporary. In chronological order they are first, the biography of Proust
by Léon Pierre-Quint which was published initially in 1925 followed
by revisions in 1928, 1936 and 1946, as well as the article prepared
in 1941 by Léon Pierre-Quint as part of a testimonial[21] honoring the
work of Henri Bergson who died on January 4th, 1941. Second, an
article prepared by Françoise Fabre-Luce de Gruson and presented in

July, 1962 at a conference on Marcel Proust. Third, the detailed and definitive study of the possible influence of Bergson on Proust written by Joyce Megay and published in 1976, and finally the equally detailed study on Bergson and his influence by Anthony Pilkington which also appeared in 1976. None of these studies invokes the digital–analogic opposition which is an underlying minor theme of the present study.

Léon Pierre-Quint

Pierre-Quint was one of the first to document the similarity between some of Bergson's philosophy and the novel of Marcel Proust. His biography of Proust was first published in 1925 before the publication of *Le Temps retrouvé*, and in this biography, he writes:

> Au droit, il (Proust) préfère la philosophie. A Condorcet, son professeur de rhétorique Darlu, lui avait donné, par son enseignement lucide, le goût des grands systèmes. Il était séduit par le prestige de Boutroux, de Lachelier, de Ravaisson, qui l'acheminaient peu à peu à comprendre Bergson. C'est à la Sorbonne qu'il devait connaître ce philosophe qui eut une influence capitale sur sa pensée . . . Les idées qui dominent l'esprit et l'oeuvre de Proust, l'écoulement du temps, l'évolution perpétuelle de la personnalité dans la durée, les richesses insoupçonnées de l'inconscient que nous ne pouvons retrouver que par l'intuition, la mémoire ou les associations involontaires . . . toutes ces idées s'inspirent de Bergson.[22]

The statement "C'est à la Sorbonne qu'il devait connaître ce philosophe" has been interpreted by some critics as indicating that Proust attended lectures delivered by Bergson at the Sorbonne, or that the two met there. However, as is well documented, Bergson never taught at the Sorbonne, for although he offered his candidacy both in 1894 and 1898 (see Chapter 8) he was never elected to a professorship there.[23] The above statement may be read as indicating that it was whilst a student at the Sorbonne that Proust became fully acquainted with Bergsonian philosophy, or that he met Bergson elsewhere during the same time period. Unfortunately, Pierre-Quint does not make an analysis of either Bergson's or Proust's writings and the chapter entitled "Le rôle de la Durée et du Temps" of the above biography contains no mention of Bergson.

His later (1941) essay on 'Bergson and Proust'[24] is lacking in critical analysis. For example, he provides only one quotation from Bergson (on art) and one from Proust (the *bottine* episode of involuntary memory). He considered that both Bergson and Proust regarded human nature and consciousness as existing in two layers (Bergson's

Les deux aspects du Moi) one of which is covered by the thick crust of habit and social necessities and niceties, but that underneath that crust there exists a real being, the true self. This true self is rarely expressed, but occasionally it does rise to the surface and becomes heard, and Pierre-Quint considered that Proust wished to multiply the frequency of these exceptional moments which he allowed to surface through Proustian involuntary memory.[25] For Pierre-Quint therefore involuntary memory is the resurgence of Bergson's *moi profond*, which expresses itself only through the reawakening of involuntary memory. He goes on to suggest that for Proust each (involuntary) memory is a sort of nebulous cloud in the center of which lies a secret treasure. The artist and writer attempts to penetrate to the center of this nebulous memory in order to capture that secret, and Pierre-Quint suggests that the Proustian hero's failure to capture that secret in the episode of *Les trois arbres de Hudimesnil*[26] is what leads to his subsequent disillusionment and disappointment. Pierre-Quint discusses briefly the language of Bergson and of Proust, emphasizing that Bergson wished to use language that is almost poetic in its imagery and rhythm in order to express thoughts without deforming them. He considers Proust's literary style to be similar to Bergson's in that through metaphor Proust depicts layers of meaning and avoids the deforming quality of rigid and habitual language. Pierre-Quint also considers that Bergson's *durée réelle* or 'Bergsonian time' is seen in Proust's novel as the slow and irrevocable change in the personality of his characters. The evolution of, for example, the hero's love for Albertine progresses through a variety of changes including sensual desire, jealousy, and (an) obsession. In a very brief discussion of Bergson's and Proust's concept of art,[27] Pierre-Quint refers to Bergson's view that the function of true art is the removal of the barriers that separate us from reality and that the joy of the revelation of reality is shown in Proust's work by, for instance, the passage describing the septet of Vinteuil. In the 1941 article, Pierre-Quint states:

> Proust, a-t-il véritablement étudié les oeuvres de Bergson? Peu importe. Il a saisi la vision bergsonienne du monde, sur laquelle il a édifié son art. En ce sens, il n'est pas excessif de prétendre que l'oeuvre de Proust est l'expression directe, sur le plan du roman, de la philosophie de Bergson. (330)

A generalization that is not supported by any critical analysis, and which is clearly incorrect, for although there are similarities between Bergson's philosophy and some elements of Proust's there is clearly not a one to one congruence. Proust's work is thus not the direct expression of Bergsonism in fictional form. Furthermore, I would not equate involuntary memory (discussed in detail in Chapter 5) with the expression of the *moi intérieur*.

Françoise Fabre-Luce de Gruson[28]

This excellent and scholarly article discusses the great similarity between Bergson and Proust's conception of (a) memory, (b) time and (c) art. Françoise Fabre-Luce de Gruson considers that the two types of memory described by Bergson (intentional and spontaneous) are identical to the voluntary and involuntary memories described by Proust, a statement which is contrary to the analysis presented in Chapter 5 of the present study.

In discussing the two writer's conception of time, Fabre-Luce de Gruson correctly maintains that Bergson's philosophy consists in contrasting our psychological and subjective notion of duration with the flow of time from that indicated by clocks. In addition she considers that these two forms of time are present in Proust's novel, for example when considering his memories of Albertine, the narrator says:

> Ma tristesse rétrospective . . . en la doublant d'une sorte d'année sentimentale où les heures n'étaient pas définies par la position du soleil, mais par l'attente d'un rendez-vous; où la longueur des jours, où les progrès de la température, étaient mesurés par l'essor de mes espérances, le progrès de notre intimité (IV 69)

Another passage that she feels illustrates Proust's notion of *la durée pure* is the narrator's statement that: "Une heure n'est pas qu'une heure, c'est un vase rempli de parfums, de sons, de projets et de climats . . ." (IV 467). In Chapter 5, we will consider this type of statement as indicating the spatial quality of Proustian time, that it often consists of small packages, or capsules (*les vases clos*) containing a particular memory suspended in spacetime and is thus spatial in character. Fabre-Luce de Gruson also considers that on occasion Proust indicates the difficulty that intelligence has in penetrating into the pure duration of Bergsonian time:

> Et comme dans la petite phrase il cherchait cependant un sens où son intelligence ne pouvait descendre, quelle étrange ivresse il avait à dépouiller son âme la plus intérieure de tous les secours du raisonnement et à la faire passer seule dans le couloir, dans le filtre obscur du son! (I 234)

She considers that Proust's notion of pure duration is intimately linked with that of memory, both voluntary and involuntary, and that the discourse of the Bergsonian *moi intérieur* takes place in pure duration.

In reviewing Bergson's and Proust's understanding of esthetics and art, Françoise de Gruson's view-point agrees with that proposed here, namely that both authors consider the main function of art as one of a revelation, of a widening of perception, but although she quotes Bergson's passage, *l'élargissement de la perception* cited in Chapter 7, and juxtaposes it with a similar quotation from Proust she does not raise the notion of an 'endogenous text.'[29] According to Françoise Fabre-Luce de Gruson there is close agreement between the notions of memory, time and art expressed by Bergson and Proust. Her article is not extensive and detailed, but she correctly analyses the views of the two writers on esthetics and art. However, I would not agree with her statements on the congruence of the two forms of memory described by Bergson and Proust. She finishes her article by stating: ". . . ayant délibérément adopté la position délicate qui vise à rapprocher deux oeuvres et deux hommes pour qui tout s'est passé comme s'ils étaient mus par une volonté commune de s'ignorer et qui pourtant se ressemblent tant, j'ai préféré . . . dénoncer par la juxtaposition des textes l'évidence de la communauté de pensée . . ." (245). Unfortunately, she does not discuss the possible reasons for this, perhaps superficial, resemblance.

Joyce Megay

This comprehensive, thorough, well documented and scholarly work ("Essai de mise au point de la question de l'influence de Bergson sur Proust") published ten years after Fabre-Luce de Gruson's essay, attempts to summarize and bring closure to previous speculations on the potential influence of Henri Bergson's philosophy on Proust's novel.

Megay consulted Proust's *Cahiers* and *Carnets* archived in the *Bibliothèque Nationale* searching for specific references to Bergson or his work and then followed up each reference to Bergson. She finds little mention of the works of Bergson in Proust's notebooks and considers that if Proust had been studying Bergson's philosophy at the time he was writing his novel, he would have referred to Bergson's texts in these notes. She thus concludes that in spite of some similarity, there is no evidence of any direct influence. For the sake of completeness, I summarize here the essential points in Megay's argument with respect to the direct contacts and correspondence between the philosopher and the novelist.

In November 1892, Proust invited Henri Bergson with Fernand Gregh to dinner at the Proust family residence at Auteuil. Gregh goes on to indicate that dinners between the Prousts and Bergson were a recurrent affair at that time, but Megay doubts that this is indeed true and suggests that Proust only saw Bergson very occasionally. She analyses five references to Bergson in Proust's early notes which I recapitulate here. First, there is Proust's preface and translation of John Ruskin's *The Bible of Amiens* which, as already mentioned, Bergson presented to the Académie des Sciences Morales et Politiques on May 28th 1904 and at which Bergson makes some complementary comments concerning Proust: "La préface est une importante contribution à la psychologie de Ruskin . . . M. Marcel Proust l'a traduit dans une langue si animée et si originale qu'on ne croirait pas, en lisant ce livre, avoir affaire à une traduction" (ML, 629–630). In spite of these flattering comments, it is only six years later (1910) in a letter to Georges de Lauris that Proust speaks of Bergson's presentation of his translation:

> Je suis content que vous ayez lu du Bergson et que vous l'ayez aimé. C'est comme si nous avions été ensemble sur une altitude. Je ne connais pas *l'Évolution créatrice* (et à cause du grand prix que j'attache à votre opinion, je vais la lire immédiatement). Mais j'ai assez lu de Bergson, et la parabole de sa pensée étant déjà assez décrivable après une seule génération pour que quelque *Évolution créatrice* qui ait suivi, je ne puisse quand vous dites Bergson, savoir ce que vous voulez dire . . . c'est même lui qui a analysé à l'Institut la *Bible d'Amiens*.[30]

Proust clearly indicates here that he has not yet read *L'évolution créatrice*, which had been published three years earlier in 1906, and was widely known. Megay considers that this statement by Proust is additional evidence that he was not actively concerned with Bergson's philosophy or his writings. Third, Proust refers, in his *Carnet* No 1, to two pages of *Matière et mémoire*, notably the first pages of the second chapter with the title "De la reconnaissance des images; la mémoire et le cerveau" and which are under the running title of "Les deux formes de la mémoire" (MM, 81–82). According to Philip Kolb's study of the note-books,[31] Proust read *Matière et mémoire* between August 1909 and December 1910, and Megay considers that it is unlikely that Proust read much more of Bergson's text, since he does not refer to them further in his notes. Fourth, in one of his *Cahiers* Proust refers to a Mme de Chemisey who spent much time reading Bergson's *Matière et mémoire* as well as other philosophy texts. Fifth and finally, Proust evokes the name of Bergson in his *Cahiers* II, and XIV in connection with the attempt of Bergotte to become member of *L'Académie*. Megay concludes that when one compares these five brief references with the twenty or more Cahiers with drafts and sketches for *Contre Sainte-Beuve* and "Du côté de chez Swann," it is unlikely that at that time Bergson's philosophy was at the center of Proust's attention.

Nevertheless, on November 13, 1913, *Le Temps* published a revealing interview with Proust which discussed the possible influence of Bergson on his work. The article coincided with the publication the previous day of *Du côté de chez Swann*, and was at the apogee of Bergson's fame and notoriety, (he was elected to l'Académie Française in 1914) and also at the height of the argument and publicity of the conflict with the Sorbonne to be discussed in Chapter 8. It was perhaps to distance himself from the famous philosopher and claim more complete originality for his work that Proust states in this interview:

> A ce point de vue, mon livre serait peut-être comme un essai d'une suite de "Romans de l'Inconscient": je n'aurais aucune honte à dire de "romans bergsoniens," si je le croyais, car à toute époque il arrive que la littérature a tâché de se rattacher—après coup, naturellement—à la philosophie régnante. Mais ce ne serait pas exact, car mon oeuvre est dominée par la distinction entre la mémoire involontaire et la mémoire volontaire, distinction qui non seulement ne figure pas dans la philosophie de M. Bergson, mais est même contredit par elle.[32]

The comparison between Bergson's and Proust's conception of memory, voluntary and involuntary will been analyzed at length in Chapter 5 of the present study. The inaccuracy of Proust's statement leads Megay to conclude, that if Proust did read *Matière et mémoire* he did not read it very thoroughly. Alternatively and following the notion of *influence* proposed by Bloom and discussed earlier, the error in Proust's rendering could perhaps be interpreted as: "an act of creative correction that is actually and necessarily a misinterpretation."

Megay considers that from 1913 onwards the contact between the two writers must have become less and less frequent; however, there is a letter from Bergson to Proust dated 30 September, 1920 which is interesting:

> Mon cher cousin,
>
> J'ai reçu votre mot hier soir en rentrant d'Oxford, à l'instant même où par une curieuse coïncidence, ma femme me disait la distinction dont vous veniez

d'être l'objet. Nous vous félicitons très cordialement. Vous savez ce que je pensais de votre livre "Du côté de chez Swann"; le dernier "À l'ombre des jeunes filles en fleurs" en est la digne continuation. Rarement l'introspection a été poussée aussi loin. C'est une vision directe et continue de la réalité intérieure. M. Jacques Rivière sera mon candidat cet après-midi. Son livre sur l'Allemand, que j'ai lu de près, est une oeuvre d'un réel talent. . . (ML 1326)[33]

One of the few documented meetings between Bergson and Proust occurred later that day when together with Barrès, Boutroux, Boylesve, Gide and Valéry, they met as members of a committee adjudicating the Prix Blumenthal. The prize was awarded that year to Proust's friend Jacques Rivière and it is presumably to this that Bergson is referring at the end of the above letter. I discuss this important meeting again in the final chapter.

The conclusion from Megay's meticulous study is that: "Il n'est pas exact de rattacher son oeuvre (de Proust) à la philosophie bergsonienne,"[34] and that there is no evidence from correspondence or notes of any direct influence of Bergson's work on Proust's novel. In the conclusion of her book, Joyce Megay writes:

. . . chaque fois qu'il est question de Bergson dans les *Cahiers*, Proust déclare son opposition aux vues du philosophe. Grâce au Carnet No 1 qui date de 1908-1910, nous savons que Proust a consulté quelques pages de *Matière et Mémoire* à l'époque où il commençait à composer *La Recherche*. Encore est-il que le nom de Bergson n'est mentionné que cinq fois dans les vingt Cahiers qui contiennent les ébauches du *Contre Sainte-Beuve* et du *Côté de chez Swann*. Visiblement, Bergson n'était pas au centre de ses préoccupations à l'époque où *La Recherche* prenait forme dans son esprit.[35]

Megay concludes by stating that in spite of the superficial similarity between certain points of the thinking of Bergson and Proust there is wide separation in their visions of the world. Having shown that any direct or conscious influence of Bergson's philosophy on Proust writing was very unlikely, she does not consider other possible reasons for their similarity.

Anthony Pilkington
This is also a well-documented and scholarly study which investigates the intellectual relationships between Bergson and four of his contemporaries: Charles Péguy (whom I briefly discuss in Chapter 8); Paul Valéry and Marcel Proust, both of whom denied any influence or closeness of their doctrines to those of Bergson, and fourth, Julien Benda, a notable adversary of Bergson.

Pilkington's views coincide with those expressed in the present analysis that valid affinities between Bergson and Proust must be sought elsewhere than in their conception of memory. He considers that Bergson and Proust have more in common in their conception of time even though there is a divergence between Bergsonian continuity and Proustian discontinuity. Pilkington considers that Proust's conception of art and his own artistic practice provide a clear example of Bergson's theory of artistic vision, but he fails to point out that Bergson's view of esthetics does not include the importance of time and memory so central in Proust's theory of art, and which will be discussed in Chapter 7.

The reasons for the apparent affinity and closeness between the work of these three writers (Péguy, Valéry and Proust) and Bergson's philosophy are not clearly delineated by Pilkington who seems to subscribe to the notion of the *Zeitgiest*[36] that Proust like Bergson was in touch with the spirit of that age, a possibility discussed in detail in the final chapter of this work.

In this study, I have accepted the position of Joyce Megay that there is no evidence suggesting a conscious incorporation by Proust of Bergson's philosophical work in his novel and my thesis supports the view of Pilkington and the statement of André Gide that both authors are expressing, in very different ways, ideas and notions that were of their period. Thus there is convergence of two independent minds in touch with the ideas and notions of their time. In addition there is a third possible cause for some allbeit not exact similarity, which is intermediate between the above two extremes and which is discussed in the final chapter.

The Origins of Bergsonian Philosophy

It is perhaps symbolic of the dichotomy that permeates Bergson's philosophy that 1889, the date of publication of the *Essai*, was also the date of the construction of *La tour Eiffel,* which symbolized the power of science and engineering over the forces of Nature, and the ability of the human intellect to tame and master the external world. Bergson's great popularity probably originated not only from his writings and charismatic eloquence as a teacher but also because his thoughts and words found resonance in the minds of many of his listeners, his words were perhaps another example of the 'endogenous text' to be discussed in Chapter 5. Tracing the origins of the philosophy of Henri Bergson necessitates outlining the intellectual and scientific climate of

Paris of the 1880–1900, which sets the stage for both Bergsonian philosophy and the Proustian novel.

The Scientific World Prior to Bergson

The mid nineteenth century was an epoch of intense scientific ferment in which the determinism of Newtonian dynamics was beginning to be challenged and displaced. The mathematics and physics of Isaac Newton (1642–1727) had been brilliantly successful, moreover the science of dynamics based on Newtonian laws of motion accurately predicted the movement of bodies, whether those of a sphere rolling down an inclined plane or the revolution of the planets around the sun. The motion of individual pieces of matter could be predicted, hence the motion of all matter could be predicted, and following Laplace, it was assumed that from the complete state of the universe at any one instant the complete state at any other instant, past or future, could be determined. Therefore an omniscient observer, whether he be God or Laplace's demon, could see all the past and all the future motions of the universe. There was theoretically no uncertainty and everything moved in predictable fashion like an intricate universal clockwork system, leaving no room for free-will. Hence the epitaph that Alexander Pope proposed for Newton (and later modified by Eddington):

> Nature and nature's laws lay hid in night.
> God said, "Let Newton be" and there was light.
> But not for long. The devil howling, "Ho!
> Let Einstein be!" restored the *status quo*.[37]

In spite of the incomparable genius of Newton and the wonders of Newtonian science it had three major philosophical flaws that did not become apparent until the nineteenth century. Briefly these may be summarized as:

- The absence of man or a human observer in the Newtonian world. Man was looking at the clockwork universe through a window, but was not part of that universe.
- The Newtonian universe was basically *atemporal* and fully reversible. Although a quantity 't' occurs in Newton's equations of motion, it is a time that has no direction and no duration. Thus motion and physical processes were fully reversible.
- It was a quantitative universe which in terms of the digital-analogic taxonomy we would classify as digital. The analogic world of the qualitative and the subjective was not apparent.

In the world of science changes were taking place that were to parallel and possibly impact both philosophy and literature. The discovery of the heat engine, which initiated the industrial revolution, was also the seed for profound changes in scientific and philosophical thinking. It uncovered an asymmetry in nature, a dissymmetry that gave a direction to time's arrow.

The first of these discoveries concerned the nature of heat and thermal motion. What is heat, what are the laws that govern its flow? Sadi Carnot (1796–1832), a French engineer, realized that whoever possessed efficient steam power would become an important industrial and military power. His work *(Reflexions sur la puissance motrice du feu*, 1824) was based on the misconception that heat was some sort of massless fluid which he termed *caloric*, which flowed from a hot body to a cooler one and caused power to be generated much as water runs from a high to a low point and turns a water-wheel. He thought that the operation of a steam engine was similar to the operation of a water mill, that caloric ran from the boiler to the condenser, and was conserved just as water flowing though a water wheel was conserved. His conception of heat as a fluid was incorrect in detail but nevertheless initiated the science of thermodynamics. He established a method of analysis that went beyond the apparently abstract notions of Newton, and developed a theoretical concept of what is now called the *Carnot Cycle*, in which a perfect gas[38] is taken through a series of completely reversible processes of having work performed on it, and the heat generated subsequently being expended as work. At the same time, Joseph Fourier (1768–1830) conducted mathematical investigations into the motion of heat in solid bodies reducing them to mathematical formulations, and developed equations governing the propagation of heat. The ideas of Carnot were developed by those of Rudolph Clausius (1822–1888) and Ludwig Boltzman (1844–1906). Boltzman applied the laws of probability and statistics to heat as energy. His image of heat related to that of the kinetic energy of individual particles oscillating about a mean point in a solid or traveling freely in a gas. The greater the temperature, the greater the kinetic energy of the particles. The image of heat had changed from that of a continuous fluid to that of discrete particles. But more important of all was the concept of entropy, that heat flow is unidirectional, from a heat source to a cold sink, otherwise work cannot be done, and in that process heat is irrevocably lost, dissipated. All these studies led to the first description of something inconceivable in classical dynamics, an irreversible process.[39] Irreversibility is linked to the fact that work involves *coherent* motion, but some of this work, or coherent motion is always lost as *incoherent* or chaotic motion, namely heat. To generalize this concept, the universe is generally considered to be moving from a state of greater organization towards a state of lower organization, ending ultimately in one of chaos or lack of any order. Negentropy, the degree of organization, is always decreasing as time progresses, and in this manner time acquires the property of direction. The profound philosophical importance of the concept of entropy and the second law of thermodynamics was clearly enunciated in 1928 by the English astronomer and philosopher, Sir Arthur Eddington:

> *The Scientific Reaction From Microscopic Analysis.* From the point of view of philosophy of science the conception associated with entropy must I think be ranked as the great contribution of the nineteenth century to scientific thought. It marked a reaction from the view that everything to which science need pay attention is **discovered by a microscopic dissection of objects**. It provided an alternative standpoint in which the center of interest is shifted from the entities reached by the customary analysis to **qualities possessed by the system as a whole,** which cannot be split up and located— a little bit here, and a little bit there. The artist desires to convey significances which cannot be told by microscopic detail and accordingly he resorts to **impressionist** paintings. Strangely enough the physicist has found the same necessity.[40] (my emphasis)

and a little later he continues:

> I think there are the strongest grounds for placing entropy alongside beauty and melody . . . Entropy is only found when the parts are viewed in association, and it is by viewing or hearing the parts in association that beauty and melody are discerned. All three are features of arrangement. (105)

These quotations are of interest for a number of reasons. First, the statement; "The scientific reaction from microscopic analysis" is of note, for the *philosophical* reaction from microscopic analysis was indeed the subject of Bergson's metaphysics. Secondly, the quotation clearly echoes the thoughts of Blaise Pascal and the concept of *l'esprit de géométrie* and *l'esprit de finesse* discussed in Chapter 2: "Il faut tout d'un coup voir la chose, d'un seul regard et non pas par progrès de raisonnement."[41] Here is science reaching the conclusion that philosophy enunciated many years previously, that often it is important to view the whole as an entity rather than dissect it into its constituent (digital) parts and loose the perception of the (analogic) whole, and that by considering the whole we gain a vision that cannot be obtained from the individual parts. Both Eddington and Pascal seem to be clearly aware of the binary opposition between the digital and the analogic modes of thought, and both are stating that the 'digital' approach alone does not provide a complete picture of either reality or of the universe, for it has to be combined with the continuous to provide that comprehensive representation. The third important point in Eddington's statement, is that he should refer to the parallel between the progress of a rather abstract science, thermodynamics, and the development of *Impressionism* in painting, indicating the parallel development between science, philosophy and art which appeared to be taking place at the end of the nineteenth century. It is an example of what Marcel Raymond, writing about Bergson and late nineteenth century poetry, describes as: "La correspondance des arts et de la philosophie, en cette fin de siècle, la curieuse convergence de diverses manifestations de l'esprit . . ."[42] and to which we will again refer in the final chapter of this study. Both Eddington and Raymond are referring to this peculiar convergence of the philosophy of science with that of art and the humanities. A movement which leads to a conflict, the collision between what has often been called the "two cultures,"[43] science against the humanities. Another great British philosopher, Sir Isaiah Berlin, refers to this question of the two visions of the universe and of man when he writes:

> The specific and unique versus the repetitive and the universal, the concrete versus the abstract, perpetual movement versus rest, the inner versus the outer, quality versus quantity, culture-bound versus timeless principles, mental strife and self-transformation as a permanent condition of man versus the possibility (and desirability) of peace, order, final harmony.[44]

This dual vision, this double choice is indeed the binary opposition that permeates Bergson's philosophy, which emerged from this conflict between the two cultures.

There were other profound changes taking place in the world of the physical sciences, those associated with the names of Max Planck, Albert Einstein, Werner Heisenberg and Erwin Schrödinger, and in which the dualism between discrete particles and continuous waves was prominent. Physical science and Bergsonian philosophy were independently moving in the same direction. A specific example of this convergence is Bergson's enunciation of a philosophical uncertainty principle that will discussed in Chapter 6 and which preceded

Heisenberg's formulation of the uncertainty principle of quantum mechanics by some thirty-eight years.

The Reaction Against the Mechanistic

The power and confidence in science, symbolized by the *Tour Eiffel* rising over Paris of the late nineteenth century, was all pervasive, and only knowledge obtained by the analytical scientific method was considered reliable.[45] Through science everything was possible, indeed everything thing might indeed be predictable. Intellect and logic were the road, not only to knowledge, but also to power, and were clearly more important than matters spiritual.

In England, Thomas Huxley (1825–1895), following on the ideas of Laplace (1749–1827), proclaimed that it was theoretically possible to predict the motions of *every* particle in the universe. The world was thus one where determinism reigned and free-will a mere figment of a religious imagination, and that nothing shall be believed "with greater assurance than the evidence warrants":

> Moreover this scientific "criticism of life" presents itself to us with different credential from any other. It appeals not to authority, nor to what anybody may have thought or said, but to nature. It admits that all our interpretations of natural fact are more or less imperfect and symbolic, **and bids the learner seek for truth not among words but among things.** It warns us that the assertion which outstrips evidence is not only a blunder but a crime.[46] (my emphasis)

The concern about the growing importance and dominance of determinism that emanated from science was clearly expressed by Anatole France (1844–1924), who, in a series of essays entitled "La morale et la science" published in *Le temps* in the summer of 1889 (the same year as the completion of the *Tour Eiffel* & the publication of Bergson's *Essai*), shows the growing concern for the determinism of Laplace and Huxley when he writes:

> Ce bonhomme (M. Adrien Sixte) est un des grands penseurs du siècle. Il a exposé la doctrine du déterminisme avec une puissance de logique et une richesse d'arguments que Taine lui-même et Ribot n'avaient point atteints . . .
> "Tout acte, dit-il, n'est qu'une addition. Dire qu'il est libre, c'est dire qu'il y a dans un total plus qu'il n'y a dans les éléments additionnés.
> "Si nous connaissions vraiment la position relative de tous les phénomènes qui constituent l'univers actuel, nous pourrions, dès à présent, calculer avec une certitude égale à celle des astronomes le jour, l'heure, la minute où l'Angleterre, par exemple, évacuera les Indes, où tel criminel, encore à naître,

assassinera son père. L'avenir tient dans le présent comme toutes les propriétés du triangle tiennent dans sa définition."
Une telle philosophie (says Anatole France) ne saurait admettre la réalité du bien et du mal, du mérite et du démérite.[47]

Traditional religious beliefs were challenged as was the dogma of the Church, and science was seen as liberating man from the shackles of medieval theology and authority. But this liberation brought with it not only the concern of determinism expressed by Anatole France above, but also the loss of wonder and mystery of the unknown that science can sometimes inadvertently destroy. In an essay entitled "Sous les galeries de l'Odéon" France expresses this longing for mysticism and mystery:

Notre littérature contemporaine oscille entre le naturalisme brutal et le mysticisme exalté. Nous avons perdu la foi et nous voulons croire encore. L'insensibilité de la nature nous désole. La morne majesté des lois physiques nous accable. Nous cherchons le mystère. Nous appelons à nous toutes les magies de l'Orient; nous nous jetons éperdument dans ces recherches psychiques, dernier refuge du merveilleux que l'astronomie, la chimie et la physiologie ont chassé de leur domaine. Nous sommes dans la boue et dans les nuages. Voilà ce que nous avons tiré d'une heure de bouquinage sous les galeries de l'Odéon.[48]

In France, the naturalistic novels of Emile Zola emphasized the importance of environmental factors and the laws of heredity in determining man's actions, rather than the existence of a free-will exercised by the inner being of man. Science was popularized and brought to the now massive reading public by publications such as Camille Flammarion's *Astronomie populaire*.[49] The novels of Jules Verne not only popularized science but illustrated the power of science in the hands of the heroic scientist-engineer such as Le capitaine Nemo (*Vingt mille lieues sous les mers*) and Cyrus Smith (*L'île mystérieuse*) to conquer and tame the powers of Nature and put them to the use of mankind.

Bergson's essay on humor, *Le rire*, in which he analyses the comic as emanating from: "du mécanique plaqué sur du vivant" (RI 29), can be seen as a reflection of humanity using the power of laughter to oppose the growing oppression of science and the mechanistic elements in Society:[50]

. . . si l'on trace un cercle autour des actions et disposition qui compromettent la vie individuelle ou sociale et qui se châtient elles-mêmes par leurs conséquences naturelles, il reste en dehors de ce terrain d'émotion et de lutte, dans une zone neutre où l'homme se donne simplement en spectacle à l'homme, une certaine raideur du corps, de l'esprit et du caractère, que la société voudrait encore éliminer pour obtenir de ses membres la plus grande élasticité et la plus haute sociabilité possible. Cette raideur est le comique, et le rire en est le châtiment. (RI, 16)[51]

As a true romantic, Bergson had a contempt for the industrial and urban character of modern society; he was convinced that mechanization and industrialization cannot bring happiness to mankind. Another contemporary example of this all pervasive opposition of humanity against the progress of science is perhaps the (1895) novel of H.G. Wells, *The Time Machine*, a book which is about time travel, but more importantly concerns the potential rift in human society between those that profit from the fruits of science, mechanization and industrialization, the privileged Eloi, and those that provide the service, the subservient Morlocks.[52]

The scientific positivism of Auguste Comte (1798–1857) was also an important element in the France of the 1870's, it sought to strengthen the social tendencies of man at the expense of the person or individual. Scientific positivism proclaimed that science was the arbiter of what was useful and not useful, and only the useful was socially acceptable. It was a movement that Bergson opposed as ignoring and denying the essential elements that became prominent in his philosophy, namely the existence of specific and unique elements of the self as something that are more than the composite of its parts and which has continuity in pure duration.

However, in the 1880–1890's a wind of change started blowing across scientific intellectualism and it began in the most philosophical of the exact sciences, theoretical physics and mathematics. It began to be realized by philosophers of science that science could only explain certain aspects of reality whilst ultimate truths remained beyond the grasp of science. Henri Bergson was to become the most eloquent and powerful spokesman of this movement, which in literature was taken up by Paul Claudel,[53] Charles Péguy, and Marcel Proust.

Bergson and l'École Normale

In order to trace further the intellectual and philosophical climate of late nineteenth century France, and the birth of Bergson's philosophy, it is helpful to review the work of the men on whose shoulders Bergson, like Newton, stood so that he could see further than they. In France there has often been a close relationship between philosophy, and mathematics as exemplified by Descartes and Pascal, and Henri Bergson who was a brilliant and naturally gifted young mathematician was to follow in these eminent footsteps. Whilst a student at the *Lycée Fontanes* (now, *Condorcet*), Bergson won four prizes in mathematics and his first publication in 1878, when only nineteen years old, was entitled "Solution d'un problème mathématique."[54] In an interview with Jean de la Harpe he speaks of his early love for mathematics: "J'aimais surtout les sciences et particulièrement les mathématiques, parce que c'était solide. Il me suffisait de suivre une démonstration au tableau noir pour la posséder: je n'ai jamais dû apprendre une leçon à la maison."[55] Bergson entered l'École Normale Supérieure in 1878 where he continued his studies of science and mathematics but came under the influence both directly and indirectly of a number of contemporary philosophers who expounded the increasingly prevalent anti-mechanistic movement. Three contemporary philosophers who probably had an influence not only on Bergson's philosophy but on the background intellectual climate of spiritualism and contra-mechanism that permeated late nineteenth century France, were Ravaisson, Lachelier and Boutroux, whose works I shall summarize briefly. Nevertheless, to what extend any of these philosophers had any direct influence on Bergson's thought is difficult to say, for Bergson was apparently jealous of his originality and disliked the notion of influence.[56] The first of these spiritual philosophers was Felix Ravaisson, who did not himself teach at l'École Normale, but whose works Bergson greatly admired.

Jean-Gaspard-Félix Ravaisson

In a paper read to *Académie des Sciences morales et politiques* in 1904, Bergson expounds on the life and works of Felix Ravaisson (1813–1900), whom he succeeded as a member of that *Académie*. In this eulogy, one can discern the beginnings of some of Bergson's philosophical notions; for example, in describing Ravaisson's ideas, Bergson distinguishes two different manners of thinking:

> Reprenant et élargissant l'idée maîtresse de son *Essai*[57] il distinguait deux manières de philosopher. La première procède par **analyse**; elle résout les choses en leurs éléments inertes; de simplification en simplification elle va à ce qu'il y a de plus abstrait et de plus vide, . . . c'est du matérialisme. L'autre méthode ne tient pas seulement compte de matérialisme mais de leur ordre, de leur entente entre eux et de leur direction commune. Elle n'explique plus le vivant par le mort, mais voyant partout la vie, c'est par leur aspiration à une

forme de vie plus haute qu'elle définit les formes les plus élémentaires. Elle ne ramène plus le supérieur à l'inférieur, mais, au contraire, l'inférieur au supérieur. C'est, au sens propre du mot, le **spiritualisme**. (PM 273) [my emphasis]

Do we not have here a re-statement of the dualism that becomes so ubiquitous in Bergsonism, of spiritualism opposed to materialism, of digital analysis as opposed to analogic intuition, of a retrograde movement to enter the reality of things? In addition, Bergson sees in Ravaisson's writings testimony of a movement that is evident both in philosophy and in the writings of scientists themselves. Although one often commenced a study with a mechanistic or geometric approach, there was an increasing tendency to move away from the purely analytical method towards a study of the integrated whole. A characteristic of the 19th century philosopher is the increasing awareness of the importance of life and living things, not merely in the biological and mechanistic sense, but also in the psychological realm of the spirit:

Maintenant, si l'on examine la philosophie française du XIXᵉ siècle, . . . voici, d'après M. Ravaisson, ce qu'on trouve. Il n'est pas rare que l'esprit s'oriente d'abord dans la direction matérialiste et s'imagine même y persister. Tout naturellement il cherche une explication mécanique ou géométrique de ce qu'il voit. Mais l'habitude de s'en tenir là n'est qu'une survivance des siècles précédents. Elle date d'une époque où la science était presque exclusivement géométrie. Ce qui caractérise la science du XIXᵉ siècle, l'entreprise nouvelle qu'elle a tentée, c'est l'étude approfondie des êtres vivants. (PM 273)

Although as previously indicated Bergson was rather jealous of the originality of his philosophical thought, he does admit that the ideas of Ravaisson have a great influence in the philosophical thinking on his contemporaries in academia: "Elles ont été pour beaucoup dans l'influence que le *Rapport*⁵⁸ exerça sur notre philosophie universitaire" (PM 275).

Jules Lachelier
Lachelier was professor of philosophy at the École Normale until 1876 and it is to Lachelier that Bergson dedicated his doctoral thesis, which became his first philosophical work, the *Essai sur les données immédiates de la conscience*. Of Lachelier, Bergson said:

Pour ce qui est de Jules Lachelier, il n'a pas été mon maître à l'École Normale, et cela pour la simple raison qu'il avait cessé d'y enseigner bien avant mon admission comme élève. Il n'en est pas moins vrai que j'ai lu sa thèse *Du Fondement de l'Induction* avec enthousiasme quand j'étais au lycée Condorcet. Elle m'a fait l'impression d'une oeuvre qui émanait d'un esprit extrêmement original.[59]

To which testimony can be added Bergson's admission: "Je dois énormémemt à la dialetique de Lachelier."[60] Lachelier's book, *Du fondement de l'induction*, was highly influential in the anti-mechanistic and spiritual movement, for it was Lachelier who revealed to many of his pupils the spiritual element of life that deterministic science could never completely analyze and comprehend in purely materialistic terms.

Emile Boutroux

According to one of Bergson's biographers, Dominique Parodi, the teachings and writings of Boutroux had a profound influence on the young Bergson. Furthermore, that Bergson read and approved Parodi's book possibly attests to the veracity of this statement.[61] It is, however, relevant that in the interview that Jean de la Harpe had with Bergson during which they discussed the latter's teachers at Normale, Bergson makes only passing reference to Boutroux, a point which de la Harpe took to be significant: "j'ai été très frappé par son silence sur Boutroux."[62] Does this indicate that Boutroux had no influence on Bergson, or as suggested by Delattre that Bergson was rather jealous of the origin of his philosophy and of the influence of others?

Emile Boutroux succeeded Jules Lachelier at the École Normale in 1876, and Bergson studied philosophy for one year under Léon Ollé-Laprune and with Emile Boutroux for two. Possibly one of the greatest influences on Bergson's philosophical development at the École Normale was Boutroux's book *De la contingence de lois de la nature*. It probably caused Bergson to question the pre-eminence of the scientific method, but in addition to his teachers at Normale, the writings of Herbert Spencer had a great influence on Bergson:

A Normale, j'avais Boutroux qui était alors tout à Kant: mes camarades me nommaient "l'anti-kantien'; on m'en raillait et je continuais à pratiquer Spencer. J'ai lu tout Spencer, tous *les Principes*; je l'aimais . . . pour l'abondance des faits invoqués. Mais *Les Premiers Principes* me chicanaient, car l'évolution suppose le temps, seulement qu'est-ce que "le temps?"[63]

The absence of duration in Spencer's conception of time was, as discussed in Chapter 3, the starting point of Bergson's study of duration which ultimately led to the dichotomy and dualism that permeates his entire philosophy.

One of the main philosophical problems discussed by Boutroux in *De la contingence de lois de la nature* was the question of determinism and free-will. It is probably not irrelevant that Boutroux was the brother-in-law of Henri Poincaré, with whom he shared some of his doubts on the pre-eminence of the scientific method:

> For Boutroux the scientific method is suspect since it fails to deal with the process and change, individuality and purpose, the very things that constitute reality. According to Boutroux, the general idea which emerges from a study of contemporary thought is that "man is more or less what he believes himself to be."[64]

Whether or not Boutroux, who was apparently a highly gifted teacher and lecturer, had any direct influence on the origins of Bergson's philosophy is not clear but he nevertheless was influential both at the École Normale and in French academic circles and in the spiritualist or counter-mechanistic movement of the late 1880's.

Claude Bernard and Henri Poincaré

Two other philosopher-scientists who, although they did not teach at the École Normale, had a profound effect on the intellectual climate in France of their time and the views of Bergson were Claude Bernard and Henri Poincaré.

Claude Bernard (1813–1878), the famed physiologist and bio-medical scientist, author of *Introduction à l'étude de la médécine expérimentale* (1865), expresses himself initially as if the interplay of mechanical forces could explain all observed facts. But when he discusses biological phenomena in details he has to hypothesize the existence of '*une idée directrice*' and even of a creative force which might be the cause of biological life. Bernard was a great believer in the value of the experimental method and the power of meticulous observation, but he also strongly believed in the power and value of intuitive insight. In his *Introduction à l'étude*, under the heading of *L'intuition ou le sentiment engendre l'idée expérimentale,* he writes:

> Nous avons dit.. que la méthode expérimentale s'appuie successivement sur le *sentiment*, la *raison* et l'*expérience* . . . Il n'y a pas de règles pour faire naître dans le cerveau, à propos d'une observation donnée, une idée juste et féconde qui soit pour l'expérimentateur une sorte d'anticipation intuitive de l'esprit vers une recherche heureuse . . . son apparition a été toute spontanée,

et sa nature est tout individuelle . . . Une idée neuve apparaît comme une relation nouvelle ou inattendue que l'esprit aperçoit entre les choses. . .

L'idée expérimentale résulte d'une sorte de pressentiment de l'esprit qui juge que les choses doivent se passer d'une certaine manière. On peut dire sous ce rapport que nous avons dans l'esprit l'intuition ou le sentiment des lois de la nature.[65]

Here, then is a clear enunciation of the value of intuitive thought in science, that logic and reason have to be accompanied by another quality which is neither of the above. The intuitive notion is difficult to predict or control, it merely appears as does artistic inspiration. These statements clearly prefigure Bergson's notions of the importance of intuition to be used in parallel with reason. In addition there is an interesting prefiguration of the inspiration of *Les clochers de Martinville* for the Proustian hero, when Claude Bernard says: "Une idée neuve apparaît comme une relation nouvelle ou inattendue que l'esprit aperçoit . . ."

For Bernard, scientific research was a dialogue between the mind and nature, in which facts and theories collaborate in the process of discovery, for facts lead to theory which in turn suggests an experiment which will confirm or modify the theory. Furthermore, Bergson was well aware of the writings and philosophy of Claude Bernard which he reviews in *La pensée et le mouvant*.[66]

The eminent mathematician Henri Poincaré presents the view that many of the most general principles of theoretical physics are merely convenient definitions and perhaps do not represent a vision of reality but rather of the interaction of the human mind with that reality. He clearly expresses his notions on the philosophy and purpose of science which opposes to the utilitarian view of Auguste Comte:

Le savant n'étudie pas la nature parce que cela est utile; il l'étudie parce qu'il y prend plaisir et il y prend plaisir parce qu'elle est belle. Si la nature n'était pas belle, elle ne vaudrait pas la peine d'être connue, . . . Je ne parle pas ici, bien entendu, de cette beauté qui frappe les sens, . . je veux parler de cette beauté plus intime qui vient de l'ordre harmonieux des parties, et qu'une intelligence pure peut saisir.[67]

and emphasizing the irreversibility of time's arrow he later writes:

Nous savons qu'en vertu du principe de Carnot, les phénomènes physiques sont irréversibles et que le monde tend vers l'uniformité. Quand deux corps de température différente sont en présence, le plus chaud cède de la chaleur au plus froid: nous pouvons donc prévoir que les températures s'égaliseront.

Mais une fois que les températures seront devenues égales, . . . nous ne pourrons pas deviner lequel des deux était autrefois le plus chaud.[68]

Thus both Claude Bernard and Henri Poincaré enunciate the belief that perhaps beauty is found in science itself, and furthermore, that some scientific ideas may originate, like artistic inspiration, from intuition. In addition, they believe that there is something beyond the utilitarian philosophy of science proposed by Comte. Before discussing further Bergson's philosophy and comparing it to the Proustian novel, we will pause to analyse the notion of the digital and the analogic opposition that seems to be so prevalent in Bergsonism.

Notes

1   Floyd Gray, 'Des *livres* (1580) aux *trois commerces* (1588),' *Montaigne: Regards sur Les Essais* (Waterloo, Ont.: Wilfrid Laurier UP, 1986) 89.

2   Subsequently referred to as the *Essai* in this book.

3   Subsequently referred to as *À la recherche* in this book.

4   The term enantiomer derives from the Greek, *entio-* meaning opposite. In chemistry the term is used to describe chemical compounds which are identical except in their configuation which differ as a right hand differs from a left.

5   Joyce Megay, *Bergson et Proust: Essai de mise au point de la question de l'influence de Bergson sur Proust* (Paris: J. Vrin. 1976) 29.

6   Jean de Pierrefeu. "Le livre de la semaine: Du Côté de chez Swann, Par M. Marcel Proust." *L'opinion* 7e année (1914): 109–121.

7   Gaston Rageot, "Romans de fin d'année," *La revue de Paris* 21ᵉ année (1914): 165–187.

8   Louis Latourrette, "Du côté de chez Swann, par M. Marcel Proust," *Les écrits Français*, 2e année (5 avril, 1914): 60–61.

9   Gladys Turquet-Milnes, *From Pascal to Proust* (London: Butler and Tanner, 1926).

10   Beatrice Watson, "Le Bergsonisme de Proust." MA Diss. (Chicago: U of Chicago, 1927).

11   Ernst-Robert Curtius, *Marcel Proust*, trans. Armand Pierhal. (Paris: Éditions de la Revue Nouvelle, 1928).

12   Anthony E. Pilkington, *Bergson and his Influence. A Reassessment.* (Cambridge: Cambridge UP, 1976).

13   Jean-Claude Demoncel, *Le symbole d'Hécate: philosophie deleuzienne et roman proustien* (Paris: Édition HYX. 1996).

14   Harold Bloom, *The Anxiety of Influence: A Theory of Poetry* 2nd ed. (Oxford: Oxford UP, 1997) 30.

15   *The Compact Edition of the Oxford English Dictionary.* Vol 1, (Oxford: Oxford UP, 1985) 1431.

16   Blaise Pascal, *Oeuvres complètes*, Présentation et notes de Louis Lafuma (Paris: Seuil, 1963) 232.

17   "If I have seen further (than you and Descartes) it is by standing upon the shoulders of giants." Letter from Issac Newton to Robert Hooke, February 5,

1675/6. Quoted in "The Campaign for Cambridge University." Cambridge: Cambridge UP. 1994. According to Edwin Hubble, *The Realm of the Nebulae*, (New Haven: Yale UP, 1936) 1; George Sarton has traced this quotation to Bernard de Chartres who died in 1126.

18   Throughout this book, references to *À la recherche du temps perdu* are in the text and refer to the 1987–89 Gallimard: Pléiade edition in four volumes, published under the direction of Jean-Yves Tadié. References are by volume number in roman numerals and page.

19   The mother of Louise Neuburger was the first cousin of Jeanne Weil, mother of Marcel Proust. See: Philippe Soulez, *Bergson: biographie* (Paris: Flammarion, 1997) 100.

20   Throughout this book, references to Bergson's work are in the text proper and use the following abbreviations: DI = *Essai sur les donnés immédiates de la conscience* (Paris: Quadrige / PUF, 1991). MM = *Matière et mémoire* (Paris: Quadrige / PUF, 1990). PM = *La pensée et le mouvant* (Paris: Quadrige / PUF, 1993). ES = *L'énergie sprituelle* (Paris: Quadrige / PUF, 1993). EC = *L'évolution créatrice* (Paris: Quadrige / PUF, 1991). RI = *Le rire* (Paris: Quadrige / PUF, 1995). ML = *Mélanges* Texte publiés et annotés par André Robinet (Paris: PUF, 1972).

21   Albert Béguin and Pierre Thévenaz, eds. *Henri Bergson: essais et témoignages recueillis* (Neuchatel: La Baconnière, 1943).

22   Léon Pierre-Quint, *Marcel Proust, sa vie, son oeuvre* (Paris: Sagitaire, 1946) 37.

23   The mistake of thinking that Proust had Bergson as a teacher, is also made by André Maurois who writes: "Enfin ses parents l'autorisèrent à suivre, sans but défini, des cours en Sorbonne, comme il le souhaitait. Ce fut là qu'il eut pour maître Henri Bergson . . ." André Maurois, *À la recherche de Marcel Proust* (Paris: Hachette, 1949) 55. It is also made by René Girard, ed. *Proust: A Collection of critical Essays* (Englewood Cliffs, Prentice-Hall, 1962) 181, who states: "[Proust] studies at the Ecole des Sciences politiques and at the Sorbonne where he attends Henri Bergson's courses."

24   Léon Pierre-Quint, "Bergson et Proust," *Henri Bergson: Essais et témoignages recueillis*, eds. Albert Béguin and Pierre Thévenaz, (Neuchatel: La Baconnière, 1943) 328–340.

25   A full discussion of the various forms of memory in Proust's and Bergson's writing is presented in Chapter 5.

26   Discussed in Chapter 7.

27   Discussed in Chapter 7.

28   Françoise Fabre-Luce De Gruson, "Bergson et Proust." *Entretiens sur Marcel Proust*, eds. Georges Cattaui and Philip Kolb. (Paris: Moutons, 1966) 234–246.

29 This notion discussed in Chapter 5 suggest that some texts are not created by the writer, for they are to some extent endogenous in the mind of the reader, from which the author or writer evokes or liberates them. In that sense, the writer discovers rather than creates.

30 Marcel Proust à G. De Lauris in G. De Lauris, *A un ami, correspondance inédite*, 1903–1922, année 1910, document LXIV, (Amiot-Dumont, Paris, 1949) 205. Quoted in Bergson, ML, 1610.

31 Megay 15.

32 Marcel Proust, *Choix de lettres*, ed. Philip Kolb (Paris: Plon, 1965) 287.

33 The book "sur l'Allemand" to which Bergson refers is presumably Jacques Rivière's *L'Allemand: souvenirs et réflexions d'un prisonnier de guerre.* (Paris: Nouvelle Revue Française, 1918).

34 Megay 150.

35 Megay 149.

36 André Gide, *Journal 1889–1939* (Paris: Gallimard, Pléiade, 1939) 782–783.

37 Arthur S. Eddington, *New Pathways in Science* (Cambridge: Cambridge UP, 1935) 325.

38 A 'perfect gas' is one which obeys Boyle's and Charles' laws.

39 Ilya Prigogine and Isabelle Stengers, *Order out of Chaos* (New York: Bantam, 1984) 12.

40 Arthur S. Eddington, *The Nature of the Physical World* (Cambrige: Camridge UP, 1942) 103.

41 Blaise Pascal, *Oeuvres complètes* (Paris: Seuil, 1963) 576; fragments 512.

42 Marcel Raymond, 'Bergson et la poesie' *Henri Bergson: Essais et témoignages*, ed. Albert Béguin and Pierre Thévenaz (Neuchatel: La Baconnière, 1943) 286.

43 C.P. Snow, *The two Cultures* (1959; Cambridge: Cambridge UP, 1993)

44 Isaiah Berlin, *Against the Current,* ed. H. Hardy (New York: Viking. 1980) xxvi.

45 R. C. Grogin, *The Bergsonian Controversy in France 1900–1914* (Calgary: University of Calgary Press, 1988).

46 Thomas Huxley, "Science and Culture," *Essays: English and American*, ed. Charles W. Eliot (Danbury: Brolier, 1985) 218.

47 Anatole France, "La morale et la science," *Oeuvres complètes illustrées de Anatole France* V2, (Paris: Calmann-Lévy, 1949) 67–68.

48 France 256.

49   Camille Flammarion, *L'astronomie populaire* (Paris: Flammarion, 1920).

50   Magnificently illustrated by the art of Charlie Chaplin.

51   Bergson's analysis of the comic as *du mécanique plaqué sur du vivant* is also evident in humorous episodes of *À la recherche*, but has not been investigated in this study. It is, to some extent, examined by Léon Pierre-Quaint, "Le comique chez Proust," *Marcel Proust, sa vie, son oeuvre*, (Paris: Sagitaire, 1946) 269–312.

52   Steven J Dick. "Science or Antiscience," *Natural History* April, 1997: 6.

53   Pierre Ganne, "Bergson et Claudel," Béguin and Thévenaz, 294–310.

54   Henri Bergson, *Nouvelles annales mathématiques*, 17 (1878): 268–276.

55   Jean de la Harpe, "Souvenirs personnels d'un entretien avec Bergson," Béguin and Thévenaz 357.

56   Floris Delattre, *Ruskin et Bergson: de l'intuition esthétique à l'intuition métaphysique* (Oxford: Oxford UP, 1947) 14.

57   "Essai sur la métaphysique d'Aristote."

58   Presumably, Bergson is referring to the latter portion of Ravaisson's "Rapport sur les archives de l'Empire et sur l'organisation de la Bibliothèque impériale," which was published in 1862.

59   Issac Benrubi, "Entretien avec Bergson," Béguin and Thévenaz 369.

60   de la Harpe 358.

61   Grogin 20.

62   de la Harpe 358.

63   de la Harpe 359.

64   Grogin 15.

65   Claude Bernard, *Introduction à l'étude de la médecine expérimentale* (Paris: Delagrave, 1921) 57–59–61.

66   Bergson, PM 229–237.

67   Henri Poincaré, *Science et méthode*, (Paris: Flammarion, 1909) 15.

68   Poincaré 71–72.

Chapter 2

The Digital and the Analogic

. . . Il faut tout d'un coup voir la chose, d'un seul regard et non pas par progrès de raisonnement, . . et ainsi il est rare que les géomètres soient fins et que les fins soient géomètres,

Blaise Pascal[1]

The brain is adapted to create and maintain human society and culture by two complementary conscious systems, ... between the intuitive, on the one side, and the analytical or rational on the other.

Colwyn Trevarthen[2]

In view of the prominence of the 'digital and analog' taxonomy and method of coding in this study, it is perhaps helpful to devote a short chapter to the salient features of these terms, which may be considered as two complementary ways of viewing reality and our way of conceiving and communicating it. Although this terminology has become well known and familiar to us in connection with computer technology, the sense and importance given to these terms in this study has more affinity to the concepts of Blaise Pascal than to those of silicon chips and word processors. The digital–analogic taxonomy, like metaphor, reveals relationships, which perhaps would not otherwise be apparent, and by distinctly indicating the relationship one clarifies an otherwise confused affinity.

Definitions[3]

Digital
As an adjective, the words digit and digital come from the Latin *digitus*, for finger and *digitalis* of or belonging to a finger or for the size of a finger, and *digitus* gave rise to the French word *doigt*. The word was also used in arithmetic in England to designate a number inferior to ten, that is the numbers (1–9 and the cipher) one can count on the

fingers of two hands, thus it refers to digital numerals. The cardiac glycoside *digitalis* is extracted from ground leaves of the foxglove, the flowers of which resemble a digital glove. The term digital became associated with mechanical adding machines in the United States (1921) and later with machines using tape punched with holes and a beam of light impinging on a photocell. More recently the term has become associated with digital computers that operate through large numbers of 'on & off' electronic gates or switches, which can be represented digitally by "0" or "1" thus enabling information to be stored in binary form. As discussed below, a digital method of coding is not necessarily binary.

Analogic

The adjective analog and the possibly more correctly analogic derives from the Latin, *analogicus* and the corresponding Greek word *analogikos* which signifies "proportional" or more precisely 'relative to an analogy or which depends on an analogy.' Analogic means proportionate, analogous to, having analogy with or founded on analogy. The related word analogy refers to an agreement of likeness between things in some circumstances or effects, when the things are otherwise entirely different. More recently the word has been used to describe analog computers, which perform calculations by means of an analogy between real, physical continuous and measurable quantities (voltage, resistance, temperature) to solve problems by physical analogy. An analog computer (examples are given below) is based on continuous variables rather than the discrete, discontinuous quantities of the digital computer. There is, of course, some similarity between the digital–analogic opposition used here and some aspects of the philosophy of Hegel,[4] particularly his belief in the unreality of separateness. Reality in Hegel's view was not a collection of separate, completely independent units, atoms or objects. The apparent contiguity of finite things was an illusion, and nothing was real except the uninterrupted whole.

Examples of the Digital and the Analogic

Digital and analog watches and clocks are obvious examples time keeping instruments that use both representations. The analog watch (which is nevertheless essentially digital in its mechanism), derives its mode of representation of time from the truly analog time-keeping qualities of the sun-dial, where the movement of the shadow across the dial is an analogy of the continuous movement of the sun across the sky and of the earth around the sun. "Man was endowed by Nature with two clocks, one digital, one analog. Our heart beat, and the rotation of the roofing of the earth."[5]

The now obsolete slide-rule, in which lengths on the ruler are proportional to the logarithm of the numbers rather than to the number itself, is a simple but excellent example of an analog calculator; a map is an example of a representation by analogy and thus coded analogic, whereas a frontier or national border which marks a binary 'in or out' 'yes or no' separation is digital. Wilden[6] presents an extensive and helpful table of the properties of the digital and analog taxonomy.

It would be totally inappropriate to consider that the difference between the digital and analogic had to wait for the invention of the computer to become apparent or be utilized. In his excellent book *River out of Eden*, on the genetic code and Darwinian evolution, Richard Dawkins highlights the digital character of the information encoded in the double helix of DNA. He emphasizes that engineers make an important distinction between digital and analog codes. For example, phonographs, tape recorders, and until recently most telephones, use analog codes, whereas compact disks, computers and most modern telephone systems use digital codes. In a digital telephone, only two possible voltages, or other discrete number of possible voltages, pass down the wire. The information lies not in the voltages themselves but in the patterning of the discrete levels. All one has to do is set the discrete levels far enough apart so that random fluctuations can never be misinterpreted by the receiving instrument as the wrong level, and this is the great virtue of digital codes. He then continues:

> Francis Crick and James Watson, the unravelers of the molecular structure of the gene, should, I believe be honored for as many centuries as Aristotle and Plato. . . . What is truly revolutionary about molecular biology in the post-Watson-Crick era is that it has become digital. . . . we know that genes themselves, within their minute internal structure, are long strings of pure digital information . . . . Our genetic system, which is the universal system of all life on the planet, is digital to the core.[7]

Although the language of the nucleic acid[8] comprising the genetic code is purely digital,[9] the protein that is produced by the decoding and transfer of the information from the base-pair sequence into amino-acid chains is essentially analogic in nature, in that it is the three dimensional, qualitative and continuous topology and shape of the protein which accounts for its important biological properties. Thus at the most fundamental structure of living things, the digital–analogic taxonomy is not only present but critically important. In general the continuous, qualitative, subjective and intuitive may be coded analog whilst the discrete, discontinuous, quantitative, objective and logical is digital. The analog conceives of the totality, it synthesizes and integrates into a whole, and can have similarities to eidetic imagery[10] in which the entirety is perceived and understood, in contrast, the digital divides, sub-divides and analyses by pulverization.

Les deux esprits of Pascal

Two hundred years before the advent of Henri Bergson and his philosophy of insight and continuity, which places intuitive thought above that of logical analysis, and some three hundred years before the unraveling of the double helix of DNA and its digital code, Blaise Pascal clearly expounded on these two different types of reasoning and communication which reflect the digital–analogic taxonomy when he wrote of the "Différence entre l'esprit de géométrie et l'esprit de finesse":

> Mais dans l'esprit de finesse, les principes sont dans l'usage commun et devant les yeux de tout le monde. . . Mais ce qui fait que des géomètres ne sont pas fins, c'est qu'ils ne voient pas ce qui est devant eux, . . . ils se perdent dans les choses de finesse, où les principes ne se laissent pas ainsi manier. On les voit à peine, on les sent plutôt qu'on ne les voit, on a des peines infinies à les faire sentir à ceux qui ne les sentent pas d'eux-mêmes. Ce sont choses tellement délicates, . . . Il faut tout d'un **coup voir la chose, d'un seul regard et non pas par progrès de raisonnement.** Et ainsi il est rare que les géomètres soient fins et que les fins soient géomètres, à cause que les géomètres veulent traiter géométriquement ces choses fines et se rendent ridicules, voulant commencer par les définitions et ensuite par les principes, ce qui n'est pas la manière d'agir en cette sorte de raisonnement.
> . . . Car le jugement est celui à qui appartient le sentiment, comme les sciences appartiennent à l'esprit. La finesse est part du jugement, la géométrie est celle de l'esprit.[11] (my emphasis)

L'esprit de finesse is intuitive thought that sees the whole as a complete, and at times eidetic, entity, while judgment (between right and wrong) is the province of finesse. On the other hand, science is the province of geometry and logic. L'esprit de géométrie, of which Pascal speaks somewhat disparagingly, is the logical analytical approach that starts with the concepts, propositions and theorems and attempts to construct truth and reality. Pascal understood that intuition was the basis of *l'esprit de finesse*, which he regarded as superior to the *esprit de géométrie* when he wrote: "Instinct et raison marques de deux natures."[12] Perhaps we could paraphrase that into *intuition et raison marques des deux esprits*. For Pascal, as for Bergson, *L'esprit de finesse,* coded analogic, is superior to *l'esprit de géométrie,* coded digital.

Language and Tropes

Language is essentially a system of arbitrary signs, and a sign is a marker of information, an assemblage of codes. The 'signifier,'[13] is objective, impersonal, and (relatively) unambiguous and is thus coded digital. The 'signified' can be digital if it is mathematical or a simple object, but usually the 'signified' of a series of words is an image, somewhat ambiguous, personal and subjective, and thus coded analogic.

Metaphor[14] is a figure of speech founded on resemblance by which a word is transferred from an object to which it properly belongs to another in such a manner that a comparison is implied though not formally expressed. It is a similarity or comparison without an 'as' or 'like,' an analogy created by substituting word for word, image for image or sign for sign. It is the illumination[15] of one part of experience by another, and there is an element of continuity rather than contiguity in metaphor. The analogy is often not a logical one, but one that is grasped intuitively by seeing the whole. Thus, metaphor is related to *l'esprit de finesse* of Pascal, and is coded analogic.

Metonymy is a trope by which one word is put for another on account of some actual relation between the things signified. It is the evocation of the whole by a connection, and consists in substituting an attribute or other suggestive word for the name of the thing meant, the imputed relationship being that of contiguity. The connection in metonymy is a logical one and is related to Pascal's *esprit de géométrie,* thus metonymy is coded digital. Related to metonymy is synecdoche, a trope in which the part is substituted for the whole or the whole for the part, and synecdoche like metonymy is coded digital.

The Nervous System[16]

At the dawn of the computer age, von Neumann[17] gave an interesting account of the analogies between the functioning of the brain and artificial computing machines as well as the digital and analog parts of the nervous system. Whilst 'sensation' is essentially continuous and qualitative, the transmission of sensation via neurons is initially digital. The neuronal impulse is a depolarization or action potential that occur on an "all or none" basis. Action potentials are identical in *amplitude*, possessing only quantity, not quality, thus the intensity of a stimulus is translated as the *frequency* of identical digital stimuli. At a neuronal synapse or junction, however, there is release of chemical neurotransmitter that then activates other neurons or by negative feedback acts on the nerve ending releasing it. The neuronal transmission then becomes partially analog in that the amount of neurotransmitter released and thus the intensity (frequency) of further neuronal impulses depends on the presence of other (inhibitory) neurotransmitters as well as negative feed-back on the auto-receptor of the releasing axon. At the level of the central nervous system and consciousness, the nerve impulse and sensation become an intimate mixture of the digital and the analog.

Hemispheric Specialization[18]

The two sides of our cerebral cortex have very different functions, and the French physician Paul Broca concluded in 1861 that "the faculty for articulate language" resides in the left hemisphere.[19] In the 130 years that have elapsed since that time, Broca's conclusion has been confirmed by many kinds of evidence. The two cerebral hemispheres, linked one with the other via the *corpus callosum*, are not identical, and neurological and psychological research, carried out initially in patients with severe epilepsy, indicate that these two portions of the brain have fundamentally different ways of functioning or thinking. One of these cerebral hemispheres (usually the left) appears to be specialized in the area of language, grammar, numbers, mathematics and all matters that are linear and logical, furthermore aphasic brains almost always show lesions in the left hemisphere. This is the discursive side of the brain, and this type of thinking is coded digital. The other cerebral hemisphere, more often the right, thinks by a process that is essentially intuitive, non-logical (but not illogical), and non-verbal. It conceives of the entirety, of continuity of the whole, and tends to function essentially in symbols and images rather than verbal language, and this method of thinking is coded analogic. Normally we think by both means simultaneously, a thought rebounding via the *corpus callosum* from one hemisphere to the other. There is some evidence that neurological lesions to portions of the cortex lead to specific defects in the perception and expression of particular literary tropes.[20] However, it is becoming clear that untangling the relationship between linguistic theories and brain structures will not be simple.[21] From the point of view of this discussion, the essential point is the distinction between the two particular *types* of thinking rather than the anatomical distinction between right and left brain.

Chance and Necessity

The digital and analogical method of coding and classification can be applied to many biological systems. For example the chance and necessity of mutations and genetic replication are examples of the digital and analogic respectively, and as mentioned above the language of the genetic code is clearly digital, although quaternary rather than binary. The protein produced by transcription of the genetic code is a substance, which may be coded analogic and where continuity, shape and topology are important. A chance mutation whereby one letter in the genome is replaced by another is a digital, unpredictable (*le hasard*) event, and is a mathematical discontinuity.[22] Chance is followed by necessity, the analogic continuity, and the altered protein, which inevitably results from that digital mutation. Necessity as a result of chance is the analogic created because of the digital change.

Bergson's Philosophy

As is discussed in the following chapters, the majority of the major topics investigated by Bergson, such as time, memory, self and thought, are described in his philosophy as existing in binaries, furthermore one element of these binary pairs is coded digital and the other analogic. The analogic is in Bergson's view always superior to the digital, and in Chapters 3 & 5, I discuss the origin of this recurrent binary opposition in Bergson's philosophy. Bergson does not, of course, use the terms digital and analogic, but his discussion of *l'analyse et l'intuition* discussed in Chapters 5, are very comparable to the digital and the analogic and resemble Pascal's two *esprits*. Perhaps even closer to the digital–analogic taxonomy, is his distinction between two kinds of multiplicity: the quantitative, discontinuous, and homogenous multiplicity, coded digital, and the qualitative, continuous, and heterogenous multiplicity coded analog:

. . . la multiplicité des états de conscience, envisagée dans sa pureté originale, ne présente aucune ressemblance avec la multiplicité distincte qui forme un nombre. Il y aurait là, disions-nous, une multiplicité qualitative. Bref, il faudrait admettre deux espèces de multiplicité, deux sens possibles du mot distinguer, deux conceptions, l'une qualitative et l'autre quantitative, de la différence entre le *même* et l'*autre*. Tantôt cette multiplicité, cette distinction, cette hétérogénéité ne contiennent le nombre qu'en puissance, . . . c'est que la conscience opère une discrimination qualitative sans aucune arrière-pensée de compter les qualités ou même d'en faire *plusieurs*; il y a bien alors multiplicité sans quantité. (DI, 90.)

Perhaps the image of *The Abacus and the Rainbow,* can represent metaphorically a quantitative, homogenous, digital multiplicity on one hand, and a qualitative, heterogenous, analogic multiplicity on the other, symbols which are themselves representative of two manners we have of thinking and of analyzing reality.

Notes

1   Blaise Pascal, *Oeuvres complètes* (Paris: Seuil, 1963) 576.

2   Colwyn Trevarthen, "The Split-Brain and the Mind," *The Oxford Companion to the Mind*, ed. Richard L. Gregory, (Oxford: Oxford UP, 1987) 740–747.

3   Alain Rey, *Dictionnaire Historique de la Langue Française* (Paris: Dictionnaires le Robert, 1978).

4   Bertrand Russell, *A History of Western Philosophy* (New York: Simon and Schuster, 1972) 730–745.

5   Julian B Barbour, "The Discovery of Dynamics," *Absolute or Relative Motion* vol. 1 (Cambridge: Cambridge UP, 1989) 42.

6   Anthony Wilden, *System and Structure* (London: Tavistock, 1972) 191–195.

7   Richard Dawkins, *River out of Eden: A Darwinian View of Life* (New York: Basic Books, 1995) 16–17.

8   James D. Watson, *The Double Helix*, (New York: New American Library 1968).

9   Although the information in the double helix of DNA is digital, it is not in a binary but a quaternary code, with each of the purine (adenine and guanine) and pyrimidine (cytosine and thymine) bases forming a symbol and the sequence of three of these designating a particular amino-acid.

10 Designating mental images that are unusually vivid and almost photographically exact. Eidetic imagery is said to have a more richly pictorial quality than other images. See: Paul A Kolers, "Imaging," *The Oxford Companion to the Mind*, ed. Richard L. Gregory, (Oxford: Oxford UP, 1987) 354.

11 Pascal, 576; fragments 512 & 513.

12 Pascal 112.

13 Ferdinand de Saussure, *Cours de linguistique générale* (1916; Paris: Payot & Rivages, 1995).

14 Andrew Ortony, ed. *Metaphor and Thought*, 2nd ed. (Cambridge: Cambridge UP, 1993).

15 Anthony Wilden, *The Rules are no Game* (London & New York: Routledge & Kegan Paul, 1987) 196.

16 Robert M., Berne, and Matthew N. Levy, eds. *Physiology*, (St. Louis & Toronto: C.V. Mosby, 1983).

17   John von Neumann, *The Computer and the Brain,* (New Haven: Yale UP, 1958) 66.

18   Joseph B Hellige, *Hemispheric Asymmetry: What's Right and What's Left.* (Cambridge: Harvard UP, 1993).

19   Steven Pinker, *The Language Instinct* (New York: William Morrow, 1994) 299.

20   Roman Jakobson, "Two Aspects of Language and Two Types of Aphasic Disturbances," *Fundamentals of Language,* Roman Jakobson and Morris Halle, eds. ('S-Gravenhage: Mouton, 1956) 55–82.

21   David Howard, & Brian Lewis Butterworth. "Neurolinguistics," *The Oxford Companion to the Mind* ed. Richard L Gregory, (Oxford: Oxford UP, 1987) 539.

22   Jacques Monod, *Le hasard et la nécessité,* (Paris: Seuil, 1970).

Chapter 3

Thinking Backwards

*Nous connaissons la vérité, non seulement par la raison, mais encore par
le coeur. . .*

Pascal[1]

*D'un être qui est durée, d'une durée qui est changement, se tisse l'étoffe
de nous-mêmes, l'étoffe de l'univers.*

Thibaudet[2]

Montaigne and Bergson

In September 1559, Montaigne was at Bar-le-Duc in Lorraine and
saw François-II receive a miniature portrait of one of his nobles. He
juxtaposes in his mind the image of the painting and that of a text and
ponders on the difference and similarities between the painted analogic
image and the written digital word, between *la chose* and *le mot*. He
writes:

> Je vis un jour à Bar-le-Duc, qu'on présentait au Roi François second, pour la
> recommandation de la mémoire de René, Roi de Sicile, un portrait qu'il avait
> lui-même fait de soi. Pourquoi n'est-il loisible de même à un chacun de se
> peindre de la plume comme il se peignait d'un crayon?[3]

Painting with words rather than with paint is precisely what
Montaigne does. He portrays in digital language the image of himself,
of his most inner thoughts, doubts and questions. So also does Henri
Bergson. Montaigne refers to the use of a pictorial representation rather
than linear words to stimulate memory and communicate attention.
Bergson does the same. The resemblance between the two philosophers is more than superficial, for both were attempting to describe,
in digital language, thoughts that were probably not verbal in the first

instance, and they both interpret what is perhaps best described as analogic, non-verbal thoughts into words. Both philosophers made extensive use of metaphors and images in their writings and it is likely that both thought to a great extent in imagery, in non-verbal form and subsequently had the task of accurately translating those images into text. Montaigne, like Bergson, was a man attentive to his interior self: ". . . qui le sent couler, qui sait que par cette durée il existe."[4] Bergson and Montaigne widen the binary of *les mots* and *les choses* to encompass the continuous triangle of words, objects and thoughts, and we will again have occasion to contrast the congruence in the thoughts of these two great French philosophers and writers.

* * *

This Chapter will summarize the method used by Bergson to develop his philosophy which is essentially an exploration and description of the qualitative essence of reality as opposed to the quantitative elements described by the physical sciences. This approach leads to a dualism and opposition between the quantitative and the qualitative, the digital and the analogic, that pervades all of Bergson's thought, such that the major elements of his philosophy which we shall discuss in Chapter 5, time, memory, being and thought occur in digital–analogic binaries, and in Bergson's philosophy, the analogic enantiomer of these elements is always the superior.

The Essence of Bergson

Bergson's philosophy was a reaction against the scientific positivism and the determinism that resulted from the outstanding success of Newtonian mathematics and physics. The tradition of Western philosophy in which Bergson was immersed and schooled was one in which 'ultimate reality,' that which we perceive with our senses, is timeless and basically unchanging. It was a reality that could only be studied by logic and science which analyzed its content and often described it mathematically. It was thus an objective and quantitative universe described in linear, quantitative and digital language. In addition, being an objective reality, it was one in which the 'observer' was absent from the actuality being studied. Bergson developed a philosophy which was based on the qualitative and continuous rather than the quantitative and discontinuous and in which the subjective is an integral and necessary part. The starting point for Bergson's philosophy was his reflection on the nature of time and movement and the difference in our subjective intuitive awareness of time as distinct from that described in the physical sciences. When Bergson entered l'École Normale Supérieure in 1878 he was keenly interested in the philosophy of Herbert Spencer which along with the philosophy of Kant dominated French universities at that period.[5] Kant discusses the notion of time in his *Critique of Pure Reason*; however for Kant,[6] time was not an empirical concept deduced from any experience: the representation of time was something given *a priori* a pure form of sensuous intuition, the form of the internal sense, and a necessary representation on which all intuition depends. Bergson was particularly interested in Spencer's work and aspired to improve on his philosophy but was struck by how the concept of time in Spencer's writings as well as in dynamics and physics ignored the notion of duration. Bergson gives us some insight into the beginnings of his philosophy, when in *La pensée et le mouvant* he writes:

> La philosophie de Spencer visait à prendre l'empreinte des choses et à se modeler sur le détail des faits. . . Nous sentions bien la faiblesse des *Premiers Principes*, . . . Nous aurions voulu reprendre cette partie de son oeuvre, la compléter et la consolider. Nous nous y essayâmes dans la mesure de nos forces. C'est ainsi que nous fûmes conduit devant l'idée de Temps. Là, une surprise nous attendait. (PM 2)

The surprise was the realization that scientific and mathematical time is one without duration, but merely a succession of markers. He elaborates on this 'discovery' in a letter written in 1908 to the American psychologist and philosopher, William James:

> Ce fut l'analyse de la notion de temps, telle qu'elle intervienne en mécanique ou en physique, qui bouleversa toutes mes idées. Je m'aperçus, à mon grand étonnement, que le temps scientifique ne *dure* pas, qu'il n'y aurait rien à changer à notre connaissance scientifique des choses, si la totalité du réel était déployée tout d'un coup dans l'instantané, et que la science positive consiste essentiellement dans l'élimination de la durée. (ML 766)

In the introduction to his recent book on Bergson, Moore states: "Bergson did what philosophers are not supposed to do. He questioned the primacy of human reason."[7] For the Bergsonian notion of pure time is not obtained by logic and reason, but rather by intuitive contemplation; it is one of the *données immédiates de la conscience,* as distinct from Kant's notion of time as an *a priori* form of sensibility.[8] From Bergson's viewpoint, the time of Newtonian physics is essentially a *dead* time, one without the essence of the continuous indivisible motion which is pure duration. Direction was also absent from Newtonian time and although the introduction of the concept of entropy and the second law of thermodynamics by Clausius (1822–1888) and Boltzmann (1844–1906) gave a direction to time, the element of 'duration' was still absent.

The essence of Bergson's methodology is thus found in the subjective and personal, in what is alive and constantly changing. In contrast, access to reality in Newtonian science and 19th century philosophy was through reason, logic, and analysis. In the nomenclature of the digital-analogic taxonomy, it was a digital science. Bergson's approach was diametrically opposite to this, for he considered that access to reality and truth could be through intuition, in the same manner that we have intuitive knowledge of duration and of our own existence and of our inner Self,[9] and he considered that inutition was infallible and superior to logic.

Throughout Bergson's writing there is a duality and opposition between the logical and the intuitive, an opposition, that can be coded as one between the digital and the analogic. As discussed in Chapter 1, this opposition was expounded by Blaise Pascal (1623–1662), is found in the philosophy of Thomas Aquinas (1225–1274) and possibly goes back to Greek philosophy. Bergson rejected the primacy of the logical approach and replaced it with the intuitive, which for Bergson, was a form of sympathy, a sort of union or fusion of self and thought with the subject under study. Intuitive thought is not logical, although clearly not illogical, it is identity of self with the essence of reality, and it grasps concepts from within and thus (according to Bergson) absolutely. Intuition is: ". . . la *sympathie* par laquelle on se transporte à l'intérieur d'un objet pour coïncider avec ce qu'il a d'unique et par conséquent d'inexprimable" (PM 181). The reverse of intuition is what Bergson calls *l'analyse*, which is perhaps the closest he approaches to the concept of the digital and of digitalization. *L'analyse* is the process of dissection, of pulverizing, of studying the parts and from them attempting to reconstruct and perceive the whole. "L'analyse est l'opération qui ramène l'objet à des éléments déjà connus, c'est-à-dire communs à cet objet et à d'autres. Analyser consiste donc à exprimer une chose en fonction de ce qui n'est pas elle" (PM 181). In *La pensée et le mouvant*, Bergson illustrates the difference between *l'analyse* and *l'intuition* by discussing the knowledge we might obtain of a town or village. We could for example, obtain detailed analytical knowledge of a town by studying a series of maps or photographs, which would give an excellent rational description of the streets and buildings. It would, however, be knowledge that is very different from the (internal) knowledge, the *sympathie* of that village or town obtained by strolling through its streets and contemplating its buildings and public places. This example illustrates two different types of understanding, two distinct levels of knowing and two contrasting forms of awareness. One form is analytical and external while the other is perception of the wholeness from within, and an example of the analogical perception of the essence of reality. The notion of *l'analyse et l'intuition* in art and artistic creation is discussed in Chapter 7.

Bergsonian Dualism

The dualism, the series of binary oppositions, which are inherent in, and pervades the entirety of Bergsonian philosophy, is an opposition between *l'intuition*, as opposed to *l'analyse*, between intuitional truth and the logical and rational, between the analogic and the digital. Bergson also defines these two realities in another manner for he says one reality is homogenous and the reality of quantity, of homogenous space in which imaginary bodies may be lined up and counted. This is the reality of quantity, of mass, and a reality in which bodies obey physical laws. However, there is another reality that is radically different in essence, a reality that is heterogeneous yet continuous, and in which elements do not obey physical laws, for they are not quantity but *quality*. This is the reality of self, thought and pure duration, of interpenetrating distinct yet continuous ideas and moments which in Proust's novel is symbolized by the continuous, eternal motion and change of the multitudinous seas, that all-pervading element which Proust creates and describes at Balbec. Since (Euclidean) space, is by definition, homogenous, time cannot exist in this space: "Car, l'homogénéité consistant ici dans l'absence de toute qualité, on ne voit pas comment deux formes de l'homogène se distinguerait l'une de l'autre" (DI 73). Thus, there are two different manners of viewing reality, one through quantitative and digital science, and the other through intuitive, analogic almost contemplative metaphysics:

> Bien différente est la relation que nous établissons entre la métaphysique et la science. L'une et l'autre portent sur la réalité même. Mais chacune n'en retient

que la moitié, de sorte qu'on pourrait voir en elles, à volonté, deux subdivision de la science ou deux départements de la métaphysique, si elles ne
marquaient des directions divergentes de l'activité de la pensée . . . Laissez-
leur, au contraire, des objects différents, à la science la matière et à la
métaphysique l'esprit. (PM 43–44)

Bergson also speaks of two form of the absolute and succinctly summarizes this opposition when he writes: "Et l'intelligence est dans le
vraie tant qu'elle s'attache . . . à la matérialité. Elle touche alors une
des côtés de l'absolu, comme notre conscience en touche un autre
. . . (PM, 104). Gilles Deleuze, expresses a similar thought when he
writes that: "la science est de l'ontologie, c'est une des deux moitiés
de l'ontologie."[10] Ontology is the knowledge of what is or exists, and
thus of the being within ourselves as well as of the universe outside
ourselves. Half of ontology is the physical and the quantitative universe external to the observer, while the other half of ontology is the
qualitative universe perceived intuitively as knowledge gained from
within, in the same manner as knowledge of Bergson's village is gained
from 'knowing' it and not by analyzing it, but as Bergson says: "Tout
le monde à remarquer qu'il est plus malaisé d'avancer dans la
connaissance de soi que dans celle du monde extérieur" (PM 40–41).

Although Bergson's philosophy is one of intuitive thought and duration, it may also be depicted as a philosophy of movement, for it is
a metaphysics of becoming rather than of static being, and permeat-
ing Bergson's ideas are those of the uninterrupted flow of time and
the continuous stream of inter-permeating thought, of the ceaseless
evolution of self which is "la création de soi par soi." It is the philosophy of *l'élan vital, le courant de la vie, le mouvement rétrograde
du vrai,* the oscillation between intuition and logic, between the duality of self, and the movement towards and into intuition by the process of 'thinking backward,' for: "Philosopher consiste à invertir la
direction habituelle du travail de la pensée" (PM 214).

Thinking Backwards

The methodology and language used by Bergson in developing his
philosophy of intuition as opposed to science and which he uses to
explore the qualitative essence of reality has affinities with the Proustian
method and as Michel Serres says: "Le succès immense du bergsonisme
a tenu à ceci qu'il partageait sans trembler les performances de la
Science, de l'Intelligence et de la pratique, de celles de l'intuition, de

l'instinct, de la Métaphysique."[11] Bergson's methodology is clearly discerned in his first major work, the *Essai sur les données immédiates de la conscience*, and although his language is often logical and scientific, and his conclusions border on those of psychology, his methodology was clearly *not* scientific. He did not carry out double-blind clinical trials with a population of subjects, nor did he develop a psychological survey to be distributed widely in order to obtain insight on people's method of thought and introspection, nor did he dissect and study the functions of the central or peripheral nervous system to study the mechanism of memory or that of sensation flowing into perception. Occasionally he does refer to scientific or psychological texts to support his arguments, but this is an exception rather than the rule. An essential criterion of the scientific method is that data and conclusions must be reproducible, and perhaps what is reproducible in Bergson's philosophy is the congruence of (some of) his reader's thought processes with Bergson's own, that his readers may follow Bergson's argument and arrive at the same conclusion. Nevertheless, in the absence of scientific verification, what is the Authority that Bergson invokes to support and give credence to his arguments, to separate the truth from the false? The Bergsonian method consists in interrogating his consciousness, his inner self, and at the same time questioning the consciousness of his reader or listener. He examines his consciousness and at the same time our consciousness, the mind of us, his readers, and perhaps he flatters us by assuming that our consciousness, our mind is similar to his, and that *les données immédiates de* sa *conscience* are the same as *les données immédiates de* notre *conscience*. For Bergson, the distinction between what is true and what is false is obtained primarily through intuition, and his Authority is intuition, *les données immédiates de la conscience,* and for Bergson, intuition is a highly refined form of common sense which is innate in all of us and does not have to be learned like logical analysis. He draws an interesting parallel between the insight of common sense and the intuition of genius when he writes:

Il y a un subtil pressentiment du vrai et du faux, qui a pu découvrir entre les choses, bien avant la preuve rigoureuse ou l'expérience décisive, des incompatibilités secrètes ou des affinités insoupçonnées. On appelle génie cette intuition d'ordre supérieur, intuition nécessairement rare. . . Mais la vie de tous les jours demande à chacun de nous, des solutions aussi nettes et des décisions aussi rapides. . . L'autorité que nous invoquons alors, celle qui lève nos hésitations et tranche la difficulté, c'est le bon sens. Il semble donc que le bon sens soit dans la vie pratique, ce que le génie est dans les sciences et dans les arts. (ML 361)

Although Bergson decried the determinism of Cartesian logic, his method has some resemblance to that of Descartes, who also placed great importance on '*le bon sens*': "Le bon sens est la chose du monde la mieux partagée: . . . la puissance de bien juger, et distinguer le vrai d'avec le faux, qui est proprement ce qu'on nomme le bon sens où la raison est naturellement égale en tous les homme."[12] In a similar vein, in the opening lines of his incisive study of *Le bergsonisme*, Gilles Deleuze writes:

> L'intuition est la méthode du bergsonisme. L'intuition n'est pas un sentiment ni une inspiration, une sympathie confuse, mais une méthode élaborée, et même une des méthodes les plus élaborées de la philosophie. Elle a ses règles strictes, qui constituent ce que Bergson appelle "la précision" en philosophie.[13]

Vieillard-Baron[14] disagrees with this and considers that "il serait tout à fait faux de prétendre que l'intuition est la méthode du bergsonisme". By this he means, not that intuition is irrelevant, but rather that Bergson's method is not one of intuition in isolation. What then is this intuition, this stroke of genius that Bergson invokes to find truth? It is: "une image fuyante et évanouissante qui hante, inaperçue peut-être, l'esprit du philosophe, qui le suit comme son ombre à travers les tours et détours de sa pensée," (PM 119–120). It is characterized by "la puissance de négation qu'elle porte en elle . . . elle souffle à l'oreille du philosophe le mot: *impossible*" (120). For Thibaudet, the authority in Bergson's philosophy is in the intuition we have of our own consciousness of our Being. "La source de la certitude est dans l'intuition que nous avons de notre être."[15] Again we have a similarity with Cartesian philosophy, for both commence with a realization of the truth of internal experience. "I am a thing with duration" was for Bergson the equivalent of Descartes' *cogito*, "I am a being which thinks,"[16] for a flowing movement of continuous change is an essential feature of Bergsonism. Following the same thought, Thibaudet writes: "M. Bergson dirait volontiers: 'Je pense, donc je change,'" and, "Le changement est donné dans l'acte élémentaire de la pensée."[17]

Inherent in the development of Bergson's philosophy by use of intuitive thinking are two important, related, and almost insurmountable difficulties that stem from the fact that, according to Bergson, intuitive, analogic, thought is non-verbal, it is what Pinker[18] calls 'mentalese.' The first of these difficulties is that, the process of focusing or concentrating on intuitive thought inevitably leads to the concept being changed and resolved into non-intuitive and verbal notions which are not identical to the original intuitive concept: "Dès qu'on cherchera à se rendre compte d'un état de conscience, à l'analyser, cet état éminemment personnel se résoudra en éléments impersonnels, extérieurs les uns aux autres, dont chacun évoque l'idée d'un genre et s'exprime par un mot" (DI 123). The second, and related difficulty, is that in order to communicate these intuitive and non-verbal ideas to pupils or colleagues, one necessarily has to use linear, digital language which itself will alter the original non-verbal thought. In particular, the use of precise, scientific language to express abstract and intuitive ideas can be misleading:

> Si l'on parlait constamment un langage abstrait, soi-disant "scientifique", on ne donnerait de l'esprit que son imitation par la matière, car les idées abstraites ont été tirées du monde extérieur et impliquent toujours une représentation spatiale: et pourtant on croirait avoir analysé l'esprit. (PM 42)

Nevertheless, Bergson overcame these difficulties brilliantly and to do this, he made extensive use of verbal imagery rather than scientific language.[19] He apparently distinguished between two kinds of images, those to help his own thinking and to test the validity of his conclusions, and the images to be used in communication to others.[20] It is unfortunate that Bergson does not give us examples of images of the former kind, for images, he says may give an indirect perception of intuition, a shadow of reality, which the skillful writer can use to communicate something of these notions: ". . . et par cela même qu'il déroule notre sentiment dans un temps homogène et en exprime les éléments par des mots, il ne nous présente qu'une ombre à son tour: seulement il a disposé cette ombre de manière à nous faire soupçonner la nature extraordinaire et illogique de l'objet qui la projette" (DI 99–100).[21] In the introduction to the *Essai* Bergson says: "nous pensons le plus souvent dans l'espace," and clearly, any images described in metaphor, are of objects in space. But how can one communicate a non-spatial concept such as pure duration by the use of spatial images? Bergson progresses and arrives at this through a dialectic, an oscillation between the intuitive notion and the image or verbal equivalent and by successive approximations arriving at language or imagery that, as nearly as possible, correctly communicates or suggests that intuitive notion.

The Dialectic between Intuitive and Verbal Thought[22]

A thought which is not expressed, or which cannot be expressed in words is not a very valuable one, and Bergson's genius lay not only in his ability to expand philosophical concepts but also in having the literary gift of translating and expressing these complex philosophical thoughts into simple language without complex jargon: "Il n'y rien en philosophie" he said, "qui ne puisse se dire dans la langue de tout le monde" (ML 939), and Michel Serres refers to Bergson's simple language as: "un assemblage ingénieux de mots usuels."[23] Bergson emphasizes that we need to express our intuitive, analogic ideas in digital words, for it is only then that the idea will crystallize and be clear enough to be inspected and studied to ensure that it is true:[24] "La dialectique est nécessaire pour mettre l'intuition à l'épreuve, nécessaire aussi pour que l'intuition se réfracte en concepts et se propage à d'autres hommes . . . la dialectique est ce qui assure l'accord de notre pensée avec elle-même." (EC 239). This dialectic between intuitive and verbal thought, is a dialectic between the analogic and the digital, and in an extraordinary passage in *L'évolution créatrice*, Bergson describes his method of using both intuitive and logical thought in the development of his philosophy and gives clearer insight into the two types of thinking required by his method. The use of intuitive thought is not a haphazard or easy method, and a philosophy which is constructed on intuition is characterized above all by hard work and intense intellectual exertion because it requires effort which is in a direction opposite to that of normal thought: "Effort douloureux, que nous pouvons donner brusquement en violentant la nature, mais non pas soutenir au delà de quelques instants" (EC 238). He describes the continuous dialectic between intuition and logic that his method necessitates:

> Le philosophe est obligé d'abandonner l'intuition une fois qu'il en a reçu l'élan, et de se fier à lui-même pour continuer le mouvement, . . . Mais bien vite il sent qu'il a perdu pied; un nouveau contact devient nécessaire; il faudrait défaire la plus grande partie de ce qu'on avait fait. En résumé, la dialectique est ce qui assure l'accord de notre pensée avec elle-même. Mais par la dialectique,—qui n'est qu'une détente de l'intuition,—bien des accords différents sont possibles, et il n'y a pourtant qu'une vérité. L'intuition, si elle pouvait se prolonger au delà de quelques instants, n'assurerait pas seulement l'accord du philosophe avec sa propre pensée, mais encore celui de tous les philosophes entre eux. (EC 239)

These two processes of thinking intuitively and logically are in opposite directions one from the other. The labor of normal thought is easy and can continue almost indefinitely. But working through intuition is difficult and has limited duration, (PM 31), for philosophizing involves reversing the normal processes of thinking, it consists of, so to speak, thinking backwards (PM 214). The process of linking one idea to another, placing them in juxtaposition and contiguity leads to the disappearance of intuitive thought. The philosopher can commence his thought process with intuition, but soon he is compelled to abandon it. He then must develop the idea using logic and verbal thought and compare the result with intuition again. The insight of intuitive thought lasts only for a few moments before disappearing in the glare of logical analysis, but if the result of logic contradicts that of intuition, then the logical conclusion has to be abandoned, for *les données immédiates de la conscience* are infallible. Throughout, language is an obstacle to struggle with and overcome because of its constrictive effect on intuitive thought. A continuous oscillation, then is necessary between intuitive reality and logical language: "La pensée sociale . . . Est-elle intelligence ou intuition? Je veux bien que l'intuition y fasse filtrer sa lumière: il n'y a pas de pensée sans esprit de finesse, et l'esprit de finesse est le reflet de l'intuition dans l'intelligence" (PM 87).

The dialectic between these two methods of thinking was developed to a studied art by Bergson. In a discussion at a meeting of *La Société Française de Philosophie* in 1909, one of the participants asked Bergson whether he agrees that intuitive thought does not necessarily exclude discursive and analytical thinking. Bergson's reply illustrates the laborious work entailed in the use of his 'intuitive philosophy':

> . . . cette manière de saisir le réel ne nous est plus naturelle dans l'état actuel de notre pensée; pour l'obtenir, nous devons donc, le plus souvent, nous y préparer par une lente et consciencieuse analyse, nous familiariser avec tous les documents qui concernent l'objet de notre étude . . . une connaissance scientifique et précise des faits est la condition préalable de l'intuition métaphysique qui en pénètre le principe. (ML 797)

The effort of intuition such as experienced in Bergson's philosophy, the march towards the inner vision, the exertion which is *pénible, mais précieux*, supersedes normal pleasure and pain. Perhaps, writes Thibaudet,[25] the resulting achievement is like the joys of child-birth! Here then is yet another form of Bergsonian movement; movement between the inner self of intuitive thought, and the logical self who writes.

The Source of Bergsonian Dualism

What is the source of the dualism that, as we shall see, pervades Bergson's philosophy, why is there a digital–analogic opposition that permeates his entire metaphysics, and why is the analogic element always dominant? The answer is, I think, related to Bergson's notion and discovery of 'pure time' and his incorporation and elaboration of this to other philosophical questions. It was, as we have mentioned, the absence of duration in Spencer's notion of time that made Bergson pause and reflect on the nature of duration, and led him to his philosophy of the difference between scientific or digital time and *la durée pure*. This distinction between the two forms of time seems to have been the starting point for much of his other philosophical notions. For in discussion with Jean de la Harpe, he says that when considering a new philosophical question: "Je me plonge dans la méditation d'un problème, je pars de la "durée" et je cherche à éclairer ce problème, soit par contraste, soit par similitude avec elle." Thus, it would seem that the dualism that Bergson 'discovered' between digital or spatial time and the continuous analogic conception of *'la durée pure'* is the starting point of much of his philosophy and the origin of the dichotomy that permeates all its important concepts. For very basic to Bergsonian philosophy is the notion that if you wish to know reality, you must immerse yourself in the flux of pure duration, and from the notion of the two forms of time there emerges intuitively the two forms of thought and the two forms of self. One form lives in spatial digital time and is concerned with the materialistic aspects of the external and immediate world, whilst the other form of self, of consciousness exists in the real analogic duration, the continuity that is reality but that is only experienced in the innermost of Bergson's *deux aspects du moi*. The two forms of memory, the continuous or analogic form that is involuntary and the digital voluntary form that resides in the present, is perhaps somewhat different in origin, but these dual forms of memory clearly have a similar derivation.

In *Le rire*, Bergson extends this dualism to society as a whole. On the one hand there is the society of reason and habit that deals with the materialistic necessities of life, the quiet humdrum life that reason and society have fashioned for us and which form an outer crust to the personality. But beneath that crust there exists the true self of the individual, the true essence of being which possesses free-will. As discussed in Chapter 5, these two forms of society and the two forms of that self are clearly seen in Proust's great novel as the opposition between the internal and creative self of the hero and the snobbish society that the superficial self frequents. Again, the dominance of the analogic form resides in the superiority of true duration as distinct from spatialised and digitalised time that is perceived in the immediate material world.

Bergson's success with this dualism led him in later life to expand his philosophy to morality and religion in *Les deux sources de la morale et de la religion*. This, Bergson's last published work, has not been analyzed in this dissertation and it does not appear to have direct relevance to Proust's *À la recherche*; however, in order to indicate the pervasiveness of Bergson's digital to analogic dichotomy, it should be pointed out that this Bergsonian dualism is also present in *Les deux sources*, albeit in slightly modified form. The two forms of society Bergson describes are one where, at the superficial level, habit social discipline, and the automatic mechanization predominate, whilst the *real* society is that ruled by open love and charity. The two forms of morality are those of social discipline, habit, and the automatic on the one hand, and the natural expression of freedom and charity, on the other. The two forms of religion may briefly be described as the dogmatic and ritualistic (digital) elements of traditional faith as opposed to the open (analogic) and mystical expression of the human mind and heart.

Notes

1   Blaise Pascal, *Oeuvres complètes* (Paris: Seuil, 1963). 512, fragment 110.

2   Albert Thibaudet, *Le bergsonisme* vol.1 (Paris: Nouvelle Revue Française, 1923) 30.

3   Michel de Montaigne, *Essai* vol. II (Paris: Gallimard, 1965) 413.

4   Thibaudet I. 23.

5   Jean Millet, "Bergsonian Epistemology and its Origins in Mathematical Thought," *Bergson and Modern Thought: Towards a unifed science*, ed. Andrew C. Papanicolau and Pete A.Y. Gunter (London: Harwood, 1987) 29–37.

6   Immanuel Kant, *Selections*, ed. Theodore Meyer Greene (New York: Scribner's. 1929) 50.

7   F. C. T. Moore, *Bergson: Thinking Backwards*, (Cambridge: Cambridge UP, 1996) 1.

8   Madeleine Barthélemy-Madaule, *Bergson adversaire de Kant* (Paris: PUF, 1966).

9   Eric Matthews, *Twentieth-Century French Philosophy* (Oxford: Oxford UP, 1966).

10 Gilles Deleuze, *Le bergsonisme* (Paris: PUF, 1966) 27.

11 Michel Serres, *Hermès IV: la distribution* (Paris: Minuit, 1977) 129.

12 René Descartes, *Discours de la méthode* (Paris: GF-Flammarion, 1966) 23.

13 Deleuze, *Bergsonisme* 1.

14 Jean-Louis Vieillard-Baron, *Bergson* (Paris: PUF, 1993) 101.

15 Thibaudet I, 197.

16 Thibaudet I, 29.

17 Thibaudet I, 29.

18 Steven Pinker, *The Language Instinct* (New York: William Morrow, 1994) 55.

19 Bergson's use of language is discussed in detail in Chapter 6.

20 Lydie Adolphe, *La dialectique des images chez Bergson* (Paris: PUF, 1951) 7.

21   The full quotation is given in Chapter 6.

22   A clear failure of Bergson's intuitive method is his totally erroneous criticism of Einstein's special theory of relativity, which Bergson elaborates in *Durée et simultanéité* (1923, Paris: PUF, 1968). Bergson's error arose because some of Einstein's results, although empirically correct, were counter-intuitive. For an excellent and recent discussion of this, see Alan Sokal and Jean Bricmont, *Impostures intellectuelles*, (Paris: Odille Jacob, 1997), 165–178.

23   Michel Serres, *Éloge de la philosophie en langue française* (Paris: Fayard, 1995) 195.

24   See also the extraordinary passage "Bergson's demon" (ES 22) quoted in Chapter 7, p. 214.

25   Thibaudet I, 180.

Chapter 4

Sesame or the Essence of Proust

Sésame, la parole magique . . . l'allégorie de la lecture qui nous ouvre la porte de ces trésors où est enfermée la plus précieuse sagesse des hommes.

Proust[1]

The analogical is the ontological.

Kristeva[2]

For Marcel Proust, certain words, particularly proper names, possess an enchanting and almost magical quality which, like 'Sesame', have the power of opening the charmed doors of creative imagination into worlds of countless riches resonant with sounds, perfumes, memories and desires. In contrast, according to Henri Bergson words can destroy and distort original non-verbal thought and reduce original ideas to the generic and commonplace. In the same way as Bergson's philosophy may be described as the exploration and description of the 'qualitative essence of reality,' so Proust's novel may be read as the search for and ultimately discovery of the analogic essence of reality, of *l'essence qualitative des choses* or *l' essence qualitative des sensations*. In the Proustian universe, as in that of Bergson, reality is of a dual nature, qualitative and quantitative, and Proust like Bergson, emphasize repeatedly that the true essence of reality cannot be acquired or discovered by logic and intelligence. For Bergson, reality is discovered through *les données immédiates de la conscience*, but for Proust these perceptions of reality are what he calls *impressions* and *l'essence*. Thus, the narrator's vocation may be described as the recreation of this analogical reality which he achieves by building bridges that create continuity and unity; a bridge with memory, a bridge with time, a connection with words, a link through metaphor. In *L'évolution créatrice* Bergson puts forward his ideas of life as continual and sometimes imperceptible change, of creation of self by self in the continuous ebb of Bergsonian time. This is depicted in *À la recherche*, where one sees the evolution and change of the characters from their early days at Balbec and Combray to their reappearance in somewhat metamorphosed nature, in the *matinée chez la princesse de Guermantes*. These are the points to be explored and discussed in this chapter, and we shall see that the digital–analogic opposition that pervades Bergson's philosophy is also present in Proust's work, although in a very different form.

* * *

The Quest for *l'essence des choses*

In the earlier portions of *À la recherche*, we learn of the hero's solitary walks through the countryside of Méséglise and Combray, where occasionally the reflection of the sun on a stone, the odor of the pathway or the sight of a roof-top causes him to pause and wonder about the reality existing beyond these perceptions. During these walks, he meditates on *l'essence des choses* and seeks something of a reality which seems hidden within normal everyday material objects. He is unsure of what he is seeking, unsure of his powers of attaining or of communicating them, if indeed he could recognize the essence of reality. Proust uses the word *essence* to describe this indescribable quality. An essence is a perfume, a smell, an entity that it is impossible to describe in linear digital words without reference to other perfumes. An *essence* is qualitative, or the essence of qualitative feelings, which the narrator clearly describes much later:

> La musique bien différente en cela de la société d'Albertine, m'aidait à descendre en moi-même, à y découvrir du nouveau: la variété que j'avais en vain cherchée dans la vie, dans le voyage, dont pourtant la nostalgie m'était donnée par ce flot sonore qui faisait mourir à côté de moi ses vagues ensoleillées. Diversité double. Comme **le spectre extériorise pour nous la composition de la lumière**, l'harmonie d'un Wagner, la couleur d'un Elstir nous permettent de connaître cette **essence qualitative des sensations** d'un autre être ne nous faisons pas pénétrer. (III 665) (My emphasis)

Note that Proust is evoking here a portion of the concept of the *Abacus and the Rainbow* by indicating that the continuous and interpenetrating colors of the spectrum are similar to the qualitative essence of sensations, the qualitative essence of reality. A concept and language that is very Bergsonian.

Where is the hero hoping to find this enigmatic essence? Not in a mathematical treatise, nor by peering through a telescope or microscope, nor in reading an encyclopedia, although each of these might indeed contain an essential quality not normally perceived. The essence of reality sought by the hero is to be found in a moist summer breeze, in the fragrance of a closed room, in the perfume of an autumnal log fire crackling in the hearth, in a glint of sunlight reflected by a pretty stone, in a quaint roof-top, or in the echo of distant church bells:

> . . . une pierre où jouait un reflet, un toit, un son de cloche, une odeur de feuilles, bien des images différentes sous lesquelles il y longtemps qu'est morte la réalité pressentie que je n'ai pas eu assez de volonté pour arriver à découvrir.
> (I 177)

What are the common properties of these Proustian images? None is easily analyzed scientifically or logically. The smell of a substance has similarities to the Raman spectrum of its molecules and there are exquisite receptors in the nasal mucosa with which these complex molecules react, and there is only one synapse in the neural pathway between these and the higher centers of the brain. But this it is not what the Proustian hero is seeking, for their essence does not lie in a scientific analysis or common denominator. They are perhaps interactions of the Bergson's *moi profond*, interactions of the inner self with elements of reality which are qualitative, heterogeneous yet continuous. They are all coded analogic and exist in pure duration, in nondigital time; in fact they may all be considered as beyond time, and not under the pressure or exigencies of time. They isolate parcels of time in its pure state, a whisper perhaps of the eternal present. Indeed much later, in *Le Temps retrouvé*, the hero become narrator realizes this when he states:

> . . . l'être qui alors goûtait en moi cette impression la goûtait en ce qu'elle avait de commun dans un jour ancien et maintenant, dans ce qu'elle avait d'extra-temporel, un être qui n'apparaissait que quand, par une de ces identités entre le présent et le passé, il pouvait se trouver dans le seul milieu où il pût vivre, **jouir de l'essence des choses, c'est-à-dire en dehors du temps.**
> (IV 450) (my emphasis)

The sea and the rainbow are images, representations of that analogic entity that is heterogeneous, continuous, qualitative, forever changing yet perpetually the same, that unifying essence of reality, that the hero calls *l'essence des choses.*

Anne Henry[3] refers to the hero's quest for what she terms Identity. Identity of pure time with the qualitative essence of reality, that is the qualitative essence, present in common everyday things which is hidden to many of us. In normal observation, we tend to glance superficially and pay attention only to that which affects our everyday needs and life. When we look, we tend to analyze, to separate ourselves from the object, to isolate ourselves from the remainder of the world, and thus tend to loose the unifying character of reality of which we, the reader or narrator, are an integral and unified part. The French word *déchiffrer* is used for this process of understanding by analysis and sub-division. *Chiffre* is the digital number, to déchiffrer is to digitalize, to analyze by subdivision and pulverization and in so doing we transform reality, we loose it's unifying essence. Habit dulls our senses, we no longer see things in their pristine purity; we can no longer perceive that stillness that comes from the continuity with all of nature, and which constitutes reality. I would like to discuss two images in the Proustian novel that illustrate that continuous qualitative essence that constitute the analogic: the sea at Balbec and the hero's journey to Balbec.

The Sea as Metaphor for the Qualitative Essence

At the beginning of *À la recherche* the topology of continuity and unity that is so prominent in Bergson's philosophy is communicated metaphorically as the recurrent emphasis on water; water of 'la Vivonne' and subsequently of the sea at Balbec. Water in the form of la Vivonne is perhaps symbolic of the youth and vigor of the hero at that stage of his development. Water is essential for life, it is the basic entity of all living matter and the Vivonne (the name echoes *vie,* and *vivacité*) nourishes the landscape and the imagination of the Proustian text. The narrator recognizes the vital importance of the waters of the sea to our past evolution and present well-being when he says: "S'il est vrai que la mer ait été autrefois notre milieu vital où il faille replonger notre sang pour retrouver nos forces" (II 178). An evocation perhaps of the image of a sea of memories into which we and the Proustian hero can immerse ourselves for refreshment, recreation and restoration. The quiet flowing waters of la Vivonne are thus a mirror for the author's and the reader's conscience and imagination. Of the reflecting symbolism of water Jean Rousset says: "Miroir ou plan d'eau, toute surface réfléchissante est conductrice de rêverie; cercle magique tracé pour notre fascination, elle insère le fantastique dans le quotidien, l'éphémère dans le stable, l'esprit dans la matière."[4] Reflection in a still mirror of water has an evocative, un-real and dream-like quality as if it were an entrance into the enchanted world of fantasy, imagination, and memory. Reflections in still water are akin to metaphors that ripple outwards in concentric rings from one domain to another, as one touches its surface. It is appropriate therefore that the entire Proustian text begins with the hero awakening from a dreamy state, rather like a swimmer calmly breaking through the water's surface, unsure of his whereabouts, and quietly bemused at seeing his own reflection. It is an overture which foreshadows the duality of reflection that is an intrinsic part of the Proustian text.

Although the Vivonne is continuously flowing, it is clearly finite in space. The second image of water in À la recherche is the far more powerful and evocative one provided by the seemingly infinite sea at Balbec. In the sea and the reflections of the sea we see not only the image of metaphor described above, so important in the entire Proustian novel, but we see also the images of Balbec and its surroundings.

The Sea at Balbec
The sea at Balbec provides an extraordinary representation of the continuos topography of the universe, the form of reality, that I have termed analogic. It provides a continuous flow of images and metaphors that illustrate that continuity of reality that the narrator (and ultimately the author) is attempting to grasp, understand and finally communicate. As Genette says: "À Balbec, le terme dominant de la métaphore est presque toujours la mer."[5] It is the sea which breaks on the beaches, and provides the atmosphere, the sounds, the images and the salty tang which permeate the town and its surrounding scenery. Above all the sea provides the images which enter the Grand-Hôtel and saturate the mind of the hero. When the protagonist first arrives at Balbec he rushes to see the church, which he imagined would be isolated and at the sea-front bravely withstanding the waves breaking at its walls, but is dismayed to find it in mid-town, at the intersection of a pair of tram-tracks:

> Mais cette **mer,**[6] qu'à cause de cela j'avais imaginée venant mourir au pied du vitrail, était à plus de cinq lieus de distance, à Balbec-Plage, et à côté de sa coupole, ce clocher que, parce que j'avais lu qu'il était lui-même une âpre falaise normande où s'amassaient les grains . . . je m'étais toujours représenté comme recevant à sa base la dernière écume des vagues soulevées, il se

dressait sur une place où était l'embranchement de deux lignes de tramways . . . (II 19)

The sea is a source of imagination and cause of deception, and it is the sea which permeates the entire hotel as well as the hero's book-case-lined bedroom:

Quelle joie . . . de voir dans la fenêtre et dans toutes les vitrines des bibliothèques, comme dans les hublots d'une cabine de navire, la **mer** nue, sans ombrages, et pourtant à l'ombre sur une moitié de son étendue . . . (II 33)

Early in the morning, the sun shines around the hotel onto the sea front below:

Quand, le matin, le soleil venait de derrière l'hôtel, découvrant devant moi les grèves illuminées jusqu'aux premiers contreforts de la **mer**, il semblait m'en montrer un autre versant et m'engager à poursuivre, sur la route tournante de ses rayons un voyage immobile et varié à travers les plus beaux sites . . . (II 34)

For Paul Claudel, the sea is also a source of imagery: "La mer," he writes, "c'est la matière en fonction de rêve produisant des images."[7] The sea at Balbec is a source of reverie, of imagery that stimulates the hero's and his reader's imagination, and is a source of joy and won-derment that evokes the thought of voyages both real and imaginary. As Genette points out, the proximity of the sea at Balbec provides a source of metaphor related to proximity, and a reservoir of metaphors based on metonymy or *métaphores diégétiques*. Not far from Balbec along the sea front is Rivebelle, whose restaurant serves as a meeting and eating place and which is a reservoir of representations and diegetic metaphors[8]:

Pareille à celle que je voyais à Combray au-dessus du calvaire quand je rentrais de promenade et m'apprêtais à descendre avant le dîner à la cuisine, une bande de ciel rouge au-dessus de la **mer**, compacte et coupante comme de la gelée de viande, puis bientôt, sur la **mer** déjà froide et bleue comme le poisson appelé mulet, le ciel du même rose qu'un de ces saumons que nous nous ferions servir tout à l'heure à Rivebelle . . . (II 161)

In this passage there is a bridge in time back to Combray to the *bon dîner qu'apprêtait Françoise* which sets the scene for the diner(s) to come. The sea also serves as a source of diegetic metaphors for *la gelée de viande*, for the gray mullet and salmon that stimulate the appetite and will soon grace the table.

Another Image of Continuity

Before the hero arrives for the first time at Balbec and the sea, and perhaps as a foreshadowing of that unity of nature and reality that the sea will provide for him, an unusual image of that harmony is provided to Marcel. On his train journey to Balbec, he sees the dawn breaking on the eastern horizon from one side of the train contrasting with the remaining darkness of night on the other:

> . . . la ligne du chemin de fer ayant changé de direction, le train tourna, la scène matinale fut remplacée . . . par un village nocturne..sous un ciel encore semé de toutes ses étoiles . . . je passais mon temps à courir d'une fenêtre à l'autre pour rapprocher, pour rentoiler les fragments intermittents et opposites de mon beau matin écarlate et versatile et en avoir une vue totale et un tableau continu. (II 15–16)

This important passage portrays the narrator seeking the harmony and oneness of reality, attempting to unite seemingly separate and opposed impressions. He is unifying not only in space but also producing a continuity in time. Perhaps this is also a symbol of artistic creation of the process of unification of binary opposites, the light with the dark, the near with the far, the brief and the eternal, the *côté de Méséglise* and the *côté des Guermantes,* and in the process of literary creation, the unification of the analogic inspiration with the verbal transcription. It is also a foreshadowing of the role that the sea is to play in the text and also perhaps an indication that the final purpose of the Proustian novel is indeed this unification.[9] In addition the train is changing direction, following a winding course reminiscent of the winding lane that Ruskin describes in *Sesame and Lilies*,[10] in which the purpose of the walk along the path is only perceived on reaching its end, and suggests that the real intention of the train journey is perhaps being withheld and will only be revealed when we reach the end of our journey, the end of the Proustian text. The winding path will appear again in different guise on the journey to *les clochers de Martinville* that is discussed in detail in Chapter 7, and, implicitly of course in the entire Proustian text. For, *À la recherche* itself has characteristics of a journey, or perhaps a walk that resembles some of the hero's walks through the countryside of Combray, completing full circle and returning in the gathering dusk, to its starting point. This

passage, of the train moving towards Balbec and the sea, may, perhaps, also be read as a metaphor for the continuous flow of (Bergsonian)
time, of the change in perspective of things and people with the ceaseless flow of time that permeates the Proustian text.

In discussing the contemporary theory of metaphor, George Lakoff
makes the point that "The metaphor is not just a matter of language,
but of thought and reason. The language is secondary. The mapping
is primary."[11] In analyzing the metaphor in the expression: 'love as a
journey', he goes on to reason that ". . . metaphor was not a figure of
speech, but a mode of thought, defined by a systematic mapping from
a source [journey] to a target domain [love]" (210). We have in the
description of the train journey and in Ruskin's path, the characteristics of the source domain of a journey, a winding path, being mapped
onto the target domain of the entire Proustian text. Ruskin uses the
same metaphor, the same mapping of the domain of a walk to the
domain of a literary text. The relationship between the hero's train
journey to Balbec and the entire Proustian text obeys what Lakoff call
the 'invariance principle' according to which: "Metaphorical mappings
preserve the cognitive topology (that is, the image-schema structure)
of the source domain, in a way consistent with the inherent structure
of the target domain"(215).

The Dual Nature of Proustian Reality

The dual nature of reality described in the philosophy of Henri Bergson
is also present in À la recherche, and Proust emphasizes the qualitative, non-quantitative world, which to him is the real world. It is the
universe of feelings, emotions and thoughts: ". . . de parfums, de sons
de projets et de climats." It is the perception of reality, of self and of
existence which intelligence and logic cannot adequately study but which
is describable by literature and art, and which the Proustian hero seeks
and the narrator describes. This view of reality is different from that
provided by science, for science deals with generalities, whilst art attempts to entrap the unique and the individual:

> Nous avons peine à croire que la science, dont l'objet est phénoménal, puisse
> jamais remplacer la métaphysique, science des noumènes, ni que la science,
> puisqu'il n'y a de science que du général, puisse jamais se confondre avec
> l'art qui a pour mission justement de recueillir ce particulier, cet individuel,
> que les synthèses de la science laissent échapper.[12]

Thus, the reality that Proust is attempting to describe is not that of logic and reason, for logical reasoning does not necessarily provide a description of reality:

> . . . si toute à l'heure je trouvais que Bergotte en avait dit faux en parlant des joies de la vie spirituelle, c'était parce que j'appelais "vie spirituelle", à ce moment-là **des raisonnements logiques qui étaient sans rapport avec elle**, avec ce qui existait en moi en ce moment—exactement comme j'avais pu trouver le monde et la vie ennuyeux parce que je les jugeais d'après les souvenirs sans vérité, (IV 450) [my emphasis]

Nor is a an accurate cinematographic record a true portrayal of the world:

> Si la réalité était cette espèce de déchet de l'expérience, à peu près identique pour chacun . . . si la réalité était cela, sans doute une sorte de film cinématographique de ces choses suffirait. Mais était-ce bien cela la réalité? (IV 468)

Rather, it is the feelings, the emotions, the sentiments, the *affect* related to the 'parfums, de sons, et projets et de climats,' that the hero and narrator is attempting to capture. As will be discussed in Chapter 7, literature and art should recover reality by removing the veil that logic and habit have placed between ourselves and reality. For Proust, as for Bergson, there are two manners of seeking truth and reality, one is the logical, analytical approach, whereby one pulverizes and dissects nature, whilst the alternative approach, is to reverse the process of logic and analysis, and enter the essence of things. Moreover, it is this *qualitative essence* of being that Proust wishes to encapsulate in words, but for Proust reality is intimately connected with memory, indeed reality perhaps only exists in memory, in the unity of the present instant with moments of past time: "soit que la réalité ne se forme que dans la mémoire" (I 182).

Although the title of *À la recherche du temps perdu* might indicate that its author or narrator was in search of time, perhaps of lost time, it is probable that Proust was seeking a form of truth. In a letter to Jacques Rivière he says: "J'ai trouvé plus probe et plus délicat comme artiste de ne pas annoncer que c'était justement à la recherche de la Vérité que je partais, ni en quoi elle consistait pour moi."[13] The hero is in search of his vocation, and of Truth as well as lost time; it is in time and memory that he finds both his vocation and Truth. But what is this Truth (Vérité is capitalized) to which Proust refers, and how does

he hope to find it. In the preface to an edition of the first book of
Montaigne's *Essais*, André Gide writes:

> Il semble qu'en face de l'atroce question de Pilate, dont l'écho retentit à travers
> les âges: "Qu'est-ce que la vérité?" Montaigne reprenne à son compte, en-
> core que tout humainement, d'une manière toute profonde et dans un sens
> très différent, la divine réponse du Christ: "Je suis la vérité". C'est-à-dire qu'il
> estime ne pouvoir véritablement connaître rien, que lui-même. "Il faut oster le
> masque aussi bien des choses que des personnes" écrit Montaigne. S'il se
> peint, c'est pour se démasquer, convaincu que "L'estre véritable est le com-
> mencement d'une grande vertu."[14]

Montaigne did not consider that he was "The Truth," but rather
that one should first seek truth within the universe of one's inner self,
and that true knowledge starts with a knowledge of oneself, of one's
Self in the absence of masks. Marcel Proust was on a similar mission,
for like Montaigne, he removes the masks of the society he describes;
he removes the mask of the narrator so that we see both society and
the narrator (and thus ourselves) as they and we *really* are.

The Narrator's Vocation is to Recreate Analogic Reality

The Proustian hero is very sensitive to the essence of reality that seems
hidden in simple objects, and he wishes to explore, capture and retain
it, perhaps in writing. He does not understand how to rediscover the
magical essence of reality he saw in his youth, and appreciates that
traveling and visiting interesting places, although exciting, is not the
method to recapture the essence of the past:

> J'avais trop expérimenté l'impossibilité d'atteindre dans la réalité ce qui était
> au fond de moi-même; que ce n'était pas plus sur la place Saint-Marc que ce
> n'avait été à mon second voyage à Balbec, ou à mon retour à Tansonville
> pour voir Gilberte, que je retrouverais le Temps perdu. . . . (IV 455)

As time goes on the hero forgets to seek truth and it is not until many
years later, during his mediation in the bibliothèque of the Prince de
Guermantes and following three shattering reminiscences (paving-
stone, napkin and spoon) that the narrator understands the nature of
what he was seeking in his youth. It is indeed these evanescent qualitative and analogic images that gave him the perception of the reality
he was seeking to capture. It is the re-creation or the re-discovery and
then the preservation of the true essence of things, the true continuous non-digitalized view of the world that is the function of true art,

and the narrator's newly found vocation. This is the *essence des choses*, *le Temps perdu* that he was seeking and wishes now to rediscover, recreate and conserve:

> . . . j'éprouvais à la fois **dans le moment actuel et dans un moment éloigné** le bruit de la cuillère sur l'assiette . . . jusqu'à faire empiéter le passé sur le présent, . . . à me faire hésiter à savoir dans lequel des deux je me trouvais . . . l'être qui alors goûtait en moi cette impression . . . n'apparaissait que quand, il pouvait se trouver dans le seul milieu où il pût vivre, jouir de **l'essence des choses**, c'est-à-dire hors du temps. (IV 450) (my emphasis)

Proust envisages his work as encompassing the totality of the universe, and his ambition is to combine within one work of literature two postulates,[15] that of the function of art together with that of a philosophy of Self and Being as part of a whole and continuous universe. A philosophy of Self is, of course precisely what Henri Bergson discusses, but Proust does not expound his philosophy in a text on metaphysics, he does so in a very different manner, by creating a work of art. For Proust's art is an example, an illustration of his philosophy. It is only through a return to the wholeness of art, says Proust, that we can have a true understanding of the essence of the universe and of self, and of the reader-narrator's place in that universe (IV 474), and it is through art that we understand, not only the world of others, but begin to comprehend the universe within ourselves.

This perception of reality, *l'essence des choses*, was whispered to him in his youth, perceived in the sea at Balbec and recognized in the paintings of Elstir, but decades later it was noticed less clearly. He is seeking his Identity within pure time and memory, and the transmittal of that identity in a manner that retains the continuous essence of pure time, of *la durée pure*: "Cette matinée . . . marquerait certainement avant tout, dans celle-ci la forme que j'avais pressentie autrefois dans l'église de Combray, et qui nous reste habituellement invisible, celle du Temps" (IV 622). It is the function of true art to recreate that lost unity, that continuity of reality that was perceived perhaps in childhood when the being was closer to reality. The narrator wishes to isolate, preserve and communicate this essence and remove it from the contingencies of time: ". . . cette contemplation de l'essence des choses, j'étais maintenant décidé à m'attacher à elle, à la fixer, mais comment?" (IV 454). The answer to the hero's question begins to be revealed in an earlier passage of *À la recherche,* commonly referred to as *Les clochers de Martinville*,[16] and it is clearly illustrated in the paintings of the sea and seascapes provided by Elstir at Balbec.

A method of communicating the continuous analogic quality of reality symbolized by the sea is disclosed to the narrator in the paintings of Elstir, which emphasize the uninterrupted constancy of the world. Elstir's paintings reveal the continuous quality in nature where barriers and separations are removed. This is perhaps best shown in the description of le Port of Carquethuit where Elstir merges the impressions of land with those of the sea in such a manner that there are no barriers and reality is viewed in its continuous qualitative whole:

> Soit que les maisons cachassent une partie du port, un bassin de calfatage ou peut-être la mer même s'enfonçant en golfe dans les terres ainsi que cela arrivait constamment dans ce pays de Balbec, de l'autre côté de la pointe avancée où était construite la ville, les toits étaient dépassés par des mâts, lesquels avaient l'air de faire des vaisseaux auxquels ils appartenaient, quelque chose de citadin, de construit sur terre, impression qu'augmentaient d'autres bateaux, demeurés le long de la jetée. . . . (II 192)

There are a number of other passages where the narrator describes the feeling of unity of continuity resulting from the removal of artificial barriers. In the dining room at Balbec when the setting sun together with the gentle sea-breeze pervades and permeates the entire dining room, the sky and the land are unified into one experience of wholeness with no obstacles or boundaries:

> . . . quand les garçons du Grand-Hôtel, en mettant le couvert, étaient aveuglés par la lumière du couchant, que les vitres étant entièrement tirées, les souffles imperceptibles du soir passaient librement de la plage . . . (III 132)

Later in *Le Temps retrouvé* we are given a similar image of the unity and continuity of reality when artificial borders and separations are eliminated:

> . . . une sensation simplement analogue à celle que j'avais à la fin de l'après-midi à Balbec quand toutes les tables étant déjà couvertes de leur nappe et de leur argenterie, les vastes baies vitrées restant ouvertes tout en grand sur la digue, sans un seul intervalle, un seul "plein" de verre ou de pierre . . . (IV 452)

Not only do these two passages illustrate the sense of unity and continuity that the narrator-writer is attempting to achieve, but read in proximity they illustrate another technique of Proust. For he wishes to communicate to his readers the continuous, qualitative nature of reality but has to use those discontinuous, quantitative, and digital elements we call words. To achieve this, Proust builds bridges, cross-linkages in time: "dans le moment actuel et dans un moment éloigné" (IV 450); bridges in the memory of the hero, cross-linkages in the text and thus in the memory of the reader, and by interlacing and connecting images with words, by the use of metaphor.

An example of the cross-linkage in the memory of the reader is illustrated above. The second passage above of the dining room at the Grand-Hôtel, quoted (IV 452) from *Le Temps retrouvé*, recalls in the mind of the reader the first passage (III 132) of a similar scene that is described many hundreds of pages earlier. A bridge in time and memory is constructed, a connection, a sense of unity is created in the reader's mind that is similar to the unity of reality that the author is attempting to create and describe.

The Qualitative Essence of Reality
is Not Revealed by Logic but by "Impressions"

Proust feels that intuitive impression, not logic or intellect, is the way to discover and penetrate the essence of reality, *l'essence des choses*. In this concept of the importance of intuition, there is a close parallel with the essential thesis of Bergson's method and indeed of his entire philosophy. The quotation reproduced below, is remarkably Bergsonian in its content and style, and worthy of close reading, although Bergson would probably have used 'intuition' or 'les données immédiate de la conscience' for Proust's 'impression':

> . . . à tout moment l'artiste doit écouter son instinct, ce qui fait que l'art est ce qu'il y a de plus réel, la plus austère école de la vie, et le vrai Jugement dernier. Ce livre, le plus **pénible** de tous à déchiffrer, est aussi le seul que nous ait dicté la réalité, le seul dont "**l'impression**" ait été faite en nous par la réalité même. . . Les idées formées par l'intelligence pure n'ont qu'une vérité logique, une vérité possible, leur élection est arbitraire. Le livre aux caractères figurés, non tracés par nous, est notre seul livre. Non que ces idées que nous formons ne puissent être justes logiquement, mais nous ne savons pas si elles sont vraies. Seule **l'impression**, si chétive qu'en semble la matière, si insaisissable la trace est un critérium de **vérité**, et à cause de cela mérite seule d'être appréhendée par l'esprit. . . (IV 458) [my emphasis]

Intuition is the source of Truth, but working with intuition can be 'pénible.' This is the same word used by Bergson ("l'effort est pénible") when describing the work of the philosopher or writer who translates intuitive inspiration and thought into a digital text (ES 22). Proust tells us that intuition or *l'impression* provides a true view of reality, whilst ideas which are logical are not necessarily Truth, moreover intuitive impressions are not something that we create, they are offered to us. This notion is almost theological in its implication and clearly reminiscent of Bergson's *données immédiates de la conscience.*

For comparison, here is Bergson expressing a very similar concept that although intuitive thought can only last a few moments, it is the final arbiter of what is Truth:

> Le philosophe est obligé d'abandonner l'intuition une fois qu'il en a reçu l'élan, et de se fier à lui-même pour continuer le mouvement . . . mais bien vite il sent qu'il a perdu pied; un nouveau contact (avec l'intuition) devient nécessaire. . . La dialectique est ce qui assure l'accord de notre pensée avec elle-même . . . il n'y a pourtant qu'une vérité. L'intuition, si elle pouvait se prolonger au delà de quelques instants, n'assuraient pas seulement l'accord du philosophe avec sa propre pensée, mais encore celui de tous les philosophes entre eux. (EC 239)

For both Proust and Bergson, then, intuitive thought rather than logic is the source of Truth and provides a contact with reality. Furthermore, when referring to Elstir's paintings, the Proustian narrator says:

> Mais j'y pouvais discerner que le charme de chacune consistait en une sorte de métamorphose des choses représentées, analogue à celle qu'en poésie on nomme métaphore, et que si Dieu le père avait crée les choses en les nommant c'est en leur ôtant leur non, ou en leur en donnant un autre, qu'Elstir les recréait. Les nom qui désignent les choses répondent toujours à une notion de **l'intelligence, étrangère à nos impressions véritables**, et qui nous force à éliminer d'elles tout ce qui ne se rapport pas à cette notion. (II, 191) (my emphasis)

The narrator is again referring to the quality in Elstir's paintings, discussed in the previous section, of removing artificial separations and of thus creating a continuity in both space and time. This, Proust says, is comparable to a metaphor, for it creates a bridge between two superficially unlike elements and thus creates a sense of continuity. Alternatively one could say that Proust's use of metaphor is attempting to achieve with words the effect that Elstir accomplishes with paint. A word, *le signifiant*, is often a barrier, for it clearly designates water as water and land as land with no ambiguities, no room for imagination. It is these barriers of quantitative identity that Proust wishes to remove so that a qualitative continuity is achieved.

Although truth can be discovered and perceived through impression of the qualitative essence, constant vigilance is necessary to protect these evanescent impressions from the destructive force of logic. The unity and continuity of the qualitative impression of the sun, land and sea at Balbec, which Elstir captures in his paintings, can rapidly be destroyed by logical analysis, which introduces artificial separations and barriers that were not present in the original intuitive and continuous thought, for the essence of analogic reality can rapidly be destroyed by pulverizing analytical intelligence:

> . . . il m'était arrivé grâce à un effet de soleil de prendre une partie plus sombre de la mer pour une côte éloignée, ou de regarder avec joie une zone bleue de fluide sans savoir si elle appartenait à la mer ou au ciel. Bien vite mon **intelligence** rétablissait entre les éléments la séparation que mon **impression** avait abolie. (II 191) [my emphasis]

Although Proust uses a positive word (rétablissait) to describe the effect of intelligence and a negative one (abolie) to describe intuitive impressions, he is stating that logical intelligence destroys the artistic message, the impression is *déchiffré,* digitalised by logic. It is the interpreting of these qualitative impressions, deciphering the hieroglyphics of the Rosetta stone of nature that is the hero's objective:

> . . . déjà à Combray je fixais avec attention devant mon esprit quelque image qui m'avait forcé à la regarder, un nuage, un triangle, un clocher, une fleur, un caillou, en sentant qu'il y avait peut-être sous ces signes quelque chose de tout autre que je devais tâcher de découvrir, une pensée qu'ils traduisaient à la façon de ces caractères **hiéroglyphiques** qu'on croirait représenter seulement des objectes matériels. Sans doute ce déchiffrage était difficile mais seul il donnait quelque vérité à lire. Car les **vérités que l'intelligence saisit directement à claire-voie dans le monde de la pleine lumière ont quelque chose de moins profond, de moins nécessaire que celles que la vie nous a malgré nous communiquées en une impression.** . . . (IV 457) [my emphasis]

I have already referred to Anne Henry's[17] statement concerning the Identity that the narrator is seeking. He is searching for Identity with pure time (la durée pure) and with the qualitative essence of the world ('temps pur: essence qualitative du monde'), and is seeking the 'sentiment de la réalité.' Logic and intelligence can discover and analyze, but such an approach is less profound in its perception, and it fails to discover and communicate the essential element that is sometimes transmitted to us directly by our senses through qualitative impressions, for the important things are often those which our intelligence discards and disdains as being irrelevant to our everyday life:

> Quant aux vérités que l'intelligence—même des plus hauts esprits—cueille à claire-voie . . . leur valeur peut être très grande; mais elles ont des contours plus secs et sont planes, n'ont pas de profondeur . . . elles n'ont pas été recréées. (IV 477)

In Proust as in Bergson, then, there is a continual opposition between *impressions* and logic, an opposition between intuitive qualitative feelings and the hard quantitative facts of logical analysis.

Bridges with Memory

The Proustian hero, become writer, wishes to recreate and communicate the analogic aspect of reality that he calls *l'impression* or *l'essence des choses*. He learns his technique partly through emulating the method of the painter Elstir, by composing bridges in time and memory with words, and thus creating an aspect of unity and continuity. At numerous points in the text there is an incident, a phrase, or a thought that takes the reader back to an event that occurred earlier in the text. These are what Gérard Genette[18] calls an internal homodiegetic analepsis [*analepses (internes) homodiégétiques*]. Sometimes these are merely a recall of a previous event, more often they are connecting, or bridging, two similar events, the second of which sometimes takes on a rather different significance.

One example of such a bridge in memory is the two descriptions of the open quality of the dining room at the Grand-Hôtel at Balbec (III 132 & IV 452) and referred to earlier. Other illustrations of this type of bridge include the numerous references to Mlle Vinteuil and her Lesbian friend at Montjouvain, an image which is gradually transformed and takes on a different signification when we learn that, at the period she was espied by the hero, Mlle Vinteuil's friend was deciphering and transcribing the manuscript of M. Vinteuil's otherwise lost masterpiece. Another example is that of the hero's mother sleeping in a small bed in his room at Combray and Albertine sleeping in a similar small bed in his room in Paris. Yet another instance is the reference to the partition between the narrator's bed and that of his grand-mother at Balbec and the later reference to a similar partition between the narrator and his mother. In addition, there are numerous recalls of the hero's walks through the countryside of Méséglise, and the sound of

the small garden gate being opened by M. Swann. A particularly striking illustration of this technique is the reminiscence of the first time
the hero saw Robert de Saint-Loup at the Grand-Hôtel:

> . . . j'étais dans la salle à manger de l'hôtel qu'on avait laissée à demi dans
> l'obscurité pour la protéger du soleil en tirant des rideaux qu'il jaunissait et
> qui par leurs interstices laissaient clignoter le bleu de la mer, quand dans la
> travée central qui allait de la plage à la route, je vis, grand, mince, le cou
> dégagé, la tête haute et fièrement portée, passer un jeune homme aux yeux
> pénétrants et dont la peau était aussi blond et les cheveux aussi dorés que
> s'ils avaient absorbé tous les rayons du soleil. Vêtu d'une étoffe souple et
> **blanchâtre** comme je n'aurais jamais cru qu'un homme eût osé en porter, et
> dont la minceur n'évoquait pas moins que le frais de la salle dà manger, la
> chaleur et le beau temps . . . Ses **yeux** . . . étaient de la **couleur de la mer**.
> (II 88)

and much later:

> Je me rappelais son arrivée, la première fois, à Balbec, quand, en lainages
> **blanchâtres**, avec ses **yeux verdâtres et bougeants comme la mer**, il
> avait traversé le hall attenant à la grande salle à manger dont les vitrages
> donnaient sur la mer. (IV 426) [my emphasis in both]

What is remarkable here, is not so much the recollection itself, but
the details of the eye color and clothing that are recalled, a recollection which in textual time (le temps de la chose racontée, temps du
signifié[19]) is many years later. In 'le temps du récit, le temps du signifiant,'
the elapsed time may also be very considerable since the second passage is over a thousand pages after the first. Clearly the detail is not
accidental, but a deliberate technique by which Proust builds a bridge
and connection in time in the reader's memory. The shuttle of time
weaves together memories and creates a texture of images, events
and people which previously seemed separate and unconnected, but
in retrospect are apprehended and comprehended through the unifying essence of memory and pure time.

This procedure in which the past memory and present perception
weave and interlaces continuously through the text rather than that of
a story-line moving in a unilateral direction is a very effective manner
of communicating continuity and unity, and is also reflected and im-
aged in the continuous movement of the sea, the surging waves of the
ocean at Balbec.

Somewhat different from the above, but also classified by Genette
as '*analepses (internes) homodiégétiques*' are the four major reminiscences related to involuntary memory. These are the three epi-

sodes at the beginning of the matinée Guermantes, and the incident of the madeleine (which Genette classifies somewhat differently since it does not take the reader back to a previous moment of the narration). These are somewhat different than those quoted above since they involve the narrator's memory, rather than that of the reader, and entails events concerning which the reader could have no knowledge when he reads the text linearly. However, these episodes also contribute to building connections back in time, and thus illustrating continuity to existence and Self and helping to depict that analogic continuity that is reality.

Bridges with Words. The Mapping of Metaphor.

Proust does with words what Elstir does with paint, and perhaps the most important bridges that Proust builds are those involving words. That is, he paints the continuous and analogic with discontinuous, discrete, digital words, for words are Proust's paint. The narrator/writer obtains the clue for this technique by observing Elstir's paintings and seeing the link between the continuity of painting and the lack of interruption that can be provided by metaphor:

> Mais les rares moments où l'on voit la nature telle qu'elle est poétiquement, c'était de ceux-là qu'était faite l'oeuvre d'Elstir. Une de ses métaphores les plus fréquentes dans les marines qu'il avait près de lui en ce moment était justement celle qui comparant la terre à la mer, supprimait entre elles toute démarcation. C'était cette comparaison, tacitement et inlassablement répétée dans une même toile qui y introduisant cette multiforme et puissante unité . . .
>
> C'est par exemple à une **métaphore** de ce genre . . . dans un tableau représentant le port de Carquethuit, qu'Elstir avait préparé l'esprit du spectateur en n'employant pour la petite ville que des termes marins et que des termes urbains pour la mer. (II 192) [my emphasis]

In a letter to Léon Daudet of November 27, 1913, Proust discusses the ideal of literary writing: ". . . où s'est accompli le miracle suprême, la transsubstantiation des qualités irrationnelles de la matière de la vie dans des mots humains."[20] In a sense, Proust is attempting the reverse, of transforming human words into the image of the irrational qualities of reality. These irrational qualities of reality are, of course, *l'essence des choses*, and it is this ideal which he would like to achieve, but knowingly cannot. However he does use words and the continuous interweaving structure of his text to achieve a genuine impression of the continuous flow of *la durée pure*. Not only does he wish to present events in continuous time, but he wishes to remove sensations and impressions, *l'essence des choses,* from the exigencies of destruction by time.

As Kristeva points out,[21] the operation which Proust refers to as 'analogy' or 'metaphor' has little connection with the same term as normally used in rhetoric to designate the replacement of a well-worn term by another. In Proust it is more like a link of reciprocal relationship or at times one of contradictions maintained between two terms:

> Même, ainsi que la vie, quand en rapprochant une **qualité** commune à deux **sensations**, il dégagera leur essence commune en les réunissant l'une et l'autre pour les soustraire aux contingences du temps dans une métaphore. (IV 468)

In the early drafts of the text Proust[22] used the term '*alliance de mots*' rather than metaphor and perhaps that term gives a clearer indication of his purpose, that of linking and uniting, creating alliances between otherwise separate images, of creating links and bridges through words and phrases. Making alliances with words is similar to the notion of *mapping* in the theory of metaphor described by Lakoff and discussed earlier in this chapter. The above quotation also emphasizes that Proust is attempting to juxtapose to unite the quality (*l'essence*) in two sensations and by thus linking them to remove that essence from the destructive power of duration—to remove them from time. The narrator, as previously discussed, also refers (II 192) to the quality in Elstir's paintings of removing artificial boundaries and thus creating a continuity in both space and time which he says, is comparable to metaphor.

Metaphor and memory are closely linked. "Les réminiscences," says Gilles Deleuze, "sont des métaphores de la vie; les métaphores sont les réminiscences de l'art. Les signes de l'art s'expliquent par la pensée pure comme faculté des essences."[23] Memory involves building a bridge back in time, mapping the past into and onto the present. Metaphor and the Proustian *alliance de mots* are providing a link, the mapping of one experience onto another so that a continuity is revealed just as memory provides a continuity in time and space. It is this unity that the Proustian hero is seeking and finds in memory and metaphor, and the bridge with words thus has a similarity to the bridge in memory, the bridge between the two representations of self, one actual in the present and one virtual in memory, that is discussed later in this chapter. The linking of the two 'Je's in memory removes the present self from the contingencies of time. The bridge with words does something similar since it links two parallel worlds of reality. If one understands metaphor as a process of mapping from a domain of origin to a target domain, one sees the parallel universes that are uncovered and which take form.

Analogy and metaphor transcend the visible to achieve an invisible unity where the essence of reality is revealed in a manner quite different from everyday logical observation, or as Kristeva states: "The analogical is the ontological."[24] One might say that the metaphor is the key to the ontological or that the analogical image provided, for example, by the sea at Balbec is a reflection of the ontological. Through changing our normally digital and quantitative perception of things, we achieve a truer sense of Self and perceive something of the true essence of reality.

The narrator, become writer-creator, must transforms those analogic impressions of memory and past reality into digital words, into *les équivalents d'intelligence*:

> Or la recréation par le mémoire, d'impressions qu'il fallait ensuite approfondir, éclairer, **transformer en équivalents d'intelligence**, n'était-elle pas une des conditions, presque l'essence même de l'oeuvre d'art telle que je l'avais conçue tout à l'heure dans la bibliothèque? (IV 621) [my emphasis]

For it is with words that the narrator-writer is to enable a fusion of self with reality, the fusion of narrator/reader, the Identity of pure time and the qualitative essence of the world. Anne Henry states the same idea in a different manner when she writes: "La métaphore, c'est à dire sur le plan stylistique l'équivalence ontologique du qualitatif, se présente donc comme la voie royale d'une esthétique de l'Identité,"[25] and somewhat later she writes in a similar vein: "Toute déconstruction de la perception fait aboutir à une saisie du **sensible pur,** cette manière unie et diverse à la fois qui est le fond commun de toute métaphore."[26] The metaphor is providing the qualitative link, the element of unity and continuity between two otherwise unrelated objects or events; it is that continuity, that qualitative equivalence which is the vision of reality provided by artistic creation. Genette evokes a very similar thought when he states that the similarity between Proustian metaphors and Elstir's (also Proustian) paintings is that both function by an accretion through proximity and a projection or mapping of an analogic relationship on something that is contiguous:

> Attribués à Elstir ou directement perçues par Marcel, ces "métaphores" visuelles, qui donnent au paysage de Balbec sa tonalité spécifique, illustrent

parfaitement cette tendance fondamentale de l'écriture de l'imagination proustiennes . . . à l'assimilation par voisinage, à la projection du rapport analogique sur la relation de contiguïté . . . **d'une coïncidence de l'analogue et du contigu;**[27] [my emphasis]

* * *

I should like to end this section on Proustian metaphor with a long quotation, which can be read as an illustration of metaphoric mapping. During the Proustian hero's first stay at the Grand-Hôtel at Balbec, he occupies a bedroom containing a glass-covered book-case which reflects the sea. One evening he enters his room as the sun is setting and observes the sunset and the sea reflected in the mahogany framed glass panels. He writes:

> J'entrais dans la chambre, le ciel violet, qui semblait stigmatisé par la figure raide, géométrique, passagère et fulgurante du soleil, s'inclinait vers la mer sur la charnière de l'horizon comme un tableau religieux au-dessus du maître-autel, tandis que les parties différentes du couchant, exposée dans les glaces des bibliothèques basses en acajou qui couraient le long des murs et que **je rapportais par la pensée** à la merveilleuse peinture dont elles étaient détachées, semblaient comme ces scènes différentes que quelque maître ancien exécuta jadis pour une confrérie sur une châsse et dont on exhibe à côté les uns des autres dans une salle de musée les volets séparés **que l'imagination seule du visiteur** remet à leur place sur des prédelles de retable. (II 160) [my emphasis]

This text contains a number of metaphors. One is that of nature perceived and reflected as a work of art, a collection of mahogany framed paintings of the moving sea and the setting sun. The image contains a series of somewhat similar yet uniquely different paintings reminiscent of Monet's many compositions of water lilies in the stream at Giverny, paintings of nature which stimulate the senses and imagination.

Perhaps there is also another metaphor here, for the reflection or image of the sea and the setting sun in the bookcase is related but not identical to the one outside the window. A mirror-image is related to the original as a right hand is to a left, it is similar but not identical. It is a view on a world that is unlike the one usually perceived. The glass of the bookcase was possibly curved or defective leading to further differences, distortions and possible omissions thus contributing an element of ambiguity and openness in the reflection. The two images are linked in space and time so that there is a component of continuity between them rather than contiguity. Perhaps most importantly, the reflected images adjacent to the window, partly through the ambiguity of the reflection, stimulate the hero's reflection and imagination to yet other images personal to the viewer and perhaps not directly related to the image. The elements of similarity, of analogy but not identity, the component of ambiguity, of continuity and the ability to stimulate further images create the sensation that the overall perception is one of an experience of reality that is greater than the direct view. It is a vision of a larger, more expansive universe.

Returning to George Lakoff's analysis of metaphor, the Proustian hero's description of the sunset reflected in the glass covered mahogany bookcase may be considered as a representation of the mapping that constitutes metaphor, the mapping of an image from the sea as the source domain to the reflection in the bookcase as the target domain. As Lakoff emphasizes, the locus of metaphor is thought, not language; it is in the way we conceptualize one mental domain in terms of another. It is a bridge between two apparently unrelated domains that are united in thought. This description[28] of the reflection of the sea and the setting sun in the book-case, which itself contains many metaphors, may be read as a poetic illustration of the process of metaphoric mapping, as a *depiction of the mapping of metaphor* and as a representation of that unity that the author is attempting to create with words. As we have said, a metaphor builds a bridge between seemingly unrelated elements, and metaphor can unveil a link and thus reveal hidden truth. One of the contemporary notions concerning metaphor is that it can provide a rational bridge from the known to the radically different and unknown, and make possible the acquisition and understanding of radically new knowledge.[29]

A Name is Sesame[30]

Proper names are particularly evocative for the Proustian hero and narrator, whereas mere words, like drawings hanging on the wall of child's class-room are quite ordinary:

> Les mots nous présentent des choses une petite image claire et usuelle comme celles que l'on suspend aux murs des écoles pour donner aux enfants l'exemple de ce qu'est un établi, un oiseau, une fourmilière, choses conçues comme pareilles à toutes celles de même sorte. Mais les noms présentes des personnes—et des villes qu'ils nous habituent à croire individuelles, uniques comme des personnes. (I 380)

Names do not recall the quantitative material things associated with the person, place or thing, rather they may evoke qualitative feelings and emotions, and arouse the analogic rather than the digital. As discussed in the previous chapter, ordinary words are, for Bergson, somewhat contrary to the flow of thought, and although words and language are essential to communication, they have the rather obnoxious property of crushing and deforming non-verbal analogic thought. For Bergson, words are generic, they lose individuality and uniqueness, and Proust's perception of words is the same as Bergson's, but he finds ways and means of using them, rather like Elstir uses paint, to depict the fundamental essence of reality through the use of metaphor. In reference to Proust's use of words, Jean Milly[31] says: "L'art de Proust est orienté, à coup sûr, beaucoup plus vers la phrase que vers le mot isolé," and obviously, sentences are normally more important than single words. Moreover, somewhat like Bergson, Proust says that words sometime fail to translate true impressions. However, proper names are different, and for Georges Poulet,[32] Proustian proper names unite a place with a person in that place, thus animating and altering both the perception of the place and the person. For example, the name Albertine evokes both the image the young member of *la petite bande* and that of the sea-front of Balbec thus metamorphosing the perception of both.

Proper names are for Proust unique and powerful in their ability to evoke the qualitative essence of reality. A name is Sesame, for its sound opens magical doors to innumerable treasures, in addition it is the seed from which wonderful images grow and flourish and which nourishes the reader's imagination and thus gives rise to other images and wonders. A proper name is also an excellent example of the opposition and contrast between the digital and the analogic. A name, *le signifiant*, is merely a linear series of digital symbols which, in itself, is nothing. But for Proust, *le signifié* associated with that proper name is wonderful and magical. *Le signifiant* is the (digital) combination which unlocks the entrance to *le signifié,* to an entire (analogic) landscape of memories. In his essay on "Proust et les noms," Roland Barthes writes:

> Le nom propre dispose des trois propriétés que le narrateur reconnaît à la réminiscence: le pouvoir d'essentialisation, le pouvoir de citation, le pouvoir d'exploration: le Nom propre est en quelque sorte la forme linguistique de la réminiscence.[33]

In addition to being a linguistic form of memory, a proper name can be the magnifying glass through which one nostalgically sees back into the past and expectantly forward into the future. Before the hero ever sees Balbec, the name has magically evocative properties which transport the hero into the future: "Dans le nom de Balbec comme dans le verre grossissant de ces porte-plume qu'on achète aux bains de mer, j'apercevais des vagues soulevés autour d'une église de style persan" (I 382). The reader experiences the magical, evocative properties of names as he follows the route of: "le beau train généreux d'une heure vingt-deux" (I 378) through real and imaginary towns and villages of Normandy and Brittany: Questambert, Pontorson, Balbec, Lannion, Lamballe, Benodet, Pont-Aven, Quimperlé.[34] The litany of names along the route are evocative and nostalgic:

> ". . . Bayeux si haute dans sa noble dentelle rougeâtre . . . Vitré dont l'accent aigu losangeait de bois noir le vitrage ancien . . . Coutance, cathédrale normande, que sa diphthongue finale, grasse et jaunissante couronne par une tour de beurre . . . Benodet, non à peine amarré que semble vouloir entraîner la rivière au milieu de ses algues" (I 382),

and:

> . . . Parme. Ce beau nom compact, verni, trop doux de Parme qui a bu en ses surfaces lisses comme certaines substances grasses le parfum des fleurs, la couleur des violettes de Parme, ce nom où ne circule pas d'air et qui fait étouffer . . . (II 1244)

These names contain that which Barthes calls "la phonétique symbolique," and for the hero or narrator, proper names, such as Parme, Bayeux, or Quimperlé do not give rise to a quantitative or statistical description of the town, its size, population, or principal industries. Rather, it is evocative, it brings forth qualitative properties, impressions, memories or anticipations. What is evoked by the digital and quantitative *signifiant* of Parme are clearly qualitative analogic properties associated with *le signifié*:

> Mais les noms présentent des personnes—et des villes qu'ils nous habituent à croire individuelle, uniques comme des personnes—une image confuse qui tire d'eux, de leur sonorité éclatante ou sombre, la couleur dont elle est peinte uniformément comme une de ces affiches. . . (I 380)

In addition to the name of a town or village, the name of a book can be a key that liberates qualitative images from spontaneous or involuntary memory. The name, for example, of *François le champi* elicits not the content of the book, rather it evokes the emotions and conditions that the hero associates with the occasion that the book was first read to him:

> C'était une impression bien ancienne, où mes souvenirs d'enfance et de famille étaient tendrement mêlés et que je n'avais pas reconnue tout de suite. . . ce livre que ma mère m'avait lu haut à Combray presque jusqu'au matin, avait-il gardé pour moi tout le charme de cette nuit-là . . . Tel nom lu dans un livre autrefois, contient entre ses syllabes le vent rapide et le soleil brillant qu'il faisait quand nous le lisions. (IV 462–3)

What is elicited is not the subject matter of the book but the circumstances and recollections of that first reading, and this is interesting, for the content of the book is clearly retained in the Bergsonian intentional memory of effort, learning, the memory which is linear, digital and which resides in the present. In contrast, the conditions associated with the episode of the reading of the book are qualitative emotions, smells and sounds: "le vent rapide et le soleil brillant qu'il faisait quand nous le lisions." associated with that occasion when the hero's mother, in the early hours of the morning, read the book. They are images and emotions that are encoded in spontaneous or involuntary memory, the Bergsonian *mémoire-image*. The name "Fançois le Champi" thus has affinities to the madeleine in evoking spontaneous or involuntary memory. However, Proust emphasizes, one must be careful not to damage the precious original memory, or that first qualitative impression will slowly be replaced with successive layers of more recent and less authentically attractive images, for the lock to the enchanted door fatigues, there is tachyphylaxis[35] to the stimulus:

> Et si j'avais encore le *François le Champi* que maman sortit un soir du paquet de livres que ma grand-mère devait me donner pour ma fête, je ne le regarderais jamais; j'aurais trop peur d'y insérer peu à peu mes impressions d'aujourd'hui jusqu'à recouvrir complètement celles d'autrefois. (IV 466)

Thus, in the hero's mind names of persons, names of people, names of things gradually become intertwined and associated, in the gray matter of memory, with qualitative impressions and recollections:

> Ainsi les espaces de ma mémoire se couvraient peu à peu de noms qui, en s'ordonnant, en se composant les uns relativement aux autres, en nouant entre eux des rapports de plus en plus nombreux, imitaient ces oeuvres d'art achevées où il n'y a pas une seule touche qui ne soit isolée où chaque partie

> tour à tour reçoit des autres sa raison d'être comme elle leur impose la sienne.
> (II 826)

These names and their associations become interwoven like so many threads of a wonderful tapestry or the interlacing themes of a great fugue. One thread, one melody, one name in itself is not very enlightening, but the total revelation becomes apparent when one perceives the entire texture of the work of art, when one reads the entire text of À la recherche.

But perhaps the most magical of all the proper names known to the hero is that of 'Guermantes.' Guermantes evokes not the geographical location, but rather the nobility, the class, the ancient historical associations so that there develops a relationship between the hero and the duchesse de Guermantes that distinctly resembles la fin'amor of the medieval troubadours and trouvères in which Ma Dame is worshipped from afar and in which carnal desire seems largely replaced by spiritual worship:

> Le nom de duchesse de Guermantes ne signifiant rien maintenant qu'il n'y a
> plus de duchés ni de principautés, mais j'avais adopté un autre point de vue
> . . . Tous les châteaux des terres dont elle était duchesse, princesse, vicomtesse,
> cette dame en fourrure bravant le mauvais temps me semblait les porter avec
> elle, comme les personnages sculptés au linteau d'un portail. (III 540)

This is emphasized by the name of Guermantes being associated with images on a stained glass window of the church at Combray and (in the hero's imagination) with sculptures in the church porch at Balbec. Moreover, the name Guermantes is ever more important, for it is the recognition of the name Guermantes amongst a large number of invitations and cartes de visite which attracts the hero's attention on his return to Paris and persuades him to attend la matinée de la princesse de Guermantes:

> Mais celle qui m'y fit aller fut ce nom de Guermantes . . . il réveillât un rayon
> de mon attention qui alla prélever au fond de ma mémoire une coupe de leur
> passé accompagné de toutes les images de forêt domaniale ou de hautes
> fleurs qui l'escortaient alors, et pour qu'il reprît pour moi le charme et la
> signification que je lui trouvais à Combray. (IV 435)

It is because of the impressions ("le charme et la signification")[36] associated with the name Guermantes that the hero attends the matinée where three shattering reminiscences and the meditation and insight they invoke are like Sesame for they opens the enchanted door of Le

Temps retrouvé. It is thus the name Guermantes which ultimately leads to the transformation of the hero—dilettante into the hero—writer, the metamorphosis of the virtual 'Charles Swann' into an actual 'Marcel Proust,' for without the name 'Guermantes' there would be no *Temps retrouvé,* there would be no *À la recherche du temps perdu.*

The *'évolution créatrice'* of the Characters

Bergson commences *L'évolution créatrice* with a very Cartesian thought: "L'existence dont nous sommes le plus assurés et que nous connaissons le mieux est incontestablement la nôtre . . ."(EC 1), but he soon leaves Descartes to venture into his notion of continuous movement and change and the evolution of Self. He evokes the concept that we are each continually changing, continuing to evolve with the flow of time, and that this continuous change of being is a characteristic both of time and life, for indeed if one ceased to change, one's time would cease: ". . . si un état d'âme cessait de varier, sa durée cesserait de couler. La vérité est qu'on change sans cesse, et que l'état lui-même est déjà du changement" (EC 2). This evolution of self, this creation of self by self is an irreversible process, just like the increase in entropy, for time has both duration and direction, a direction that we cannot reverse:

> L'objet de la vie humaine est une création qui, à la différence de celle de l'artiste et du savant, et susceptible de se poursuive à tout moment et change tous les hommes: **la création de soi par soi,** l'agrandissement de la personnalité par un effort qui peut tirer beaucoup de peu, quelque chose de rien, et ajouter sans cesse à ce qu'il y avait déjà de richesse dans le monde.[37] [my emphasis]

To exist in pure time implies a process of change of maturation, of evolution, it suggests a process of which we are not often conscience, but nevertheless like spontaneous memory, it is a procedure which is continually taking place, and is: "la création de soi par soi."

As we think, and act, so our being changes and evolves, but unlike the creation of a work of art, this process is continual and leads to a deepening and widening of personality thus increasing the value and richness of the world. This notion of the continual change of personality and appearance, of evolution and change of self with time is clearly and vividly reflected in *À la recherche,* although this is not unique to Proust. Proustian characters do not remain the same, they evolve and change with the passage of time. We witness this change, this development which sometimes has an interesting redemptive quality, and at the matinée de la princesse de Guermantes the hero sees the transformation that time can, does and will produce in many of his former acquaintances in the autumn of their days: "Les parties blanches de barbes jusque-là entièrement noires rendaient mélancolique le paysage humain de cette matinée, comme les premières feuilles jaunes des arbres alors qu'on croyait encore pouvoir compter sur un long été" (IV 505).

When, at le Bal de têtes, the protagonist sees his former enemy M. d'Argencourt he ponders: "Combien d'états successifs ne me fallait-il pas traverser si je voulais retrouver celui du d'Argencourt que j'avais connu!" The états successifs are the succesive states of self, the layers of our moi, that we ourselves create as we think, live and act:

> Et de même que le talent du peintre se forme ou se déforme, en tout cas se modifie, sous l'influence même des oeuvres qu'il produit, ainsi chacun de nos états, en même temps qu'il sort de nous, modifie notre personne . . . nous nous créons continuellement nous-mêmes. . . . (EC 7)

Bergson then continues to explain that existence implies le vieillissement, a flow of being in real time and that a knowledge of human beings involves knowledge of their duration and flowing continuity in real time, and not merely their perception at a mathematical point in time:

> L'évolution, elle, implique une continuation réelle du passé par le présent, une durée qui est un trait d'union. En d'autres termes, la connaissance d'un être vivant . . . est une connaissance qui porte sur l'intervalle même de durée, tandis que la connaissance d'un système artificiel ou mathématique ne porte que sur l'extrémité. (EC 22)

Thus M. d'Argencourt thus reveals and renders visible to the hero his creation of self by self and the passage of Time. More important and subtle than the change in their physical appearance produced by the flow of time is the change in the personality and character of the major individuals in the Proustian novel. Some change much as one might expect, others in a quite unexpected direction. We see Albertine evolve from a lovely vivacious and sportive young girl running and cycling along the beach at Balbec to a rather worldly and somewhat unpleasant, sedentary and stagnant individual. We see Gilberte develop in a rather different manner from the spoilt, gesticulating and slightly rude young girl in the garden at Tansonville to the self-assured but disillusioned marquise de Saint-Loup. However, there is clearly an element of redemption in the evolution of many Proustian characters. For example, the evolution of the Lesbian friend (who is never graced with a name) of Mlle Vinteuil to the person who transcribed and thus saved from oblivion the magnificent sonata of M. Vinteuil. We see la Berma fall from grace whilst 'Rachel quand du Seigneur' moves gradually and imperceptibly from being a common prostitute to the mistress of Robert de Saint-Loup to displacing la Berma in high society, so that eventually, la Berma is forced to ask Rachel to be invited to the *matinée* de la princesse de Guermantes. Even the old reprobate, M. de Charlus, evolves and mellows into a figure reminiscent of King Lear. Thus, we see in Proust's novel the image of Bergson's *création de soi par soi*, of two opposing forces, the creative evolution of the self and the irreversible flow of time, the second law of thermodynamics exerting its effect on the personages of *À la recherche* whilst they create themselves.

Pierre-Quint, writing on the role of duration and of Time in Proust's novel states that Proust's psychology leads to the notion that:

> Le monde de nos sentiments est un écoulement ininterrompu . . . Notre moi se modifie à tout instant, chaque sensation, chaque sentiment vieillissent par le fait même qu'ils durent. Et c'est la second grande idée de Proust: notre vie consciente et inconsciente est en évolution perpétuelle.[38]

Unfortunately, Pierre-Quint does not give any citations to illustrate his statements, but clearly these notions, implicit in Proust's text and discussed above, are explicitly stated by Bergson in *L'évolution créatrice*, and again confirms the correspondence and convergence of portions of Proust's novel with many aspects of Bergsonian philosophy.

The Fusion of the Digital and the Analogic

The quantitative and the qualitative, the discontinuous and the continuous, the particle and the wave, the two worlds of Henri Bergson are also the two worlds of Marcel Proust and of ourselves. Reality is their unity, and that reality is perceived in a work of true art where words and ideas are combined, unified, and fused together. The real Proustian *anneau* is that between the words and the evoked image, between *le signifiant* and *le signifié*. In a paragraph which describes one of the essential elements and a recurring theme of this study, the importance of the fusion of the digital with the analogic in any work of art, Gérard Genette in discussing metonymy in Proust writes:

> La solidité indestructible de l'écriture, dont Proust semble chercher ici la formule magique ("la métaphore seule peut donner une sorte d'éternité au style" dira-t-il dans son article sur Flaubert), ne peut résulter de la seule liaison horizontale établie par le trajet métonymique; mais on ne voit pas non plus comment pourrait y pourvoir la seule liaison verticale du rapport métaphorique. Seul le recoupement de l'un par l'autre peut soustraire l'objet de la description, et la description elle-même, aux "contingences du temps," c'est-à-dire à toute contingence; seule la croisée d'une trame métonymique et d'une chaîne métaphorique assure la cohérence, la cohésion "nécessaire" du *texte*.[39] (Genette's emphasis)

That is, for literature to create images that are beyond the destructive properties of time it is necessary that the horizontal elements represented by metonymy be conjoined with the vertical elements represented by metaphor, and thus there must be: "coïncidence de l'analogue et du contigu" (54), for then and only then does the textual interweaving result in the multi-dimensional text that recreates reality.

At the outset of *À la recherche* there are two areas which are as separate in the narrator's mind as east is from west and also very different in nature. Speaking of the "les deux côtés" he says:

> Mais surtout je mettais entre eux, bien plus que leurs distances kilométriques, la distance qu'il y avait entre les deux parties de mon cerveau où je pensais à eux, une de ces distances dans l'esprit qui ne font pas qu'éloigner, qui séparent et mettent dans un autre plan. Et cette démarcation était rendue plus absolue encore parce que cette habitude que nous avions de n'aller jamais vers les deux côtés un même jour, dans une seule promenade, . . . les enfermait pour ainsi dire loin l'un de l'autre, inconnaissable l'une à l'autre, dans les vases clos et sans communication entre eux. (I 133)

He considers that the two *côtés* will always be separated, the qualitative and the quantitative, the poetic and the snobbish can never be united. Yet as time passes, and only with the passage of considerable time and perhaps like the reversal of the process of continental drift, the *deux côtés,* the two continents of the Proustian world move slowly towards each other. Finally, the unity and the fusion of the *deux côtés* is consummated, and *À la recherche* is created by the union of *Du côté de chez Swann* and *Le côté de Guermantes*, by blending of the qualitative and the quantitative, by the successful fusion of the analogic imagery of *Du côté de chez Swann* with the more digital (in or out, yes or no,) world of *Le côté de Guermantes*.[40] *À la recherche* is ultimately created by the union of the analogic and poetic elements of Méséglise, Combray and Balbec, of *Du côté de chez Swann* with the digital, snobbish and exclusive, elements of high society symbolized by *Le côté de Guermantes*. Gilberte Swann, through her union with Robert de Saint-Loup, becomes la marquise de Saint-Loup and ultimately la duchesse de Guermantes. Tansonville thus becomes fused with Guermantes, and the seemingly impossible does occur, for as in *Macbeth*, where Birnam Wood eventually comes to Dunsinane, so in *À la recherche*, Tansonville eventually becomes Guermantes. A clear symbolic representation that *les deux côtés* have become fused into one, the metonymic metaphor of the digital–analogic union.

Conclusion

Many aspects of Bergsonism can be perceived in Proust's novel, and both works reflect, are permeated by and enunciate comparable, though not identical, concepts. Although some elements of Bergson's philosophy are clearly discernible in Proust's writing, it would be an incorrect oversimplification to state, as does Pierre-Quint: ". . . l'oeuvre de Proust est l'expression direct, sur le plan du roman, de la philosophie de Bergson."[41] For such a generalization implies a congruence of thought and probably a direct influence of Bergsonian philosophy on Proust. However, there appears to be neither exact correspondence of thought nor, if one accepts Megay's conclusion, direct influence of Bergson on Proust. Rather there appears to be convergence of two independent thinkers in tune with the pulse and ideas of their time. For, as discussed in Chapter 8, the two writers were contemporaries, had a similar education, lived in the same city and were related by marriage, so that it is perhaps not entirely surprising that there should be similarity in their philosophy. But perhaps, as discussed in the final chapter, there is more to this subtle similarity than independent convergence.

Notes

1   Marcel Proust, Footnote 1; John Ruskin, *Sésame et les lys*, trans. Marcel Proust, (Paris: Mercure de France, 1906) 61.

2   Julia Kristeva. *Proust and the Sense of Time*. Trans. Stephen Bann (New York: Columbia UP, 1993) 65.

3   Anne Henry, *Marcel Proust: théories pour une esthétique* (Paris: Klincksieck, 1981) 263.

4   Jean Rousset, *L'intérieur et l'extérieur* (Paris: José Corti, 1968) 197.

5   Gérard Genette, "Métonymie chez Proust," *Figures III* (Paris: Seuil, 1972) 53.

6   In the following four quotations, the word **mer** is highlighted to emphasis its pervasiveness.

7   Paul Claudel, *Oeuvres complètes* vol. XXV (Paris: Gallimard, 1965) 181.

8   Genette 52.

9   Georges Poulet, *L'Espace proustien* (Paris: Gallimard, 1982) 101–102.

10   See quotation in Chapter 8.

11   George Lakoff, "The contemporary theory of metaphor," *Metaphor and Thought,* ed. Andrew Ortony (Cambridge: Cambridge UP, 1993) 208–210.

12   Marcel Proust, *Contre Sainte-Beuve: précédé de pastiches et mélanges* (Paris: Gallimard, Pléiade, 1971) 495.

13   Marcel Proust, *Choix de lettres,* ed. Philip Kolb (Paris: Plon, 1965) 197.

14   André Gide, préface, *Essais*, vol 1, by Michel de Montaigne, (Paris: Gallimard, 1962) 8.

15   Henry 260.

16   The reading of this passage as an fable of artistic inspiration is discussed in Chapter 7.

17   Henry 262–265.

18   Genette 95.

19   Genette 77.

20   Proust, *Lettres* 195.

21   Kristeva 58.

22   Jacques Robichez, notes, *Le Temps retrouvé* by Marcel Proust, (Paris: Gallimard, 1990) 416.

23   Gilles Deleuze, *Proust et les signes* (Paris: PUF, 1993) 70.

24   Kristeva 65.

25   Henry 267.

26   Henry 296.

27   Genette 53–54.

28   Poulet, *L'Espace proustien* 129–130, describes this as a metaphor of the entire Proustian novel, with the separate parts framed and together making the whole.

29   Hugh G. Petrie, and Rebecca S. Oshlag, "Metaphor and learning," *Metaphor and Thought* ed. Andrew Ortony, (Cambridge: Cambridge UP, 1993) 584.

30   See, footnote 1.

31   Jean Milly, *Proust et le style* (Genève: Slatkine, 1991) 125.

32   Poulet, *L'Espace proustien* 121.

33   Roland Barthes, *Le degré zéro de l'écriture suivi de nouveaux essais critiques* (Paris: Seuil, 1972) 124.

34   All are real towns except for Balbec.

35   Physiological term originating from the Greek for swift or rapid, and meaning rapid reduction in the response to repeated stimuli, or habituation to a stimulus.

36   *La signification* is, of course, *le signifié*.

37   Henri Bergson, "Page écrite par Bergson pour l'album de M. I. Benrubi," *Henri Bergson: essais et témoignanges*," eds. Albert Béguin & Pierre Thévenaz (Neuchatel: Baconnière. 1943) frontispiece.

38   Léon Pierre-Quint, *Marcel Proust: sa vie, son oeuvre* (Paris: Sagittaire, 1946) 153.

39   Genette 60.

40   It can be argued that *Du côté de chez Swann* may be read as metaphor, for the entire area, the poetic feelings and emotions evoked by Méséglise and Combray, the *aubépines* and the *cocliquots*. *Le côté de Guermantes* is inherently different in character, perhaps metonymy rather than metaphor, for it represents the Nobility, the titles, a world characterized by barriers and frontiers of yes/no or in/out which is thus quantitative or digital in character.

41   Léon Pierre-Quint, "Bergson et Proust," *Henri Bergson: essais et témoignages* ed. Albert Béguin & Pierre Thévenaz (Neuchatel: Baconnière, 1943) 330.

Chapter 5

The Duality of the Common Themes

La durée est essentiellement mémoire, conscience, liberté . . .

Deleuze[1]

Une heure n'est pas qu'une heure, c'est un vase rempli de parfums, de sons, de projets et de climats. Ce que nous appelons la réalité est un certain rapport entre ces sensations et ces souvenirs qui nous entourent simultanément . . .

Proust[2]

A number of key concepts in Bergson's philosophy are clearly discernible in *À la recherche*, particularly the notions of time, memory, self and thought. These four major Bergsonian themes occur in binaries, one enantiomer of these binaries may be coded digital and the other analogic, or in Bergson's terminology one is quantitative and the other qualitative. Furthermore, there is opposition between these two forms, and in Bergson's philosophy, the analogic or qualitative enantiomer is always the dominant, a consequence which seems to be inherent in the Bergsonian method. Binaries of memory, self and thought similar, but not identical, to those described by Bergson also occur in Proust's novel and here also, the analogic element is the dominant. In contrast however, Proust's concept of time is distinct from Bergsonian time.

Time

Bergsonian Duration
The notion of *la durée pure* is perhaps one of the most novel and striking features of Bergson's philosophy, and he develops this concept of pure duration in the *Essai*, and further in *L'évolution créatrice*, and *Introduction à la métaphysique*.[3] As we have seen, it seems to

have been the absence of the notion of duration in the philosophy of Herbert Spencer, and Bergson's subsequent reflections on the nature of time and the difference between our subjective intuitive awareness of the passage of time as distinct from that described in the physical sciences, which was the starting point for his philosophy:

> Mais cette durée, que la science élimine, qu'il est difficile de concevoir et d'exprimer, on la sent et on la vit. Si nous cherchions ce qu'elle est? Comment apparaîtrait-elle à une conscience qui ne voudrait que la voir sans la mesurer . . . Telle était la question. Nous pénétrions avec elle dans le domaine de la vie intérieure, dont nous nous étions jusque-là désintéressé. . . Mais comment la philosophie de Spencer, doctrine d'évolution, faite pour suivre le réel dans sa mobilité, son progrès, sa maturation intérieure, avait-elle pu fermer les yeux à ce qui est le changement même? (PM 4)

Bergson repeatedly elaborates on the differences between pure duration and scientific or astronomical time, which are merely markers while real time, pure duration, is the interval between those markers which physical science does not discuss:

> Mais ces unités de temps, qui constituent la durée vécue, et dont l'astronome peut disposer comme il lui plaît parce qu'elles n'offrent point de prise à la science, sont précisément ce qui intéresse le psychologue, car la psychologie **porte sur les intervalles eux-mêmes, et non plus sur leurs extrémités.** (DI 147) [my emphasis]

In *L'évolution créatrice*, he expands further on the difference between *l'intervalle* of pure duration and the scientific markers at each end of an interval of pure time:

> Quand le mathématicien calcule l'état futur d'un système au bout du temps *t*, rien ne l'empêche de supposer que, d'ici là, l'univers matériel s'évanouisse pour réapparaître tout à coup. C'est le $t^{ième}$ moment seul qui compte,—quelque chose qui sera un pur instantané. **Ce qui coulera dans l'intervalle, c'est-à-dire le temps réel**, ne compte pas et ne peut pas entrer dans le calcul. . . Que s'il divise l'intervalle en parties infiniment petites par la considération de la différentielle *dt*, il exprime simplement par là qu'il considéra des accélérations et des vitesses, . . . l'état du système à un moment donné. (EC 22) [my emphasis]

Time, in science and physics, is that represented by the quantity 't' in the classical equations of Newtonian dynamics, such as:[4]

$$a = d^2s/dt^2$$
$$s = ut + \tfrac{1}{2}at^2$$

This 't' is the time that accurately describes and predicts the trajectories and orbits of objects moving with uniform acceleration, but this time has no duration, it is merely a digital marker which ignores the duration in the interval between the markers. Yet, pure time is precisely that which exists between the markers, not the markers themselves, and the only way to understand the concept of pure duration, says Bergson, is through intuition; for time is not space, nor *in* space, nor can it be accurately represented by images in space. For the same reason, it is perhaps misleading and somewhat irrelevant to state that time is merely the fourth dimension of space (x, y, z , & ict[5]), although this is mathematically correct and gives us important insight into the interrelationship between space and physical time. However, such a fourth dimension fails to communicate the notion of duration, the subjective and intuitive knowledge of the *continuous flow* of time, a quality which does not exist in (even imaginary) space.

Bergson's notion of pure duration is opposed to the familiar concept of time, which is usually perceived as spatial and digital and represented by, for example, the ticking of a clock. In the *Essai*, he clearly indicates that the usual, but incorrect, conception of duration is that of time projected in space: "Nous juxtaposons nos états de conscience de manière à les apercevoir simultanément, non plus l'un dans l'autre, mais l'un à côté de l'autre; bref, nous projetons le temps dans l'espace" (DI 75). When I (Bergson) turn my thoughts to within myself, I see a number of things. First I see perceptions coming from the external world and these perceptions are distinct and clear and tend to group themselves into what we call *objects*. Second, I perceive within myself my accumulated memories which may be related or evoked by my perceptions and help in my understanding of them. These elements are organized and focused from within towards the exterior, from my inner self towards the external world. If, however, I reverse the process and work from the outside towards my innermost self and seek that which is the most uniform, the most constant, the most consistently myself, I find something quite different:

> C'est, au-dessous de ces cristaux bien découpés et de cette congélation superficielle, une continuité d'écoulement qui n'est comparable à rien de ce que j'ai vu s'écouler. C'est une succession d'états dont chacun annonce ce qui suit et contient ce qui précède. (PM 183)

Bergson then analyses more closely this flow of duration, the succession of conscience states or thoughts and comes to the conclusion that they are of two distinct types, one quantitative and the other qualitative:

> Mais une autre conclusion se dégage de cette analyse: c'est que la multiplicité des états de conscience, envisagée dans sa pureté originelle ne présente aucune ressemblance avec la multiplicité distincte qui forme un nombre. Il y aurait là, disions-nous, une multiplicité qualitative . . . il faudrait admettre deux espèces de multiplicité, deux sens possibles du mot distinguer, deux conceptions, l'une qualitative et l'autre quantitative. (DI 90)

and

> Distinguons donc, pour conclure, deux formes de la multiplicité, deux appréciations bien différentes de la durée, deux aspects de la vie consciente. Au-dessous de la durée homogène symbole extensif de la durée vraie, une psychologie attentive démêle une durée dont les moments hétérogènes se pénètrent; au-dessous de la multiplicité numérique des états conscients, une multiplicité qualitative; (DI 95)

The imagery that Bergson uses to express in words that which is inexpressible, that which "est difficile de concevoir et d'exprimer," provides perhaps an image of *la durée pure*. But images are merely symbols[6] representing portions of reality and should not be confused nor be substituted with reality itself: "La conscience, tourmentée d'un insatiable désir de distinguer, substitue le symbole à la réalité, ou n'aperçoit la réalité qu'à travers le symbole" (DI 96). Often, we fully understand only if we can visualize, hence we tend to make images in space in order to visualize and help us comprehend and rationalize concepts which are not spatial. Symbols are of great importance, says Bergson, but no image, symbol or concept will communicate the notion of true duration to the individual who does not already possess intuitive knowledge of it. One of the disadvantages of symbols and images is that they tend to generalize, they indicate a common denominator between things and thus represent something by making it similar to a large number of other objects. That is, they tend to represent something by what it is not, and to generalize is to make common that which is unique and the uniqueness of individuality, of self and being, is often lost in the symbol. Philosophy, says Bergson, has occasionally to use symbols and images, but in general, philosophy is truly itself only when it surpasses rigid concepts in order to create notions that are quite different from those we normally use, and Bergson uses the imagery of fluids and motion when he says that philosophy has to use: "des représentations souples, mobiles, presque fluides, toujours prêtes à se mouler sur les formes fuyantes de l'intuition" (PM 188).

To illustrate and communicate the notion of pure duration as opposed to spatialized digital time, Bergson analyses the sounds of a church bell chiming the hour, and the sound of the repetitive blows of a hammer,[7]:

> Ainsi, quand nous entendons une série de coups de marteau, . . . nous découpons ce progrès en phases que nous considérons alors comme identique; et cette multiplicité de termes identiques ne pouvant plus se concevoir que par déploiement dans l'espace, nous aboutissons encore nécessairement à l'idée d'un temps homogène, image symbolique de la durée réelle. . . Ce qui prouve bien que notre conception ordinaire de la durée tient à une invasion graduelle de l'espace dans le domaine de la conscience pure, . . . car le sommeil, en ralentissant le jeu des fonctions organiques, modifie surtout la surface de communication entre le moi et les choses extérieures. Nous ne mesurons plus alors la durée, mais nous la sentons; de quantité elle revient à l'état de qualité; l'appréciation mathématique du temps écoulé ne se fait plus; mais elle cède la place à un instinct confus. (DI 93–4)

Bergson emphasizes that pure duration is: "une multiplicité non-numérique, une multiplicité qualitative," while digitalized, quantified time is a *quantitative* multiplicity and spatial in character, thus a mere symbolic depiction, and not a faithful representation of the *qualitative* multiplicity of pure duration with is real time.

I have already suggested that the rainbow with its interpenetrating series of changing colors provides an example, or symbol of a *multiplicité qualitative*, in addition perhaps, the continuous, interpermeating, and ever-changing flow of images provided by the sea and its movement and which pervade the Proustian novel at Balbec, provides another image of a qualitative multiplicity.

Duration and Memory

Pondering about duration naturally leads one to reflect on memory, for duration and memory are intimately linked, so that it is perhaps not surprising that *Matière et mémoire* (1896) was the first book Bergson published after the *Essai*. Writing of Bergson's philosophy and his concept of time, Bertrand Russell says:

> Pure duration is what is most removed from externality and least penetrated with externality, a duration in which the past is big with a present absolutely new. . . Duration is the very stuff of reality, which is perpetual becoming, never something made. It is above all in *memory* that duration exhibits itself, for in memory the past survives in the present. [8]

Clearly the Bergsonian concept of time is closely linked with that of memory, for without memory we can have no concept of the flow of time, of duration, although we might conceive of mathematical time and have an intuitive idea of space. Gilles Deleuze enunciates the same idea when he writes: "La durée est essentiellement mémoire, conscience, liberté. Et elle est conscience et liberté, parce qu'elle est d'abord mémoire . . . identité de la mémoire avec la durée même."[9] Thus inherent in the Bergsonian notion of duration are two other concepts; that of memory and that of the direction or arrow of time. The Bergsonian arrow of time is linked to memory since for a conscious person two moments of time cannot be identical, because each moment contains the memory of the preceding one. The only consciousness which could perceive two identical moments, is a consciousness without memory which would, in fact, be the unconscious. Not only is memory closely linked with the idea of *la durée pure* but without memory there can be no sense of self, since without memory I do not exist as a conscious being, for my memory is me, it provides my uniqueness and differentiates me from other beings. A being without memory, if one can conceive of such, would be an instantaneous being which could conceive of space and possibly of mathematical time, but have no sense of duration. Gilles Deleuze says: "C'est donc la mémoire qui fait que le corps est autre chose qu'instantané, et lui donne une durée dans le temps."[10]

The Arrow of Time
Memory thus provides a direction to Bergsonian duration, but there is another arrow of time to which we have already referred, namely entropy and the entropy-gradient. Eddington, whose writing is cited[11] by Bergson in *Durée et simultanéité*, also discusses the two forms of time and refers to a hypothetical but fascinating discussion[12] on the nature of time between the Astronomer Royal (as the keeper of scientific time) and Prof. Bergson. Later, Eddington says:

> In any attempt to bridge the domains of experience belonging to the spiritual and the physical sides of our nature, Time occupies the key position. I have already referred to its dual entry into our consciousness—through the sense organs which relate it to the other entities of the physical world, and directly through a kind of private door into the mind. (91)

Eddington's 'private door into the mind' is, of course, Bergsonian intuition. He then discusses the possibility that these two 'arrows of time;' first, that provided by the entropy-gradient and second, that provided by consciousness and memory might be related:

It seems to me, therefore, that consciousness with its insistence of time's arrow and its rather erratic ideas of time measurement may be guided by entropy-clocks in some portion of the brain . . . Entropy-gradient is then the direct equivalent of the time of consciousness in both its aspects. (101)

A discussion of the relationship between these two arrows of time is well beyond the scope of this study, but it is not irrelevant that Eddington, whose work is occasionally referred to by Bergson, should consider them affiliated. The discussion of pure duration linked to memory leads us into the Bergsonian duality of memory, but first we shall consider the Proustian conception of time.

Time in Proust

Georges Poulet concisely summarizes Proust's view on time when he states: "le temps proustien est du temps spatialisé, juxtaposé."[13] Proust's notion of time is different from Bergson's notion of *la durée pure*, and is rather similar to the normal spatial visualization of the flow of time, and thus resembles that spatialized perception of time that Bergson says is incorrect: "Lorsque nous parlons du temps, nous pensons le plus souvent à un milieu homogène où nos faits de conscience s'alignent, se juxtaposent comme dans l'espace, et réussissent à former une multiplicité distincte" (DI 67).

We cannot visualize time, but can visualize the flow of a stream; hence we tend to spatialize time, incorrectly but helpfully. We need to distinguish between the concept of 'time flowing' from 'time the epoch,' that is an element of time past. Proust intermingles space and memory with time, and one of his principal and recurrent metaphors to represent a past epoch of time is that of *vases clos* filled with qualitative images:

Mais surtout je mettais entre eux, . . . une de ces distances dans l'esprit qui ne font pas qu'éloigner, qui séparent et mettent dans un autre plan. Et cette démarcation était rendue plus absolue encore parce que cette habitude que nous avions de n'aller jamais vers les deux côtés un même jour, [et] les enfermait pour ainsi dire loin l'un de l'autre, inconnaissable l'un à l'autre, dans les vases clos et sans communication entre eux . . . (I 133)

and

—le geste, l'acte le plus simple reste enfermé comme dans mille vases clos dont chacun serait rempli de choses **d'une couleur, d'une odeur, d'une température** absolument différentes; sans compter que ces vases, disposés sur toute la hauteur de nos années pendant lesquelles nous n'avons cessé de

changer . . . sont situé à des altitudes bien diverses, et nous donnent la sensation d'atmosphères singulièrement variées . . . mais entre le souvenir qui
revient brusquement et notre état actuel, de même qu'entre deux souvenirs
d'années, de lieux, d'heures différentes, la distance est telle que cela suffirait,
en dehors même d'une originalité spécifique, à les rendre incomparables les
uns aux autres (IV 448) [my emphasis]

Not only are memories of past time, distinct separate one from another, but they are separated by a (spatial) distance, which is also a
difference in nature, so that Proustian memories appear to be in separate and discrete universes.

The above citations indicate three separate properties of Proust's
notion of time-epoch. First, time-epoch is digital, it is an interval of
time that can be parceled and separated from other epochs and the
continuous flow of time. Second, these intervals are somehow situated in space not only because of the reference to *hauteur* and *alti-
tude* and *distances*, but because of the *vases* which are separate,
evidently identical, countable and clearly elements, likes beads of an
abacus, in Bergson's homogenous space. Third, these epochs of time
are in some manner separated by a distance which is in a certain way
measurable. The narrator quite often refers to distance as implying a
separation in time of past events: "Non pas une figuration de ce clocher,
ce clocher lui-même, qui, mettant ainsi sous mes yeux la distance des
lieues et des années" (IV 275). Thus, times past and geographical
locations are separated by a similar type of distance, and this
spatialization and digitalization of time into discrete parcels separable
by a spatial distance is quite contrary to Bergson's notion of the continuous flow of time. A number of times Proust uses the metaphor of
a telescope to describe the process of recall, the perception and reminiscence of times past, these *vases clos* which resemble islands isolated in spacetime:

Même ceux qui furent favorable à ma perception des vérités . . . me félicitèrent
de les avoir découvertes au "microscope," quand je m'étais au contraire servi
d'un télescope pour apercevoir des choses, très petites en effet, mais parce
qu'elles étaient situées à une grande distance, et qui étaient chacune un monde.
(IV 618)

Thus, there is in Proust's conception of time and memory the notion of a time-capsule that is somehow suspended in space, or
spacetime, and viewable from a great distance but not always attainable. Proust verbalizes this notion even more clearly in a letter written

in 1922 to Camille Vettard, in which he says that he created his text by the use of an instrument resembling a telescope which was focused on elements of time past, and which again illustrates the spatialization of Proutian time-epochs:

> . . . mon livre . . . est sorti tout entier de l'application d'un sens spécial . . . ce sens spécial c'est peut-être celle d'un télescope qui serait braqué sur le temps, car le télescope fait apparaître des étoiles qui sont invisibles à l'oeil nu, et j'ai tâché . . . de faire apparaître à la conscience des phénomènes inconscients qui, complètement oubliés, sont quelquefois situés très loin dans le passé.[14]

Bergson also makes use of a spatial representation of time-epochs in discussing memory when he uses the metaphor and image of an inverted cone (MM 169 and 181). The apex of the cone represents the *moi* and resides at *now*, the present moment of time, while the entire cone fanning out in time represents the totality of past reminiscences accumulated in memory. A section through the cone, representing a certain group of memories, remains immobile, whilst the apex moves continually and inexorably forward with the flow time. There is an element of similarity between Proust's telescope and Bergson's cone, although for Bergson, memory of past epochs does not appear to be wrapped in individual and independent 'packages' like Proust's *vases clos*.

Cinematography is an image or metaphor that both Proust and Bergson use, albeit in rather different contexts. Proust makes use of this to illustrate the passage of time, but the cinema is not, he admits a faithful reproduction of the flow of time:

> Une heure n'est pas qu'une heure, c'est un vase rempli de parfums, de sons, de projets et de climats. Ce que nous appelons la réalité est un certain rapport entre ces sensations et ces souvenirs qui nous entourent simultanément— rapport qui supprime une simple vision cinématographique, laquelle s'éloigne par là d'autant plus du vrai qu'elle prétend se borner à lui—rapport unique que l'écrivain doit retrouver pour en enchaîner à jamais dans sa phrase les deux termes différents. (IV 467)

Here Proust agrees with the Bergsonian concept of time in that the succession of digital images of the cinema does not, he says, give a faithful representation of reality. Memory and epochs of past time seem to be represented as discrete digital encapsulated entities, awaiting to be recovered. Reality, says Proust, is that mysterious relationship between the unique present moment, and past experience encapsulated in the *vases clos*, and this unique relation, this annular link between the present experience and past recollections are not communicated by cinematography, by an endless sequence of discontinuous, digital images, indeed, these discrete images tends to suppress the true essence of reality. The above quotations contain another important point; they indicate what is contained in the *vases clos* of memory is "parfums, sons, projets et climats," while in the earlier quotation the content of the vases is "choses d'une couleur, d'une odeur, d'une température," and we will return to these points when discussing Proustian memory. Although Proust agrees with Bergson that an unending sequence of separate digital images is not a good representation of the flow of time, he unfortunately does not state in positive terms what might be a true depiction of duration or time. Yet the metaphor of cinematography does have some merit, for it is an image of the technique that a writer should use to link digital words so that they appear to be a non-ending sequence, a continuity that resembles reality.

Bergson uses the same metaphor, that of cinematography, not to illustrate the flow of time, but rather to emphasize that thoughts are not a sequence of distinct digital moments or elements. In *L'évolution creatrice*, he makes the point that:

> La science moderne, comme la science antique, procède selon la méthode cinématographique . . . Il est de l'essence de la science, en effet, de manipuler des *signes* qu'elle substitue aux objets eux-mêmes. Ces signes diffèrent sans doute de ceux du langage par leur précision plus grande et leur efficacité plus haute; ils ne sont pas moins astreints à la condition générale du signe, qui est de noter sous une forme arrêtée un aspect fixe de la réalité. (EC 328)

Reality viewed by science is a transposition into digital symbols which are then rapidly processed in some linear fashion like a ciné film or, we would now say, a digital video. Clearly this is not Bergson's view of reality. A few paragraphs later, he again emphasizes that the resemblance between the flow of thought and of time is *not* like a cinematographic film, for the latter always ignores *l'intervalle,* the duration between the markers that science calls time:

> La science pourra considérer des réarrangements de plus en plus rapprochés les unes des autres; elle fera croître ainsi le nombre des moments qu'elle isolera, mais toujours elle isolera des moments. Quant à ce qui se passe dans l'intervalle, la science ne s'en préoccupe pas plus que ne font l'intelligence commune, le sens et le langage. (EC 329)

Spacetime

Reality may be found in Nature, says Proust, but it is reproduced only in the unison and unity of two separate but related events, for example: "midi à Combray que dans le bruit de ses cloches, les matinées de Doncières que dans les hoquets de notre calorifère" (IV 468). By linking two events in space and time, Proust considers that they are then removed from the erosive quality, the destructive property of time. Thus, time is not a continuum, but a series of isolated events, a plurality of discontinuous moments separated in time and space.

The linking of two events in time and space leads to an interesting parallel, for the relationship between time and space for Proust is rather like the relativistic concept of 'spacetime.'[15] In the same way as memory can localize images in past time, so too it can localize them in space, or more correctly in spacetime. For to each event in time there is a space coordinate and a corresponding time coordinate in the four-dimensional spacetime continuum.

A reality that is unbounded yet finite in volume, is like the four dimensional surface of a hypersphere described by Einstein in his theory of relativity. Thus, a voyager on a globe traveling in one direction never reaches a boundary or edge, for the surface is unbounded, yet finite, and the traveler may voyage endlessly ultimately returning to the starting point. Is this not the essence of the Proustian novel? Is this not a form of *mise en abyme*, like the perpetual reflection in a pair of parallel mirrors, with the Proustian narrator and reader returning to the starting point after circumnavigating the globe of spacetime, after completing the text and returning to: "Longtemps, je me suis couché de bonne heure." The surprise at the end of Ruskin's metaphorical winding path[16] would thus be finding oneself again at the beginning. This experience of a circular journey and somewhat unexpectedly finding oneself at the starting point is wonderfully illustrated in the episode from *Combray* of the family's walk around Méséglise, and when all but Marcel's father feel totally lost, he reaches into his pocket and with seeming magic takes out of the key to the small gate at the bottom of the garden which is now in front of them:

> Tout à coup mon père nous arrêtait et demandait à ma mère: "Où sommes nous?" Épuisée par la marche, mais fière de lui, elle lui avouait tendrement qu'elle n'en savait absolument rien. Il haussait les épaules et riait. Alors, comme s'il l'avait sortie de la poche de son veston avec sa clef, il nous montrait debout devant nous la petite porte de derrière de notre jardin qui était venue avec le coin de la rue du Saint-Esprit nous attendre au bout de ces chemins inconnus. (I 113)

In that sense, the Proustian universe is very contemporary and even relativistic. But perhaps an even more contemporary view of Proust's concept of time and memory would be that of hypertext, in which segments of text are situated in hyperspace and can be accessed and explored in random sequence:

> Hypertext is a termed coined by Nelson in the 1960's and refers also to a form of electronic text, [hypertext] means *nonsequential writing,*—text that branches and allows choices to the reader, best read on an interactive screen, . . . it denotes a series of text chunks connected by links which offer the reader different pathways.[17]

Each passage of text is a separate world, a separate monad, and a distinct piece of reality. In each *vase clos* the world and text are ordered and time is uni-directional. However, one can move from one world, one text, to another in almost random fashion, eventually returning perhaps, to the starting point. Thus time need not be entirely uni-directional, for the sequence in which one visits the portions of hypertext may be random. That *À la recherche* may be considered a form of hypertext is also suggested by Landow,[18] who cites Georges Poulet's observation that in Proust, time does not appear as Bergsonian duration but as: "a succession of isolated moments," and points out that readers of Proust: "find themselves taking leaps and jumping into a different time and different characters." The following quotation illustrates the hypertextual quality in the Proustian concept of spacetime as discrete elements of reality floating in space and time:

> Ainsi se déroulait . . . une de ces causeries où la sagesse non des nations mais des familles, s'emparant de quelque événement, . . . et le glissant sous le verre grossissant de la mémoire, lui donne tout son relief, dissocie, recule et situe en perspective à différents points de l'espace et du temps ce qui . . . semble amalgamé sur une même surface, les noms des décédés, les adresses successives, les origines de la fortune et ses changements, les mutations de propriété. (IV 253–4)

Time and Personalities

The perception of the movement of time in Proust is indicated both in retrospective memory and in the change of the major characters, a factor which was discussed in Chapter 4. These changes are not gradual like the uninterrupted flow of time; they tend to be digital, discontinuous. An excellent example of this are the changes seen by the hero when he attends la matinée de Guermantes, *le Bal de têtes,* and encounters M. d'Argencourt and other former acquaintances. The changes of being are perceived not as successive but rather as discontinuous and digital, as a succession of discrete representations or layers of self and events:

> On dit et c'est ce qui explique l'affaiblissement progressif de certaines affections nerveuses, que notre système nerveux vieillit. Cela n'est pas vrai seulement pour notre moi permanent, qui se prolonge pendant toute la durée de notre vie, mais tous nos moi successifs qui, en somme le composent en partie. (IV 1145,[19])

The hero clearly realizes that his self, his Being is a succession of layers of his selves, each layer, each self being only a portion of his complete being. Furthermore, the successive *moi*'s still seem to have a discrete and digital quality rather than being a flowing continuum. Yet, the narrator clearly understands that within himself there is a continuity of being, of successive states that are united in one whole entity which is his Being:

> Pour tâcher de l'entendre de plus près, c'est en moi-même que j'étais obligé de redescendre. C'est donc que ce tintement y était toujours, et aussi, entre lui et l'instant présent, tout ce passé indéfiniment déroulé que je ne savais pas que je portais. Quand elle avait tinté, j'existais déjà, et depuis pour que j'entendisse encore ce tintement, il fallait qu'il n'y eût pas eu discontinuité, que je n'eusse pas un instant cessé . . . de ne pas exister, de ne pas penser, de ne pas avoir conscience de moi, (IV 624)

Consequently, the narrator can descend (a spatial image) to whatever level of his (involuntary) memory he chooses and everything, the totality of past experiences, is there to be found and indicates the continuity of memory and therefore of Being. This is clearly reminiscent of Bergson's *deux aspects du moi*, which is discussed more fully later in this chapter.

Memory[20]

Before entering into a detailed discussion of the types of memory described in Bergson's philosophy and comparing them with those in Proust's novel, I should emphasize two points. First, in order to simplify and clarify the distinction between some of Bergson's terms and Proust's and particularly to avoid the unconscious identification and congruence of Bergson's *mémoire volontaire* with the *mémoire volontaire* of Proust, I have avoided, in what follows, the use of the terms 'voluntary' and 'involuntary' when referring to the memories described by Bergson, preferring to use the designations of 'intentional' and 'spontaneous,' whereas the terms *volontaire* and *involontaire* are used in discussing the types of memory described by Proust. Second, it should be noted that the process of memory and recollection may, for simplicity, be divided into three phases with the self-explanatory titles of: encoding or registration, consolidation, and retrieval or recall, and when referring to memory, it is helpful to specify whether the adjectival terms 'spontaneous' or *volontaire* apply to the process of encoding or to that of retrieval.

Bergson
Intentional Memory: Encoding & Retrieval
Bergson clearly describes and delineates two forms of memory (see Table 1) which are quite distinct. The first form of memory is deliberate or intentional, it is quantitative, discontinuous, requires effort to acquire and lies in the forefront of our attention. The second is spontaneous, continuous, qualitative and essentially in images. While this latter memory requires no effort to acquire, it may be inconsistent and capricious in its retrieval. Bergson starts the analysis of these two forms of memory in *Matière et mémoire*, by giving the example of someone learning a lesson, say, memorizing a poem, or learning a piece of music. On the first day, he or she perhaps partially memorizes the poem and on the next occasion, he or she repeats the process until after two or three sessions, the lesson, the poem is learnt or memorized. The lesson is words, or symbols of some form, and the process of learning is intentional and deliberate, furthermore the retrieval is also deliberate and intentional and when I recite the lesson, my mind is concentrating, is in the present, and looking forwards to the future:

> Le souvenir de la leçon, en tant qu'apprise par coeur, a *tous* les caractères d'une habitude. Comme l'habitude, il s'acquiert par la répétition d'un même effort. Comme l'habitude, il a exigé la décomposition d'abord, puis la recomposition de l'action totale. (MM 84)

This memory is one of a task or lesson learned by habituation; it is a memory relating to action rather than representation, imagery, or contemplation, and is deliberate or intentional in that both encoding and retrieval are intentional and under the control of the will. Bergson uses the terms *souvenir acquis, mémoire volontaire,* and *mémoire habitude* (MM 93) to describe this intentional memory of effort, intelligence, logic, and things learned: "La première conquise par l'effort, reste sous la dépendance de notre volonté; la seconde, toute spontanée, met autant de caprice à reproduire que de fidélité à conserver" (MM 94).

Spontaneous Memory: Encoding
There is another form of memory linked to learning that lesson or poem, which involves the recollection, the reminiscence of the events surrounding the learning of the poem. For example, it might involve the recollection of the day one first read the poem, perhaps sitting at one's desk by the open window through which came the sound and perfume of summer, or perhaps the sound of the rain on the road outside mixing the smell of the dusty wet road with the odor of the waxed hardwood floor. All these latter impressions form what Bergson calls: "le souvenir pur, la mémoire spontanée, ou mémoire vraie, la mémoire par excellence,":

> . . . le souvenir de telle lecture particulière, la seconde ou la troisième par exemple, n'a *aucun* des caractères de l'habitude. L'image s'en est nécessairement imprimé du premier coup dans la mémoire, puisque les autres lectures constituent, par définition même, des souvenirs différents. C'est comme un événement de ma vie; il a pour essence de porter une date, et de ne pouvoir par conséquent se répéter. (MM 84)

This Bergsonian *souvenir spontané,* the *mémoire-image* is thus spontaneous, impromptu, unpremeditated and automatic in the sense that encoding requires no conscious effort or deliberate act, the process is spontaneous and effortless:[21] ". . . l'enregistrement, par la mémoire, de faits et d'images uniques en leur genre se poursuit à tous les moments de la durée" (MM 88).

While intentional memory requires effort and at times considerable concentration both to encode and retrieve, the spontaneous memory requires no deliberate exertion to encode or register. It is the memory in which the past is totally enveloped, totally encompassed and in which the process of recognition normally occurs by a comparison of present perception with the bank of images consolidated and held in this spontaneous memory:

> . . . on pourrait se représenter deux mémoires théoriquement indépendantes. La première enregistrerait, sous forme d'images-souvenirs, tous les événements de notre vie quotidienne à mesure qu'ils se déroulent; elle ne négligerait aucun

Table 1 Some characteristics of the types of memory described by Bergson and Proust.

	BERGSON				
INTENTIONAL		**SPONTANEOUS**			
		SPONTANEOUS–I		**SPONTANEOUS–II**	
Digital. Words, numbers, symbols, movements. Habit. *Mémoire volontaire.*[1] *Souvenir acquis. Mémoire habitude.*		Analogic. Visual images and episodes. *Images-souvenirs. Souvenir spontané. Mémoire spontané. La mémoire par excellence. Mémoire vraie.*		Analogic. Visual images combined with smell. Not described in detail. *Je respire l'odeur d'une rose, et aussitôt des souvenirs confus d'enfance me reviennent à la mémoire.*	
Encoding	Retrieval	Encoding	Retrieval	Encoding	Retrieval
Intentional. Requires mental effort.	Intentional. *Duration* fixed and order of retrieval critical. May be necessary for present action.	Spontaneous, requires no effort. Occurs continually during waking state	Voluntary, daydreaming. May be interrupted by intentional retrieval. *Duration arbitrary, je lui assigne une durée arbitraire. Order is elective*	Spontaneous.	Only example: Smell of rose recalls childhood. Duration not specified. Bergson's experience not as overwhelming as that of Proust's hero

Table 1 Continued

INTENTIONAL	PROUST			
	VOLUNTARY		**INVOLUNTARY**	
	Encoding	Retrieval	Encoding	Retrieval
No comparable memory described by Proust.				
Retrieval		Analogic. Visual images in monochrome, an inaccurate and incomplete reproduction. Only visual modality is retrieved. *Mémoire volontaire.*[1] *Mémoire de l'intelligence et des yeux. Des instantanés.*		Analogic. Visual images fully integrated with smell, taste, sound, touch and emotion. Complete and accurate retrieval of all aspects of past reality. *Mémoire involontaire. Souvenir involontaire.*
Encoding	Spontaneous, but not discussed in detail.	Presumably voluntary. *Duration arbitrary . . . on peut prolonger les spectacles de la mémoire volontaire.* Images in monochrome, not the full retrieval of reality.	Spontaneous but not discussed in detail.	Involuntary. Requires ancillary, rare, non-visual cue, e.g. taste of madeleine, feel of starched napkin, unusual sound. An overwhelming occurrence with similarities to a profound religious experience. *Le souvenir..venait à moi comme un secour d'en haut.. Duration brief.*

[1] Note that Bergson and Proust use the term *mémoire volontaire* to describe different forms of memory.

détail; . . . elle emmagasinerait le passé par le seul effet d'une nécessité naturelle. Par elle deviendrait possible la reconnaissance intelligente, ou plutôt intellectuelle, d'une perception déjà éprouvée; (MM 86)

The word *emmagasinerait* used here is characteristically Bergsonian, and not infrequently used by him. It evokes a vivid impression and describes in this context the ability of memory to encompass and envelop the past completely while more often it is used to describe the all-embracing, the all-containing power of language over thought.

Spontaneous Memory: Retrieval
The retrieval of the images in spontaneous memory is more difficult than that of intentional memory. Bergson suggests that perhaps this is because, except in the process of recognition, the content of this spontaneous memory is not normally useful or helpful to our everyday existence or survival, and therefore its retrieval takes a secondary place to that of intentional memory. Bergson associates the retrieval of spontaneous memory, to a sort of reverie, when our mind can wander back in time without concern for the present necessities. The only requirement for its retrieval, says Bergson, is the removal of the inhibitory effect of intentional memory, for these images of spontaneous memory are always present in our mind, but resident behind the veil of data and information that comprises learned intentional memory that we need for our everyday activities. The images of spontaneous memory may break through at occasional unsuspecting moments when we are less concerned with recitation and repetition of learned tasks, that is, when we are day-dreaming:

> Ce souvenir spontané, qui se cache sans doute derrière le souvenir acquis, peut se révéler par des éclairs brusques: mais il se dérobe, au moindre mouvement de la mémoire volontaire. (MM 93)

and:

> Mais si notre passé nous demeure presque tout entier caché parce qu'il est inhibé par les nécessités de l'action présente, il retrouvera la force de franchir le seuil de la conscience dans tous les cas où nous nous désintéresserons de l'action efficace pour nous replacer, en quelque sorte, dans la vie du rêve (MM 171)

This is perhaps why important things which are essential to our every-day survival have to be laid down in the intentional memory of action and habit where the information can rapidly be retrieved at will:

. . . les images emmagasinées par la mémoire spontanée ont encore un autre usage. Sans doute ce sont des images de rêve; sans doute elles paraissent et disparaissent d'ordinaire indépendamment de notre volonté; et c'est justement pourquoi nous somes obligés, pour *savoir* réellement une chose, pour la tenir à notre disposition il faut l'apprendre par coeur. (MM 90)

Comparison between Bergson's Intentional and Spontaneous Memory[22]

Their is an important difference between Bergson's two forms of memory that is relevant to their relation with the two forms of Proustian memory and this relates to their duration:

> . . . la conscience nous révèle entre ces deux genres de souvenir une différence profonde, une différence de nature. Le souvenir de telle lecture déterminée est une représentation, et une représentation seulement; il tient dans une intuition de l'esprit, que je puis, à mon gré, allonger ou raccourcir; je lui assigne une durée arbitraire: rien ne m'empêche de l'embrasser tout d'un coup, comme dans un tableau. Au contraire, le souvenir de la leçon apprise, . . . exige un temps bien déterminé, le même qu'il faut pour développer un à un, ne fût-ce qu'en imagination, tous les mouvements d'articulation nécessaires: ce n'est donc plus une représentation, c'est une action. Et, de fait, la leçon une fois apprise ne porte aucune marque sur elle qui trahisse ses origines et la classe dans le passé; elle fait partie de mon présent au même titre que mon habitude de marcher ou d'écrire; elle est vécue elle est "agie," plutôt qu'elle n'est représentée; (MM 85)

The duration of Bergson's spontaneous memory, the *souvenir d'image*, is arbitrary: "je puis, à mon gré, allonger ou raccourcir; je lui assigne une durée arbitraire: rien ne m'empêche de l'embrasser tout d'un coup, comme dans un tableau," it does not have a finite or quantitative duration in the sense that the learned poem occupies a fixed interval of time, one can wander about in the memory of images for as long as one wishes. In addition to having continuity, this memory has an all embracing property, an eidetic quality of encompassing the totality of the experience in an uninterrupted whole, "Le souvenir [image] . . . rien ne m'empêche de l'embrasser tout d'un coup, comme dans un tableau."[23] By comparison, the memory of the lesson learned is linear and uni-dimensional, and, in a sense, resembles a magnetic tape wound on a spool, or a fishing-line wound on a reel. One draws the memory out in a linear fashion, it has a beginning, an end, and a direction, for the order of events, like the words of a poem or the notes of a musical composition, is highly significant if not crucial. Our consciousness moves along the tape with time as our memory pulls out the information. Not only is the tape of this intentional memory linear, but it is uni-dimensional, at any one moment one can only be at one portion of the thread, one place of the poem. It is a memory symbolized by the abacus, of independent contiguous objects lined up in imaginary space. Thus intentional memory is very different from the *mémoire-image*, the pure Bergsonian memory which is multidimensional, without beginning and without end, where one image flows imperceptibly into the next and which can, perhaps, be symbolized by the rainbow.

It is of note that Bergson's intentional memory is often a memory of words, language or mathematical digits, and it is thus a memory of *le signifiant*. The spontaneous memory, the *mémoire-images* is not a retrieval of words or digits, but of the images that perhaps are evoked by those words and symbols and is thus a memory of *le signifié*.

In summary (see Table 1), for Bergson there are two radically different forms of memory. First there is the recollection of the poem learned or the task acquired, which is *intentional* memory and the adjective *intentional* applies both to the process of encoding and to that of retrieval, it requires effort and logic to learn, is linear, digital, quantitative and has a defined time span. It is a memory of habit and experience that resides in the forefront of our attention, such that it is rapidly accessible and can be put to immediate use, and is coded digital. The second form of memory, *la mémoire par excellence,* is spontaneous in that the process of encoding is unpremeditated and unconscious. It is the totality of one's past preserved in images which are qualitative and have no definite time span, nor direction in time, it has an eidetic quality in that it can be encompassed in its totality; ("rien ne m'empêche de l'embrasser tout d'un coup, comme dans un tableau"). This Bergsonian *mémoire par excellence, mémoire-image, mémoire spontané, mémoire vraie* is coded analogic, and is in Bergson's view, the superior or dominant.

Proust

In *À la recherche* Proust refers to two types of memory which I will denote as voluntary and involuntary memory and which we will later compare to Bergson's two forms of memory.

Voluntary Memory

An excellent description of what Proust understands by memory, *mémoire* or *mémoire volontaire* is given in the early part of 'Combray' when the sleepless and meditating narrator states:

> C'est ainsi que, pendant longtemps, quand, réveillé la nuit, je me ressouvenais de Combray, je n'en revis jamais que cette sorte de pan lumineux, découpé au milieu d'instincts ténèbres, pareil à ceux que l'embrasement d'un feu de Bengale ou quelque projection électrique éclairent et sectionnent dans un édifice dont les autres parties restent plongés dans la nuit: à la base assez large, le petit salon, la salle à manger, l'amorce de l'allée obscure . . . ma chambre à coucher avec le petit couloir à porte vitrée pour l'entrée de maman; en un mot, toujours vu à la même heure, isolé de tout ce qu'il pouvait y avoir autour, se détachant seul sur l'obscurité, (I 43)

This type of memory is one of reverie in a half-awake, half-asleep state when the mind can wander back in time. The memory is clearly incomplete; it includes a portion of the family home in Combray in which only fragments are visible and seemingly in only two dimensions, comparable perhaps to a stage set, while surrounding areas are obscure or not retrievable to the mind. It is a still and motionless picture, in which Combray is always perceived at the same time of day. That this memory is one involving voluntary recall is emphasized in an early draft of this portion of 'Combray' which again indicates the motionless, and lifeless quality of the image recalled and that only one period in time is retrieved:

> . . . et tout cela à neuf heures du soir, en un mot le décor indispensable comme celui qu'on indique en tête des vieilles pièces, pour le drame de mon déshabillage, avec l'heure où il avait lieu. Je ne revoyais jamais que cela, toujours dans la même lumière . . . est-ce que les jours à Combray n'avaient qu'une heure ou deux, de neuf heures à onze heures du soir? . . . En tout cas, présentées à l'appel de ma **volonté par ma mémoire consciente**, je me les serais rappelées, sans les revivre avec une apparente exactitude et sans vérité, sans charme, sans désir de les décrire. (I 695 [Esquisse XIII]) (my emphasis)

Another draft, which has important differences from the final text, further clarifies Proust's understanding of voluntary memory, emphasizing the monochrome and dull quality of the retrieved image that clearly is not a faithful resurrection or reproduction of past experience, and emphasizes that the retrieval of this memory is under the control of the intellect:

> Pendant bien des années je ne me souvins jamais de notre maison de Combray. Je savais que j'y avais passé une partie de mon enfance. Quand je voulais retrouver quelque image, je la demandais à l'intelligence, à cette **mémoire volontaire** qui ne nous rend nullement notre passé, car elle le peint tout entier d'une couleur uniforme et faussée qu'elle emprunte au présent. En réalité, Combray était mort pour moi. Mort à jamais? C'était possible. (I 1045. [Variante])[24] (my emphasis)

Proust usually uses the unqualified noun *mémoire* to describe this rather dull recall of images of the past. Nevertheless, in the final text of *À la recherche*, he uses the term *mémoire volontaire* on three occasions to describe the memory which, like that cited above, contains images of past events and people and does not appear to be encoded by a deliberate act of volition but whose retrieval is entirely under the control of the conscious will:

> . . . j'aurais pu répondre à qui m'eût interrogé que Combray comprenait encore autre chose et existait à d'autres heures. Mais comme ce que je m'en serais rappelé m'eût été fourni seulement par la **mémoire volontaire, la mémoire de l'intelligence**, et comme les renseignements qu'elle donne sur le passé ne conservent rien de lui, je n'aurais jamais eu envie de songer à ce reste de Combray. Tout cela était en réalité mort pour moi.
> Mort à jamais? C'était possible. (I 43)[25] (my emphasis)

and again:

> . . . nous pouvons tirer, comme des petits tubes dont on se sert pour peindre, la nuance juste, oubliée, mystérieuse et fraîche des jours que nous avions cru nous rappeler, quand, comme les mauvais peintres, nous donnions à tout notre passé étendu sur une même toile les tons conventionnels et tous pareils de **la mémoire volontaire**. (II 311)

Again, in *le Temps retrouvé*, the narrator tells us that voluntary memory requires no effort to recall and resembles casually glancing through a album of pictures:

> Certes, on peut prolonger les spectacles de la **mémoire volontaire** qui n'engage pas plus des forces de nous-mêmes que feuilleter un livre d'image. Ainsi jadis, par exemple le jour où je devais aller pour la première fois chez la princesse de Guermantes, de la cour ensoleillée de notre maison de Paris j'avais paresseusement regardé, à mon choix, tantôt la place de l'Église à Combray, ou la plage de Balbec, comme j'aurais illustré le jour qu'il faisait en feuilletant un cahier d'aquarelles prises dans les divers lieux . . . .(IV 452)

Proust's *mémoire* or *mémoire volontaire* is a memory of images, events and episodes and not of things or actions leaned, but these pictures and images are not faithful reproductions, but rather as might be inaccurately depicted by *les mauvais peintres*. It is voluntary in the sense that although the encoding has been carried out spontaneously (although this is not specified by Proust), the retrieval is *à mon choix*.

"La mémoire volontaire procède par instantanés," writes Deleuze,[26] for although Proust's *mémoire volontaire* may contain images usually, these are motionless images, which: "ne conservent rien de lui" and which: "ne nous donne du passé que des faces sans vérité." They are lifeless, monochrome images that one can examine rather like turning the pages of an old family photograph album: "J'essayais maintenant de tirer de ma mémoire d'autres "instantanés," notamment des instantanés qu'elle avait pris à Venise, mais rien que ce mot me la rendait ennuyeuse comme une exposition de photographies" (IV 444).

It is interesting to explore further Proust's notion of voluntary memory and its difference from the involuntary memory to be discussed below. In the interview published in *Le temps*, and mentioned in Chapter 1, Proust expands further on his conception of voluntary memory, and emphasizes that it retrieves images of past events which are incorrect or incomplete in that they do not evoke all the details of reality:

> Pour moi, la **mémoire volontaire**, qui est surtout une **mémoire de l'intelligence et des yeux**, ne nous donne du passé que des faces sans vérité; mais qu'une odeur, une saveur retrouvées dans des circonstances toutes différentes, réveille en nous, malgré nous, le passé, nous sentons combien ce passé était différent de ce que nous croyions nous rappeler, et que notre mémoire volontaire peignait, comme les mauvais peintres, avec des couleurs sans vérité.[27] [my emphasis]

He again states (I 43, quoted above) that voluntary memory is a memory of the intellect, although its retrieval requires little effort or concentration, but then goes on to add an important and often overlooked fact that voluntary memory is *une mémoire . . . des yeux*. Proust's voluntary memory is merely the retrieval of that portion of past perception that was encoded through the visual system. In addition, only a fragment of the encoded visual images are recalled, while those portions of experience perceived through the other sensory modalities are totally omitted. Reality involves the fusion, the complete integration, of data from all of our five senses; visual, olfactory, auditory, tactile and gustatory, intermixed with the emotions and memories they evoke. But our normal memory of past events is almost entirely visual, for although we can easily *recognize* a smell or taste, it is difficult to *recall voluntarily* or *imagine* a smell, a taste or a touch. We can, of course, recall the sound of a musical composition, but we do this through the uni-dimensional retrieval of digital memory, with fixed order and duration, rather than through the retrieval of an analogic quality.

Proust's *involuntary* memory appears to involve the retrieval of all the data encoded through visual perception as well as the information obtained through the other four sensory modalities in such a manner that there is a complete and faithful replication of the entirety of past reality. It is this retrieval, full integration and unison of data from all the sensory modalities that makes the recall of Proust's involuntary memory such a powerful, unique, and literally awesome, experience.

Involuntary Memory

Although Proust uses the term *mémoire involontaire* in his interview quoted above with the newspaper *Le Temps*, the term strangely does not occur anywhere in the published text of *À la recherche*, so that although the word '*mémoire*' occurs many times[28] none of these are followed by the qualifier '*involontaire.*' On two occasions, however, the Proustian text contains the term '*souvenir involontaire,*' but these are relatively minor occurrences. One of these is the *bottine* episode, when the hero, exhausted after his journey to Balbec, is unlacing his boots and the touch of his shoe is the cue for a sudden recollection of his dead grandmother:

> Mais à peine eus-je touché le premier bouton de ma bottine, ma poitrine s'enfla, remplie d'une présence inconnue, divine . . . Je venais d'apercevoir, dans ma mémoire, penché sur ma fatigue, le visage tendre préoccupé et déçu de ma grand-mère, telle qu'elle avait été ce premier soir d'arrivée; le visage de ma grand-mère, non pas de celle que je m'étais étonné et reproché de si peu regretter et qui n'avait d'elle que le nom, mais de ma grand-mère véritable dont, pour la première fois depuis les Champs-Élysées où elle avait eu son attaque, je retrouvais dans un souvenir involontaire et complet la réalité vivante. Cette réalité n'existe pas pour nous tant qu'elle n'a pas été recréée par notre pensée. . . . (III, 152–3)

Although this incident may not be a major dramatic event comparable to the other involuntary recalls, it is clearly the resurrection and retrieval of *la réalité vivante,* a more complete retrieval of the past than the normal *mémoire.* The second use of the phrase *souvenir involontaire* is merely a sorrow that resembles, but is not the retrieval of involuntary memory:

> Ma mère devait arriver le lendemain. Il me semblait que j'étais moins indigne de vivre auprès d'elle, que je la comprendrais mieux, maintenant que toute une vie étrangère et dégradante avait fait place à la remontée des souvenirs déchirants qui ceignaient et ennoblissaient mon âme . . . Je le croyais; en réalité il y a bien loin des chagrins véritables comme était celui de maman

. . . à ces autres chagrins, passagers malgré tout comme devait être le mien,
qui s'en vont vite comme ils sont venus tard, qu'on ne connaît que longtemps
après l'événement parce qu'on a eu besoin pour les ressentir de le
"comprendre;" chagrins comme tant de gens en éprouvent et dont celui qui
était actuellement ma torture ne se différenciait que par cette modalité du
souvenir involontaire. (III 165)

Proust's involuntary memory (*le souvenir* and *souvenir involontaire*)
seems to be encoded spontaneously, and would appear to be termed
'involuntary' because its retrieval is not under the control of the will or
of the intelligence which indeed seems to have a detrimental effect on
its retrieval:

. . . la moindre parole que nous avons dite à une époque de notre vie, le geste
le plus insignifiant que nous avons fait était entouré, portait sur lui le reflet de
choses qui logiquement ne tenaient pas à lui, en ont été séparées par
l'intelligence qui n'avait rien à faire d'elle pour les besoin du raisonnement.
(IV 448)

All the efforts of intellect, and concentration are not able to secure the
recall of these complete images of the past, although the information
seems to be fully encoded in the labyrinths of the mind:

C'est peine perdue que nous cherchions à l'évoquer, tous les efforts de notre
intelligence sont inutiles. Il est caché hors de son domaine et de sa portée, en
quelque objet matériel, (en la sensation que nous donnerait cet objet matériel),
que nous ne soupçonnons pas. Cet objet, il dépend du hasard que nous le
rencontrions avant de mourir, ou que nous ne le rencontrions pas. (I 44)

The *souvenir involontaire* is a memory whose content is hidden
and out of the reach of will-power, logic and intelligence, its retrieval
is dependent on a chance occurrence or cue, for example the fortuitous congruence of a non-visual sensation with an element of a past
event stored in involuntary memory, a serendipitous encounter that
perhaps will never occur. The images of *mémoire involontaire* are
quite distinct from those ordinary images of the past that we evoke
daily in our *mémoire volontaire*:

Sur l'extrême différence qu'il y a entre l'impression vraie que nous avons eue
d'une chose et l'impression factice que nous nous en donnons quand
volontairement nous essayons de nous la représenter, . . . je comprenais trop
que ce que la sensation des dalles inégales, la raideur de la serviette, le goût
de la madeleine avaient réveillé en moi n'avait aucun rapport avec ce que je
cherchais souvent à me rappeler de Venise, de Balbec, de Combray, à l'aide
d'une mémoire uniforme; (IV 448)

This fortuitous cue or chance occurrence is the necessary requirement for the opening of the Proustian *vases clos* and the emergence and liberation of the visions and reality of the past, of the *Temps retrouvé*.

Both types of memory described by Proust are analogic in nature, hence there is no digital–analogic opposition as in Bergson. Nevertheless for Proust, the involuntary memory is clearly the dominant and entirely superior of the two forms.

Comparison of the Two Forms of Memory Described by Bergson and Proust

The two forms of memory described by Bergson (Table I) are distinct from the two forms described by Proust, although they appear to overlap in the case of spontaneous memory. Much has been written concerning the resemblance, or lack of, between Proust's *mémoire volontaire* and *involontaire* and the two Bergsonian forms of memory. The controversy between the forms of memory described by these two authors was to some extent sparked by Proust's own statements on the subject in the interview published in *Le temps* in 1913. This statement possibly implies that Proust did not read carefully Bergson's *Matière et mémoire*, for although Proust is correct is stating that Bergson does not make the distinction that he, Proust, makes between *mémoire volontaire* and *mémoire involontaire*, nowhere does Bergson contradict their possible existence. In similar vein, Pilkington[29] says: "The most useful starting-point is to ask whether Proust was right in maintaining that his distinction between involuntary and voluntary memory was not only absent from Bergson but positively contradicted by him; there has been a move to the opposite extreme and a tendency to identify unreservedly the Proustian distinction with a distinction worked out in *Matière et Mémoire*." In her article on "Bergson et Proust," Françoise Fabre-Luce de Gruson states that the forms of memory described by the two writers are identical:

> De l'analyse de ces textes il semble que nous pouvons conclure que la distinction des deux mémoires, dont Proust a fait l'obstacle majeur à toute tentative de rapprochement entre son oeuvre et celle de Bergson, existe de façon formelle dans les textes bergsoniens.[30]

On the other hand, Pilkington suggests that this is not the case:

> All depends upon an identification of the Proustian concept of 'mémoire involontaire' with the Bergsonian 'souvenir spontané,' and a parallel identifi-

'mémoire-habitude.' It should be evident . . . that there is no basis for this identification.[31]

Indeed the present analysis clearly indicates that Pilkington is correct while Françoise Fabre-Luce de Gruson is not, and that the two memories of Bergson are not equivalent to those of Proust. The confusion arises partly from the uncritical use of the terms *volontaire* and *involontaire*, since there is indeed, as we have seen, a voluntary and involuntary components in Bergson's two forms of memory, but these are not the same as in Proust's. This confusion is increased by both writers use the term *mémoire volontaire* to denote a different type of memory (Table 1).

In summary, the two forms of Bergsonian memory are: first, the *mémoire habitude* or *souvenir acquis*, which I have termed intentional memory, the memory of things learned intentionally and whose retrieval is also intentional and deliberate, and a second type of memory, a *mémoire image*, *la mémoire vraie*, which I have termed spontaneous memory, a memory of images and episodes whose encoding is continuous and spontaneous but whose retrieval is voluntary albeit at times difficult:

> Il y a, disions-nous, deux mémoires profondément distincts: l'une, fixée dans l'organisme, n'est point autre chose que l'ensemble des mécanismes intelligemment montés qui assure une réplique convenable aux diverses interpellations possibles. . . . Habitude plutôt que mémoire, elle joue notre expérience passée, mais n'en évoque pas l'image. L'autre est la mémoire vraie. Coextensive à la conscience . . . se mouvant bien réellement dans le passé définitif, et non pas, comme la première, dans un présent qui recommence sans cesse. (MM 167–8)

Proust does not describe the intentional and digital form of memory discussed by Bergson and the two forms of memory described in *À la recherche* seem to be sub-divisions of Bergson's spontaneous memory, for they are both memories encoded spontaneously and both are a memory of imagery, of events and faces.

Proust's voluntary memory is one of colorless, motionless imagery which corresponds perhaps to Bergson's normal spontaneous memory, although Bergson does not mention this colorless and lifeless quality. The *mémoire involontaire* is by contrast the full retrieval and replication of past reality. The difference in the two Proustian forms of memory is in the process of retrieval in that the Proustian *mémoire volontaire* is amenable to voluntary retrieval, whereas the Proustian *mémoire involontaire* is a rare event, not under the control of the will and

which requires the congruence of some other, usually rare and serendipitous, non-visual event which acts as a cue or trigger.

The recollection that in Bergson's writings resembles most closely
Proust's *mémoire involontaire* is his experience, describes in the *Essai*,
of the scent of a rose which evokes images of his childhood, but
which Bergson unfortunately does not discuss in *Matière et mémoire*,
or elsewhere in his writings:

> Je respire l'odeur d'une rose, aussitôt des souvenirs confus d'enfance me
> reviennent à la mémoire. A vrai dire, ces souvenirs n'ont point été évoqués
> par le parfum de la rose: je les respire dans l'odeur même; elle est tout cela
> pour moi. (DI 121)

The two forms of Proustian memory also differ in the duration of
the retrieval, the *mémoire volontaire* has a duration that can be extended at will: "Certes, on peut prolonger les spectacles de la mémore
volontaire qui n'engage pas plus de forces de nous-mêmes que feuilleter
un livre d'image" (IV 452). It is here that we see a similarity between
Proust's voluntary memory and Bergson's spontaneous memory whose
recall (Table 1) can also have indefinite duration: "je lui assigne une
durée arbitraire," although it may be interrupted by an urgent appeal
for action from intentional memory. In contrast, Proust's *mémoire
involontaire* has a brief and evanescent duration that it does not appear possible to prolong. Gilles Deleuze tells us that Proustian involuntary memory is: "l'image instantanée de l'éternité," lasts only an
instant, and that:

> La réminiscence nous livre le passé pur, l'être en soi du passé. Sans doute cet
> être en soi dépasse-t-il toutes les dimensions empiriques du temps . . pour
> avoir une image de l'éternité. Ce passé pur est l'instance qui ne se réduit à aucun
> présent qui passe, mais aussi l'instance qui fait passer tous les présents . . .[32]

This evanescent quality of Proust's involuntary memory is thus a distinction from the duration of Bergson's spontaneous memory. The
process of retrieval of Proustian *mémoire involontaire* is such a striking, important and almost traumatic event that it deserves more careful analysis.

The Proustian Recall

The episode of the madeleine may be considered as the annunciation
of the Proustian hero's vocation, for it is the incident that begins to
make manifest to the hero his calling and his future life. The retrieval

of involuntary memory as recounted in the madeleine episode is a mixture of concentration, emotion and astonishment that is reminiscent of a profound religious experience, or in more prosaic terms perhaps of the process of childbirth.

The madeleine incident commences in an atmosphere of sadness and depression, for Combray is dull, gray and mournful. Then as the hero tastes the madeleine moistened in warm tea, he trembles: ". . . à l'instant même. . . Je tressaillis . . ." (I 44 onward), this is followed by a warm feeling of pleasure: ". . .un plaisir délicieux". Worries and concerns of this life begin to melt away: ". . . rendu les vicissitudes de la vie indifférentes," and there is a remarkable feeling of confidence: "J'avais cessé de me sentir médiocre, contingent, mortel." Until this point, the experience has required no effort, but at this stage, the hero begins to question the cause and nature of the emotions and feelings that are sweeping over him: ". . . d'où venait-elle? Que signifiait-elle?" Intense and concentrated thought does not help to clarify what is happening. The hero then attempts relaxation: ". . . je le force au contraire à prendre cette distraction que je lui refusais, à penser à autre chose." Then rather like the pause following the uterine contractions in childbirth, he concentrates again and even more like childbirth he feels something moving within himself: ". . . et je sens tressaillir en moi quelque chose qui se déplace . . ." After a number of such concentrated contractions of his intellect, the hero realizes the origin of the similarity: "Et tout d'un coup le souvenir m'est apparu . . . Et dès que j'eus reconnu de goût du morceau de madeleine . . ." and the full revelation occurs, the full essence of memory with all its anecdotal emotions, sensations, smells, sounds and color emerges from the gray shadows of the former Combray. A new life is born, the life of the new Combray, and the new hero. This is the Proustian epiphany, the beginning of the revelation of the hero's future life and vocation.

That the madeleine episode was largely autobiographical, with a *madeleine*[33] replacing perhaps a more mundane *biscotte* seems highly plausible. Another autobiographical passage by an English-speaking author has many similarities to the madeleine episode although the context is very different. This is another epiphany announcing and revealing a future life and vocation:

> We walked down the path to the well-house, attracted by the fragrance of the honeysuckle with which it was covered. Some one was drawing water and my teacher placed my hand under the spout. As the cool stream gushed over one

hand she spelled into the other the word water, first slowly, then rapidly. I stood still, my whole attention fixed upon the motions of her fingers. Suddenly I felt a misty consciousness as of something forgotten—a thrill of returning thought; and somehow the mystery of language was revealed to me. I knew then that "w-a-t-e-r" meant the wonderful cool something that was flowing over my hand. That living word awakened my soul, gave it light, hope, joy, set it free!

. . . As we returned to the house every object which I touched seemed to quiver with life . . . I saw everything with the strange, new sight that had come to me.[34]

Although the attendant conditions of this passage are essentially different from the madeleine episode, there is a basic similarity between the two which is striking. In both cases, there is an unexpected sensory stimulation (taste and touch), the significance of which is not initially recognized. This causes attention and concentration and there is the notion of a forgotten memory: ". . . as of something forgotten—a thrill of returning thought." There is an unsuspecting link between that sensory stimulation and another related sensory event, (the tea with Tante Léonie, and the message being tapped in Helen's other hand). Then suddenly there is the burst of recognition (of Combray and of language), the revelation of reality that leads to joy and euphoria. Helen Keller was blind and deaf hence data from the visual and auditory senses could not be evoked; it is of note, therefore, that reference to the senses of smell and touch are prominent in the above citation.

After the revelation, the world appears totally different and it would never again be the same for either individual. Both the Proustian hero and Helen Keller still had a long journey ahead of them, but the wonder of language and a new world of memory had been revealed by a remarkably similar process. For Proust, the retrieval of involuntary memory is like the tide of flowing water that carries the young blind and deaf girl out of darkness and enables her and him to rise from obscurity into the light of reality: ". . . le souvenir . . . venait à moi comme un secours d'en haut pour me tirer du néant d'où je n'aurais pu sortir tout seul" (I 5). Gilles Deleuze describes the sudden revelation of involuntary memory as a glimpse of the timeless, a revelation of reality or a vision of eternity that lasts only for a brief instant: "La mémoire involontaire nous donne l'éternité, mais de telle manière que nous n'ayons pas la force de la supporter plus d'un instant, ni le moyen d'en découvrir la nature. Ce qu'elle nous donne, c'est donc plutôt l'image instantanée de l'éternité."[35]

All of the Proustian hero's experiences of involuntary memory are not so shattering as the madeleine episode or those at the *matinée de Guermantes*. There are some cases when the retrieval is clearly 'involuntary' in that it is not instigated by an act of the will, but is caused by the sight of a familiar object, nevertheless, the retrieval is relatively un-traumatic. The thought of a settee belonging to his Tante Léonie that the hero wishes to give to the proprietor of the *maison de passe,* where *Rachel quand du Seigneur* plied her trade, arouses a mildly erotic recollection:

> D'ailleurs, comme notre mémoire ne nous présente pas d'habitude nos souvenirs dans leur suite chronologique, je me rappelais seulement beaucoup plus tard que c'était sur ce même canapé que, bien des années auparavant j'avais connu pour la première fois les plaisirs de l'amour avec une de mes petites cousines . . . (I 568)

Even in the *bibliothèque du Prince de Guermantes*, involuntary memories need not be world shattering. The sight of the book *François le champi* in the bookcase produces an involuntary recall which is qualitative and sensuous but not of the same intensity as the experience of the madeleine or the other recalls at the *matinée de Guermantes*:

> . . . la douloureuse impression que j'avais éprouvée en lisant le titre d'un livre dans la bibliothèque du prince de Guermantes; titre qui m'avait donné l'idée que la littérature nous offrait vraiment ce monde de mystère que je ne trouvais plus en elle . . . C'était une impression bien ancienne, où mes souvenirs d'enfance et de famille étaient tendrement mêlés . . . Aussi ce livre que ma mère m'avait lu haut à Combray presque jusqu'au matin, avait-il gardé pour moi tout le charme de cette nuit-là . . . Tel nom lu dans un livre autrefois, contient entre ses syllabes le vent rapide et le soleil brillant qu'il faisait quand nous le lisions. (IV 462–3)

and:

> . . . si je reprends dans la bibliothèque *François le Champi*, immédiatement en moi un enfant se lève qui prend ma place, qui seul a le droit de lire ce titre: *François le Champi*, et qui le lit comme il le lut alors, avec la même impression du temps qu'il faisait dans le jardin, les mêmes rêves qu'il formait alors sur le pays et sur la vie, (IV 464)

Memory as One of the Faculties which Modifies Perception

Not only is time intermixed with memory, but memory is intermingled with perception. Possibly more important in the Proustian novel than involuntary memory itself is the effect that memory has on perception or the interaction of recognition on recollection, and recollection on perceiving. Our perception of the external world is modified and modulated by previous experience as laid down in memory. Bergson says, "Perception et souvenir se pénètrent toujours, échangent toujours quelque chose de leurs substances par un phénomène d'endosmose." (MM 69). Perception is never an exact representation of the external world, of external reality. Perception consists of images that are filtered, chosen, and selected. The central nervous system plays an important role in percolating and refining only those aspects of the external world that are of interest to the self at a particular moment. An example of the filtering action of mind over perception is the way in which we can focus our attention and hearing on particular conversations in a room crowded with people and voices. The mind consciously, unconsciously and sub-consciously filters, selects, suppresses and amplifies.

In discussing the effect of memory on perception, Bergson starts with the simple example of someone who overhears two individuals speaking in what is, to the observer, a foreign language:

> J'écoute deux personnes converser dans une langue inconnue, . . . Les vibrations qui m'arrivent sont les mêmes qui frappent leurs oreilles. Pourtant je ne perçois qu'un bruit confus où tous les sons se ressemblent. Je ne distingue rien et ne pourrais rien répéter . . . la conversation que j'entends n'est pour moi qu'un bruit, (MM 120)

The unknown language is mere noise to the untrained ear. But should the observer return having learned that language, and thus with that tongue in his memory, the noise now will be transformed into information, communication, and perhaps even poetic images.

The most obvious effect of memory on perception is related to the process of recognition. Normally, says Bergson, we see things in mere outline, but should that outline fit a memory, should the sketch find resonance and congruence with an image in our memory, then retrieval is triggered and a complete image emerges:

> Nous n'apercevons de la chose que son ébauche; celle-ci lance un appel au souvenir de la chose complète; et le souvenir complet, dont notre esprit n'avait pas conscience, qui nous restaient en tous cas intérieur comme une simple pensée, profite pour s'élancer dehors. C'est cette espèce d'hallucination, insérée dans le cadre réel, que nous nous donnons quand nous voyons la chose. (ES 99)

Of importance in the above is the clear statement that there are elements of memory, perhaps very large ones, of which we are not conscious and these unconscious memories may be retrieved by a suitable cue. This is clearly relevant to the Proustian phenomenon of recollection, as is the suggestion that if there is a close relation between the initial sensory stimulus that precedes the conscious perception and a memory trace, then that conscious perception and experience may be modified. Thus although we might normally say that *la saveur d'une madeleine* was the cue for the retrieval of large amount of encoded information, the existence of which the hero was unaware, equally one would be correct in stating that memory had altered the taste of the madeleine, that is memory had modified perception and experience:

> Mille et mille évocations de souvenirs par ressemblance sont possibles, mais le souvenir qui tend à reparaître est celui qui ressemble à la perception par un certain côté particulier, celui qui peut éclairer et diriger l'acte en préparation. Et ce souvenir lui-même pourrait, à la rigueur, ne pas se manifester: (ES 145)

Bergson gives another example of sensations evoking and thus becoming intimately intermixed with memories, when he recounts the experience, quoted earlier, of the fragrance of a rose evoking vivid memories of his childhood. There is an obvious similarity here between Bergson stating: ". . . ces souvenirs n'ont point été évoqués par le parfum de la rose: je les respire dans l'odeur même," and Proust's statement, quoted in the next section, that: "la meilleur part de notre mémoire est . . . dans un souffle pluvieux," as if the memory were somehow in the cue itself. Bergson says that there are two ways of thinking of the effect of memory on perception. Either one can take a mechanistic view and say that sensation, the smell of the rose, is a trigger for memory, a password which opens the door into memory banks. Or one can take a more qualitative approach and say that the memory is *in* the odor of the rose. He expounds further on this fusion of perception with memory, of the unity of the perfume of a rose with the childhood memory:

> D'autres la sentiront différemment.—C'est toujours la même odeur, direz-vous, mais associée à des idées différentes.—Je veux bien que vous vous exprimiez ainsi; mais n'oubliez pas que vous avez d'abord éliminé, des impressions diverses que la rose fait sur chacun de nous, ce qu'elles ont de personnel; vous n'en avez conservé que l'aspect objectif, ce qui, dans l'odeur de rose, appartient au domaine commun . . . A cette condition seulement, d'ailleurs,

on a pu donner un nom à la rose et à son parfum. Il a bien fallu alors, pour distinguer nos impressions personnelles les unes des autres, ajouter à l'idée générale d'odeur de rose des caractères spécifiques. . . Mais l'association dont vous parlez n'existe guère que pour vous, et comme procédé d'explication. (DI 122)

Bergson is suggesting here that 'the smell is the perfume of child-hood,' not just a trigger of memory, but rather that in the mind of the inner self, cause and effect are not necessarily separable, they are not contiguous but often continuous. The association of the perfume of the rose with one's childhood is something very special and personal. One cannot treat this as a generalized association of rose-perfume with childhood memories. To do that would be to universalize the relationship between cause and effect, which are subjective, personal and totally intermixed so that one is not separable from the other. Thus, the perception of the perfume of a rose, according to Bergson, is greatly modified by memories of childhood.

In every-day life affection and memory, modify our perception. This is particularly the case when the perception is the sight, the glimpse of a loved one, who we rarely see as they *really* are because their image is often modified for and by us, the window of our perception is clouded by the veil and mist of affection and memories:

Nous ne voyons jamais les êtres chéris que dans le système animé, le mouvement perpétuel de notre incessante tendresse, laquelle, avant de laisser les images que nous présente leur visage arriver jusqu'à nous, les prend dans son tourbillon . . . (II 438)

For the Proustian hero and narrator, perception and memory are of-ten totally intertwined and woven inseparably together. Thus, on one occasion the hero inadvertently sees a loved one as she really is rather than as he normally sees her through the eyes of his memory, and his actual perception of his grandmother becomes disassociated from memory. He returns to his grandmother's apartment unannounced and metaphorically before his memory has the chance to catch up with him and hide the reality of present actuality: ". . . quand quelque cruelle ruse du hasard empêche notre intelligence et pieuse tendresse d'accourir à temps pour cacher à nos regards ce qu'ils ne doivent jamais contempler" (II 439). Accordingly, he sees his beloved grand-mother, not through the window of memory and affection which soft-ens and mellows her image, but perhaps as others see or saw her, perhaps as she *really* was, when perception was not altered by memory:

. . . moi pour qui ma grand-mère c'était encore moi-même, moi qui ne l'avais
jamais vue que dans mon âme, toujours à la même place du passé, à travers
la transparence des souvenirs contigus et superposés, tout d'un coup, dans
notre salon qui faisait partie d'un monde nouveau, celui du Temps, celui où
vivent les étrangers, . . . pour la première fois et seulement pour un instant
car elle disparut bien vite, j'aperçus sur le canapé, sous la lampe, rouge,
lourde et vulgaire, malade, rêvassant, promenant au-dessus d'un livre des
yeux un peu fous, une vieille femme accablée que je ne connaissais pas. (II
439)

The clearest and most dramatic interaction of perception with memory,
of recollection with sensation, in the Proustian novel are the four shattering reminiscences which are such key events in *À la recherche*.
There is first, the episode of the madeleine, which like Bergson's rose,
is associated with a host of images of childhood and adolescence. The
others are described in *Le Temps retrouvé* when the significance of
these reminiscences eventually becomes clear to the hero. To these
we might add the less shattering episode of *la bottine* mentioned
earlier in which memory influences the hero's perception of his shoe.

There are two important scientific paradigms that are related to
these Proustian events of involuntary retrieval. One is chance and the
other is resonance. Chance is not, of course, unique to science, but it
is often crucially important in scientific investigations. Louis Pasteur,
whose career was greatly influenced by serendipity, very rightly said:
"Dans les champs de l'observation, la chance ne favorise que les esprit préparés."[36] Both Marcel Proust and his hero were eventually prepared to see the significance of the chance tasting of a madeleine
dipped in a cup of tea, or of stumbling on a cobblestone in the court
yard. But perhaps a more dramatic scientific paradigm involved here
is that of resonance. Resonance is a relatively large, sometimes cata-
strophic selective response of a system that vibrates in step with an
externally applied oscillatory force. Resonance occurs when the frequency of the driving force coincides exactly with the natural frequency
of the assemblage being driven. A resonant response is totally out of
proportion to the size of the stimulus. The madeleine dipped in the
tea-cup may be considered as the stimulus, the natural properties of
which coincided exactly with the olfactory images that lay dormant in
the hero's memory. The response was enormous and totally out of
proportion to the size of the stimulus:

. . . toutes les fleurs de notre jardin et celles du parc de M. Swann, et les
nymphéas de la Vivonne, et les bonnes gens du village et leurs petits logis, et

l'église et tout Combray et ses environs, tout cela qui prend forme et solidité, est sorti, ville et jardins, de ma tasse de thé. (I 47)

We might also add that the impact of the resonance of the madeleine is much greater than this quotation itself might imply, for the totality of À la recherche, and the millions of pages of commentary and criticism that have ensued, were the resonant response to that minute stimulus of a *biscotte* in a tea-cup.

Where is Memory?

Another apparent similarity between Bergson and Proust concerns their notion of the location of memory, the site where the encoding and recall occur. Here, Bergson seems to drift away from the neuroscience of his age and his usual precision and analysis to enter a vague realm of spiritualism. He cannot understand how memory, the essence of self, can be located in matter, that is in the brain. For Bergson, mind and memory are somehow external to matter and brain: "D'où l'étrange hypothèse de souvenirs . . . nous ramèneraient au passé par un processus mystérieux" (MM 95), and more specifically: ". . . le cerveau contribue à rappeler le souvenir utile, mais plus encore à écarter provisoirement tous les autres. Nous ne voyons pas comment la mémoire se logerait dans la matière" (MM 198). Proust's view on the location of memory is somewhat more poetic, implying that memory is actually located in a drizzly gust of wind or in the aroma of a crackling fire:

. . . la meilleure part de notre mémoire est hors de nous, dans un souffle pluvieux, dans l'odeur de renfermé d'une chambre ou dans l'odeur d'une première flambée, partout où nous retrouvons de nous-mêmes ce que notre intelligence, n'en ayant pas l'emploi, avait dédaigné, la dernière réserve du passé, la meilleure, celle qui, quand toutes nos larmes semblent taries, sait nous faire pleurer encore. (II 4)

Indeed, he is suggesting that the trigger for the retrieval of involuntary memory is located in these qualitative sensations. Proust does not appear to be more precise on the location of memory, and the similarity between him and Bergson in this respect is perhaps more superficial than actual.

Bergson's inability to rationalize the relationship between memory, mind and brain is not surprising. The Nobel winning and pioneer neurophysiologist, Sir Charles Sherrington wrote: "That our being should consist of two fundamentally elements offers, I suppose, no greater inherent improbability than that it should rest on one only. We have to regard the relation of mind to brain as still not merely unsolved, but still devoid of a basis for its beginning." At the end of a discussion on the physical basis of mind, Sherrington said: "Aristotle, 2,000 years ago, was asking how is the mind attached to the body? We are asking that question still."[37] So was Henri Bergson.

Self

Bergson's "Les deux Aspects du Moi"

The third aspect of Bergson's philosophy I would like to compare with Proust's is that of self or being. There are two perceptions of time, and two kinds of memory. Linked to these two perceptions of time and memory, and thus of reality, are two aspects of ourselves, of our Self, two perceptions of our Being which Bergson calls: "les deux aspects du moi."

In the *Essai*, Bergson starts his description of *les deux aspects du moi* (DI 95) by recapitulating the two perceptions of time in a paragraph, quoted earlier in this chapter, which is dense in imagery and thought and which summarizes much of his philosophy. He reminds us that time exists in both a quantitative and a qualitative form and goes on to suggest that associated with each of these forms of time there is: "au-dessous du moi aux états bien définis, un moi où une succession implique fusion et organisation" (DI 95). Bergson uses the term *moi superficiel* to designate the consciousness that exists in spatial time and the *moi profond*[38] for the consciousness that exists in pure time: "Mais comme ce moi plus profond fait qu'une seule et même personne avec le moi superficiel, ils paraissent nécessairement durer de la même manière" (DI 93). The word *superficiel* gives a spatial representation to the form of being, and also signifies that this self is indeed superficial, in the sense of being trivial, perfunctory, flimsy and shallow. This superficial self may be precise in its thoughts, but these are not continuous but separate, in contiguous order and expressed in digital impersonal words, which are generic and somewhat commonplace. In contrast the thoughts and feelings of the *moi profond* are not digitalized and generic, but are continuously flowing, changing like the colors of the rainbow or the image of the flowing, ever-changing waves of the sea. In order that the ideas and emotions of the *moi profond* may be communicated, they have to be transposed to the superficial self and at that point, the flowing and fluid

thoughts solidify into words. Habit and social necessities of expressing ourselves result in the unique and personal thoughts changing
their character and being transformed into words, which are non-spe-
cific, but these words crush and deform original thoughts and make
them fit into the mold of commonplace social discourse. In order to
protect this inner self, it is to our advantage not to remove that cover-
ing layer of social conventions that protects our true being, for to do
this would reveal and expose our inner self which will then change
and loose its uniqueness. Clearly, the superficial self which is verbal
and exists in spatial time can be coded digital, while the deeper self,
whose ideas are interweaving and continuous, has the character of the
analogic and is the dominant and genuine being. Moreover, it is not
possible to analyze precisely this *moi profond*, for as soon as one
focuses one's attention on this aspect of being, and attempts to analyze these intimate, personal and non-verbal thoughts and concepts,
they melt away and the *moi profond* reverts to the superficial self, the
non-verbal thoughts and emotions are transformed into the generic
and verbal. This is the Bergsonian 'uncertainty principle' that is discussed in Chapter 6.

The Two Aspects of Self and the
Voices of the Proustian Hero[39]

Proust is clearly very much aware of the existence of a superficial and
a deeper self although this clearly does not imply that his awareness
arises from a knowledge of Bergson's writings. In *Contre Sainte-Beuve*
he says:

> . . . qu'un livre est le produit d'un autre *moi* que celui que nous manifestons
> dans nos habitudes, dans la société, dans nos vices. Ce moi-là, si nous voulons
> essayer de le comprendre, c'est au fond de nous-mêmes, en essayant de le
> recréer en nous que nous pouvons y parvenir.[40]

Representations of the Bergsonian *deux aspects du moi* can be
seen in the voice(s) of the hero or protagonist in *À la recherche*, and
at times the hero represents the superficial *moi* of Bergson, while at
other times the hero also takes on the voice of the *moi profond*.
Although the two Bergsonian aspects of being are clearly present in
the Proustian hero, this does not imply that the Proustian treatment
of the two selves is specifically or uniquely Bergsonian.

The superficial voice of the hero is seen when the protagonist is in
action and clearly living and thinking in the present and looking in

anticipation towards the future. At these times the hero's self is often united with other members of the family so that his uniqueness is fused with that of others and he looses something of his single subjective self. In these cases, he occasionally refers to himself either as 'on' or 'nous' indicating that the unique qualities of the *moi profond* have been fused with that of others, and that it is the social *moi* who is speaking or thinking. One example of the hero's 'je' becoming a 'nous', is cited by Marcel Muller, namely the arrival of Swann in the evening when the family is gathered together in the garden at Combray: "Nous étions tous au jardin quand retentirent les deux coups hésitants de la clochette. On savait que c'était Swann; néanmoins tout le monde se regarda d'un air interrogateur et on envoya ma grand-mère en reconnaissance" (I 23). Another example of the hero's self melting in with other family members and thus remaining at the superficial and social level, is given in the elegantly playful description of *le samedi asymétrique*:

> Cette avance du déjeuner donnait d'ailleurs au samedi, pour nous tous, une figure particulière, indulgente, et assez sympathique. Au moment où d'habitude on a encore une heure à vivre avant la détente du repas, on savait que, dans quelques secondes, on allait voir arriver des endives précoces, une omelette de faveur, un bifteck immérité. (I 109)

Here, the hero is clearly living in the present looking, with anticipation, at the immediate future and refers to himself as *nous* and *on*. It is perhaps not surprising that it is the superficial self speaking to us on this occasion, for *le samedi asymétrique* is not a profound philosophical discourse.

There are other times when the self of the hero takes on another form and he becomes the Bergsonian *moi profond*. An example is when the young hero is impatiently awaiting his mother's good-night kiss:

> C'est que les soirs où des étrangers, ou seulement M. Swann, étaient là, maman ne montait pas dans ma chambre . . . ce baiser précieux et fragile . . . il me fallait transporter de la salle à manger dans ma chambre . . . que je le prisse, que je le dérobasse brusquement, publiquement, sans même avoir le temps et la liberté d'esprit nécessaires pour porter à ce que je faisais cette attention des maniaques qui s'efforcent de ne pas penser à autre chose. (I 23)

This is very much the interior self, the inner being, talking, feeling and thinking. Other examples, are the times when the hero is taking his solitary walks through the countryside of Combray and Méséglise, and we hear the pensive and reflective soul-searching for the philosophical and artistic essence of reality:

> Alors, bien en dehors de toutes ces préoccupations littéraires et ne s'y rattachant en rien, tout d'un coup un toit, un reflet de soleil sur une pierre, l'odeur d'un chemin me faisaient arrêter par un plaisir particulier qu'ils me donnaient, et aussi parce qu'ils avaient l'air de cacher au-delà de ce que je voyais, quelque chose qu'ils invitaient à venir prendre et que malgré mes efforts je n'arrivais pas à découvrir. (I 176)

The episode of *Les clochers de Martinville,* which is discussed at length in Chapter 7, is also an example of the discourse of the hero's *moi profond* as distinct from his superficial self.

When the hero is with his family group, as in the examples cited above, or attending an elegant social function, he becomes more gregarious and in those cases the superficial and socially necessary self usually but not invariably predominates. Solitude seems to be an essential requirement for the emergence of the *moi profond* and the beauty of the external world is perceived more clearly when seen by the inner rather than through the senses of superficial self whose perception is dulled by habit. This is clearly seen in the remarkable passage of *la belle laitière,* in which the hero on his solitary train journey perceives, as the dawn is breaking, the natural beauty of the countryside and one of its inhabitants, who he hopes also experiences solitude and a seclusion which he would like to share. His perceptions of *la belle laitière* are as fresh and unique as the pink of the dawn reflected on her cheeks and are equally different from those that he would normally perceive through his superficial self, for they are a brief perception of a reality that is usually dulled and hidden by the habits of convention:

> . . . la grande fille que je vis sortir de cette maison et, sur le sentier qu'illuminait obliquement le soleil levant, venir vers la gare en portant une jarre de lait. . . elle ne devait jamais voir personne que dans ces trains qui ne s'arrêtaient qu'un instant. Elle longea les wagons, offrant du café au lait à quelques voyageurs réveillés. Empourpré des reflets du matin, son visage était plus rose que le ciel. Je ressentis devant elle ce désir de vivre qui renaît en nous chaque fois que nous prenons de nouveau conscience de la beauté et du bonheur. Nous oublions toujours qu'ils sont individuels et, leur substituant dans notre esprit un type de convention . . . (II 16)

He continues his introspection by specifying the two aspects of self, which the hero here calls his 'complete' as opposed to his 'reduced' self:

> Mais ici encore la cessation momentanée de l'Habitude agissait pour une grande part. Je faisais bénéficier la marchande de lait de ce que c'était mon être au complet, apte à goûter de vives jouissances, qui était en face d'elle. C'est d'ordinaire avec notre être réduit au minimum que nous vivons; la plupart de nos facultés restent endormies, parce qu'elles se reposent sur l'habitude . . . (II 17)

It is the *moi profond*, the full and complete inner self that rises to the surfaces to experience and become part of this new world which usually is not seen by the faculties of perception which are dulled by routine and custom, and it is because of this uncovering of his deeper self, that the hero is able to experience, for few moments, the sight of *la belle laitière* and her surroundings in their true beauty, untarnished by the perceptions and conventions of everyday life.

The hero also realizes that solitude is an essential quality for the emergence of his *moi profond* and is well aware of these two aspects of being, of the two levels of his inner self and at dinner with the Prince de Guermantes he thinks to himself:

> Dans un dîner, quand la pensée reste toujours à la surface, j'aurais pu sans doute parler de *François le Champi* et des Guermantes sans que ni l'un ni l'autre fussent ceux de Combray. Mais quand j'étais seul, comme en ce moment, c'est à une profondeur plus grande que j'avais plongé . . . (IV 462)

Here, the hero is quite conscious of both his superficial self that converses with words in a social context and also of that other being that exists at greater depths and in which the qualitative memories of Combray and of his first reading of *François le champi* are entrapped under those protective layers that Bergson terms: "la croûte extérieure de faits psychologiques" (DI 126). The two Bergsonian aspects of being are thus clearly discernible in the Proustian hero, who like all of us, has two aspects of being that are described in the text.

The Doubling of Self in Memory

There is another duality of self in Bergson's writings that should not be confused with the two aspects of being discussed above. This second duality of self is the reflection we have of ourselves in the memory of our immediate past, or the immediate doubling of self in actuality and in memory. Therein lie these two *additional* forms of being, as Bergson puts it, one self is *actual* while the other, mirrored in memory, is *virtual*:

> Notre existence actuelle, au fur et à mesure qu'elle se déroule dans le temps, se double ainsi d'une existence virtuelle, d'une image en miroir. Tout moment de notre vie offre donc ces deux aspects: il est actuel et virtuel, perception d'un côté et souvenir de l'autre.
>
> Celui qui prendra conscience du dédoublement continuel de son présent en perception et en souvenir . . . se comparera à l'acteur qui joue automatiquement son rôle, s'écoutant et se regardant jouer. (ES 136 & 139)

As we shall see, these latter two forms of Being, the twinning of self into the 'I' who exists at the present moment and the 'I' who acts in the past are also ubiquitous and omnipresent in À la recherche.

Our spontaneous memory is continually recording the events of our existence, our perceptions of the outside world, thus our life is incessantly being doubled. At the moment of intersection of past, present and future an interesting situation occurs when it is difficult to differentiate present perception from immediate past memory. How long does the present last? How long, how many seconds, milliseconds or microseconds, does current perception endure before it exists only in past memory? How long does present perceiving continue before it survives only in former recollection? At that mysterious frontier between the present and the past, memory and perception are inextricably intermixed. In L'énergie spirituelle, Bergson discusses the continual doubling of our self, of our consciousness, in involuntary memory. Our self is continually twinned like an object placed in front of a mirror. This doubling takes place ceaselessly and without our being aware of the process.

This twinning of self from actual in the present, to virtual in past memory takes place at the present instant, at the present moment. An epoch which is always moving forward, and stands at the intersection between past and future, the demarcation between the immediate past which is no more and the near future which doesn't yet exist. It is what Marcel Muller calls the junction between: "l'éternel présent, appuyé sur un passé immédiat et orienté vers un proche avenir."[41] "L'instant présent," says Bergson with his remarkable use of words, is: ". . . le miroir mobile qui réfléchit sans cesse la perception en souvenir" (ES 136).

The person who is aware, says Bergson, and conscious of this continual doubling of self into memory, will see himself as an actor who plays his role automatically whilst listening and observing himself on the stage of life. All perception is thus doubled into memory and perception, the actual in the present and the virtual in the past. There are thus two 'I's, one in the present looking forward and back and the 'I' who is in the past and observed by the 'I' in the present: "C'est plutôt une oscillation de la personne entre deux points de vue sur elle-même, un va-et-vient de l'esprit entre la perception qui n'est que perception et la perception doublée de son propre souvenir" (ES 139). These two aspects of the 'I' are clearly different from the superficial and deeper self described by Bergson in his *Essai* as *les deux aspects du moi* and discussed earlier in this Chapter. On the one hand the 'I' knows full well what he was, a being who thinks and acts, but at times the memory of that being past makes him think that he repeats what he already has said, and he sees again things already seen, the sensation of *déjà vu*, and seems to transform the 'I' into an actor who recites his role (ES 139): "De là une compénétration d'états qui se fondent et même s'identifient ensemble dans la conscience immédiate . . . et que la conscience réfléchie se représentera dès lors par un dédoublement du moi en deux personnages différents . . ." (ES 140). The two 'I's are thus a twinning, a doubling of my self into two seemingly different beings. These two aspects of my self are inseparable and distinguishable with difficulty one from the other. One is the 'I' in the immediate present, whilst the other is the image of the 'I' in memory and in the past.

I suggest that this doubling of self into the 'I' who exists at the present moment and the 'I' who acts in the past is constantly and perpetually present in *À la recherche* as the doubling of 'Je' into Narrator and Hero. In *La place de la madeleine*, Doubrovsky[42] indicates that the doubling of the 'Je' becomes apparent from the opening line of *À la recherche*: "Longtemps, je me suis couché de bonne heure." The doubling is indicated by the use of 'Je' together with the verb in the perfect tense. There is the 'Je' who is speaking to us, who is enunciating and the 'Je' who is spoken about. Doubrovsky, following Benveniste[43] says: "Il y a donc, dans ce procès, une double instance conjugués: instance de *je* comme référent[44], et instance de discours contenant *je*, comme référé."[45] The use of the *passé composé* indicates that the 'Je' is speaking of an action of the 'Je' in the past, preceding the present moment of narration, and the *passé composé* also indicates perhaps a prolongation of the past into the present, an echo of a past action prolonging into the present.

The opposition between the 'Je' speaking, and the 'Je' spoken about is the same duality which pervades the entire Proustian text, the inter-relationship between the many guises of the narrator and that of

the hero or protagonist. This interdependence of narrator and hero in
À la recherche resembles that existing between the *process* of narration and the *content* of narration, between *le signifiant* and *le signifié*.
The narrator is recounting, he is in the process of narration, and his
discourse is *le signifiant*. The hero is the actor seen and described by
the narrator, he is the other aspect of self, seen in the past acting and
speaking on the stage of past time. The hero thus represents *le signifié*,
or *le référé*.

Returning to the Bergsonian mirror image of the self reflected in
memory, the narrator is thus the 'I' standing in the present and dis-
coursing whilst perceiving the mirror of himself, as the hero in memory.
The narrator is, so to speak, watching and perceiving the image of
himself in memory as someone observing and recounting the perception of himself acting on the stage of life reflected in the mirror of time
and memory. The two I's of the Proustian text, like Bergson's actual
and virtual selves are inseparably entangled, interwoven and intermingled, one cannot exist without the other. As textual time (*le temps
de l'histoire, le temps du signifié*) progresses the 'Je' hero and the
'Je' narrator come closer and closer in time until at some mysterious
moment towards the end of *Le Temps retrouvé*, the two coincide.

Kristeva emphasizes a similar point when she writes: "Let us emphasize this two-faced 'being' which Proust seeks to name in his writing—perception is always in a state of being stretched between the
world of the present and the historical self,"[46] that is why: "cette essence est en partie subjective et incommunicable" (IV 464).

The Bergsonian concept of the doubling of self in memory is inherent in the entire Proustian text. Just as it is difficult to discern whether
one is seeing perception in actuality or merely virtual perception
doubled in memory, so it is difficult to differentiate in the Proustian
text between the various narrative voices of the 'Je'. This continuous
interaction of the two identities of the 'Je' and the difficulty of stating
with any degree of certainty the moment of enunciation leads to this
reflection and oscillation between the two forms of the 'Je', which
Doubrovsky calls the 'Copernican revolution' of the Proustian text.

As distinct from the 'Je' in the immediate past, the 'Je' in the distant past is, for Proust, entrapped in the *vases clos* of spontaneous or
involuntary memory awaiting liberation and perception. Here again,
Proust indicates the opposition between intelligence and true impressions that was discussed previously. For intelligence and reasoning
resurrect the mere *impression factice* which does not have the

magical powers of 'Sesame,' of opening the doors of memory and
Time:

> Sur l'extrême différence qu'il y a entre l'impression vraie que nous avons eue
> d'une chose et **l'impression factice** que nous nous en donnons quand
> volontairement nous essayons de nous la représenter, je ne m'arrêtais pas;
> me rappelant trop avec quelle indifférence relative Swann avait pu parler au-
> trefois des jours où il était aimé, parce que sous cette phrase il voyait autre
> chose qu'eux. (IV 448)

Conscious effort and will-power are not sufficient to open these *vases
clos*. The images of voluntary memory are perhaps logical and analytical but do not contain the true essence of reality entrapped in
involuntary memory, they do not have the power to unlock the *vases
clos* of time past.

> . . . la moindre parole que nous avons dite à une époque de notre vie, le geste
> le plus insignifiant que nous avons fait était entouré, portait sur lui le reflet de
> choses qui logiquement ne tenaient pas à lui, en ont été séparées par
> **l'intelligence** qui n'avait rien à faire d'elle pour les besoins du **raisonnement,**
> (IV 448) [my emphasis]

Although the 'Je' in the present will change with time, the 'Je
'entrapped in the *vases clos* of spontaneous or involuntary memory
will not change, he (or she) remains the identical self and awaits the
possibility of starting to act his/her part and play his role on the stage
of memory whilst being observed by the 'Je' in the present. It is the
reuniting of these two forms of the 'Je' that is the essence of the
Proustian work, the oneness of the 'Je' narrator observing and the
'Je' the liberated hero being perceived. The key to the *vases clos* is
provided by the identity of present perception doubled in past memory:

> . . . l'être que j'avais été était un être extra-temporel, par conséquent insoucieux
> des vicissitudes de l'avenir. Il ne vivait que de **l'essence des choses**, et ne
> pouvait la saisir dans le présent où l'imagination n'entrant pas en jeu, les
> sens étaient incapables de la lui fournir . . . Cet être-là n'était jamais venu à
> moi, ne s'était jamais manifesté, qu'en dehors de l'action, de la jouissance
> immédiate, chaque fois que le miracle d'une analogie m'avait fait échapper au
> présent. Seul, il avait le pouvoir de me faire retrouver les jours anciens, le
> temps perdu, devant quoi les efforts de ma mémoire et de mon **intelligence
> échouaient** toujours. (IV 450) [my emphasis]

The bridge in time is made between the two 'I's' so that both narrator
and hero, the observer and the observed are again united, beyond the

contingencies of time, in 'des fragments d'existence soustraits au temps' (IV 454) residing in the eternal present. It is the 'Je' in the present that is the controller, the commander, for he has the power to resurrect the past, but it is clearly the 'Je' in the past, entrapped in the *vases clos* of memory that is the most exquisite and precious:

> Toujours . . . le lieu lointain engendré autour de la sensation commune s'était accouplé un instant, comme un lutteur, au lieu actuel. Toujours le lieu actuel avait été vainqueur; toujours c'était le vaincu qui m'avait paru le plus beau; si beau que j'étais resté en extase sur le pavé inégal comme devant la tasse de thé. (IV 453)

Proust's language in the above citation sounds almost Bergsonian as he speaks of two beings, one in the past, one in the present, real and actual. Images of perception past which were seemingly lost are revived, liberated from the *vases clos*. At times the 'Je' in the past seems to come forward in time and meet his older self who does not immediately recognize his younger ego:

> Je m'étais . . . demandé avec colère quel était l'étranger qui venait me faire mal. Cet étranger, c'était moi-même, c'était l'enfant que j'étais alors, que le livre venait de susciter en moi, car le moi ne connaissant que cet enfant, c'est cet enfant que le livre avait appelé tout de suite . . . (IV 462)

Again these are the two 'I', the narrator and the young hero seeing and conversing with each other. The narrator also refers to the Bergsonian layers of being, when he says:

> J'ai superposé trop d'images de moins en moins aimées, pour pouvoir retrouver la première, moi qui ne suis pas le moi qui l'ai vue et qui dois céder la place au moi que j'étais alors . . . (IV 466)

These are the various successive layers of self that have over the years been superposed over that of the young hero that was and that the narrator would like to recall. These layers are comparable to a succession of mirror images like those between parallel and facing mirrors, but the narrator wants to see only the original. Muller[47] points out an interesting case when the 'Je' narrator imitates the 'Je' hero at the beginning of *À la recherche*, when the narrator is awakening yet still half asleep recalls when he was a guest of Mme de Saint-Loup at Tansonville:

> Puis renaissait le souvenir d'une nouvelle attitude; le mur filait dans une autre direction: j'étais dans ma chambre chez Mme de Saint-Loup, à la campagne;

mon Dieu! il est au moins dix heures, on doit avoir fini de dîner! J'aurai trop
prolongé la sieste que je fais tous les soirs en rentrant de ma promenade avec
Mme de Saint-Loup, avant d'endosser mon habit. Car bien des années ont
passé depuis Combray. (I 7)

As Muller indicates there are three 'Je's in this passage, first, the hero
guest of Mme de Saint-Loup, second, the older, insomniac hero looking back and recollecting his visits to Tansonville and third, the narrator describing the insomniac hero, who in turn remembers his earlier
self. Thus the *actual* narrator is looking backwards to the *virtual* insomniac hero, who himself is recollecting his *virtual* self at Tansonville.
For a brief moment, the narrator speaks in the present tense, as if he
were the hero at Tansonville, and thus seems to impersonate his virtual self. The narrator watching himself acting on the stage of memory,
speaks as if he were that actor. The Bergsonian actual self pretends he
is the virtual self, thus the narrator and his mirror image in memory
have temporarily become fused into one being.

Thought

Linked to the two aspects of self, *les deux aspects du moi*, there are
two types of thought. The concept of the two forms of thought and
two distinct sources of knowledge, is not unique nor original with
Bergson, for it is explicitly stated in the writings of Saint Thomas
Aquinas (1275–1274)[48] and in his *Pensées*, Pascal clearly distinguishes
between intuitive and logical thought:

> Nous connaissons la vérité, non seulement par la raison, mais encore par le
> coeur. C'est de cette dernière sorte que nous connaissons les premiers
> principes, et c'est en vain que le raisonnement, qui n'y a point de part essaie
> de les combattre. . . . Car les connaissances des premiers principes: Espace,
> temps, mouvement, nombres sont aussi fermes qu'aucune de celles que nos
> raisonnements nous donnent et c'est sur ces connaissances du coeur et de
> l'instinct qu'il faut que la raison s'appuie et qu'elle y fonde son discours.[49]

With a slight change of language, this statement could be Bergson
speaking to us of time, space and movement, and of the two sources
of knowledge, *le coeur* and logic. By *le coeur*, Pascal evidently means
intuitive wisdom, or that which Bergson calls *les données immédiate
de la conscience*. In another *Pensée*, Pascal elaborates on these two
forms of thought as *l'esprit de finesse* et *l'esprit de géométrie* which
is quoted and discussed in Chapter 2.

Thought Creates Being

Throughout Bergson's philosophy there is the movement of being and becoming, the creation of self by self, the notion that in time everything is changing and evolving, which is the essence of *L'évolution créatrice*. Change and creation is thus the essential quality of existence, of Becoming. Our thoughts and actions create and in so doing they change us. Evoking the image of an artist painting and improving his technique and skills as he paints, Bergson writes:

> Et de même que le talent du peintre se forme ou se déforme, en tout case se modifie, sous l'influence même des oeuvres qu'il produit, ainsi chacun de nos états, en même temps qu'il sort de nous, modifie notre personne, étant la forme nouvelle que nous venons de nous donner. (EC 7)

Just like a painter's skill and talent changes, evolves and is modified by the work that he performs, so do our own thoughts and actions change our self and alter our being. For our thoughts become part of our memory and 'my memory is my being, it is my essence.' The above passage from Bergson's *L'évolution créatrice* evokes the thoughts of an earlier great French philosopher and writer. At the beginning of his first book of essays, Michel de Montaigne uses an image and metaphor similar to Bergson's, that of the artist painting his own portrait, when he writes: ". . . car c'est moi que je peins. . . Ainsi, lecteur, je suis moi-même la matière de mon livre."[50] Later, he even more explicitly identifies himself with his own thoughts and writings when, again using the metaphor of painting his own likeness, he says: "Me peignant pour autrui, je me suis peint en moi de couleurs plus nettes que n'étaient les miennes premières. Je n'ai pas plus fait mon livre que mon livre m'a fait, livre consubstantiel à son auteur . . ."[51] Although the use of the image of the painter by Bergson and Montaigne is not identical, in both there is the clear notion of *la création de soi par soi*. In writing Montaigne not only transcribes the content of his inner self, but he transcribes *into* his inner self, which in turn becomes transcribed into text and self. There is an interesting form of *mise en abyme* here, for we are what we think and write, and at the same time we write what we are and what we think. We create a text from our thoughts and in so doing we re-create ourselves which we then re-transcribe in our text. The text then does indeed become consubstantial with self, thought and memory.

Each moment of our existence contains the memory of all preceding moments and this includes, of course, thoughts whether they are transcribed into text or not. Thus the process of thinking and of transcription into writing, paint or music creates not only the thoughts and the work, but it creates and recreates the Self. We have previously mentioned Thibaudet's statement that Bergson would probably say: "I think, therefore I change."

In the same way that language helps crystallize thought and thought helps construct language, so the oscillation between self and thought and thought and self creates and re-creates the self. There is thus an endless swaying to and fro, the oscillation of Montaigne's scales, the *va-et-vient* to which Bergson (EC 240) refers, like an image being perpetually reflected between two facing and parallel mirrors.

It should perhaps be emphasized that both Montaigne and Bergson make use of the reverberation between the analogic and the digital. The transcription of the analogic image, the painted portrait or the continuos thought into the linear digital word of the text. As surely as the Proustian hero at Martinville was a different person after transcribing his first text, so his text was a transcription of his vision, his experience and himself. In the same way that Marcel Proust created *À la recherche*, then also the process of writing *À la recherche* re-created Marcel Proust.

The Endogenous Text

A number of times in *Le Temps retrouvé*, the narrator tells us that a great literary text does not have to be created, for it already exists in each of us. The writer has merely to discover this 'endogenous text' and translate it into words, thus the work of an author is similar to that of a translator:

> Je m'apercevais que ce livre essentiel, le seul livre vrai, un grand écrivain n'a pas, dans le sens courant, à l'inventer puisqu'il existe déjà en chacun de nous, mais à le traduire. Le devoir et la tâche d'un écrivain sont ceux d'un traducteur.
> (IV 469)

Moreover when a reader reads a text he or she is actually interpreting his or her own personal text, reading the textual passages of himself, of his or her self. The writer is thus not only a translator but a sort of optical instrument which Proust sometimes refers to as telescope, and sometimes as a microscope or magnifying glass. An instrument which enables the reader to study and perceive aspects of himself[52] which perhaps he did not know existed, and interpreting the text is thus, in part, a recognition of portions of himself of his self:

> En réalité, chaque lecteur est quand il lit le propre lecteur de soi-même. L'ouvrage de l'écrivain n'est qu'une espèce **d'instrument optique** qu'il offre au lecteur afin de lui permettre de discerner ce que sans ce livre il n'eût peut-être pas vu en soi-même. La reconnaissance en soi-même, par le lecteur, de ce que dit le livre, et la preuve de la vérité de celui-ci, (IV 489–490)

The text will only appear to be true if such a recognition, if a congruence is found to exist between the external text and the one internal to the reader. One could say, therefore, that the text has to fit into 'receptors'[53] which are already present in the mind of the reader. If the text does not conform, is not congruent with these 'receptors' then it does not appear to be true. Thus, says the narrator (who here seems to be the author himself), my readers are not really readers of my book, but readers of themselves and it is through my text that they become capable of reading themselves, the words of my text are those within themselves:[54]

> Car ils ne seraient pas,. . . mes lecteurs, mais les propres lecteurs d'eux-mêmes, mon livre n'étant qu'une sorte de **ces verres grossissants** comme ceux que tendait à un acheteur l'opticien de Combray; mon livre, grâce auquel je leur fournirais le moyen de lire en eux-mêmes . . . si les mots qu'ils lisent en eux-mêmes sont bien ceux que j'ai écris. (IV 610.) [my emphasis]

This thought repeated at least three times has of course similarities to Montaigne's notion that in writing one paints oneself, one's inner self and that in creating a text, one creates one's self.[55] This concept that there is in the mind of the reader the essence of a text with which a great literary work must find congruence and resonance is also clearly stated by Bergson in "La Perception du changement," when discussing the role of the artist or poet:

> A quoi vise l'art, sinon à nous montrer, dans la nature et dans l'esprit, hors de nous et en nous des choses qui ne frappaient pas explicitement notre sens et notre conscience? Le poète et le romancier qui expriment un état d'âme ne le créent certes pas de toutes pièces; ils ne seraient pas compris de nous si nous n'observions pas en nous, jusqu'à un certain point, ce qu'ils nous disent d'autrui. Au fur et à mesure qu'ils nous parlent, des nuances d'émotion et de pensée nous apparaissent **qui pouvaient être représentées en nous depuis longtemps**, mais qui demeuraient invisible: telle l'image photographique qui n'a pas encore été plongée dans le bain d'où elle se révélera, le poète est ce révélateur. (PM 149–150)[56] [my emphasis]

For Bergson as for Proust, a text is only real and true if a notion akin to it is already present in the mind of the reader although perhaps not in his or her consciousness.[57]

The truth of a text and hence the quality of the literature will become apparent if congruence and resonance occur between the exogenous written text and that 'endogenous text' already present in the mind of the reader. Art and literature are only exceptional or outstanding if they are true, if they reflect a reality in the mind of the reader, and for a text to be enduring it must enunciate such a truth. This notion of a text, a truth already present in the mind does not seem to have been original with Bergson or Proust, for it was clearly implied by Pascal:

> Quand un discours naturel peint une passion ou un effet on trouve dans soi-même la vérité de ce qu'on entend, laquelle on ne savait pas qu'elle y fût, de sorte qu'on est porté à aimer celui qui nous la fait sentir, car il ne nous a point fait montre de son bien mais du nôtre. . . .[58]

Conclusion

Bergson's philosophy of the intuitive as opposed to the logical emerged in late nineteenth century France to some extent in the forefront of a general reaction against the deterministic elements in science that appeared to leave little room for free-will and the individual.[59] The duality of the analogic as opposed to the digital, the qualitative as opposed to the quantitative, *la multiplicité qualitative* as opposed to *la multiplicité quantitative* pervades all the four elements of Bergson's philosophy that we have explored, namely time, memory, self and thought and in all cases the qualitative or analogic element is the dominant. These four elements are also of great importance in Proust's great novel although not in a direct or congruent manner. Time is clearly a outstanding factor and component in Proust's mind and novel, for he seemed to be greatly concerned with the destructive property of time that nullifies and demolishes the enchanting properties of the present, contemplative, essence of reality. But the Time of Proust is not Bergson's *la durée pure*, it is a time with spatial characteristics so that for Proust, past events are rather like people and events encapsulated and suspended in spacetime in such a manner that they can be accessed in random order. This gives a very contemporary character to Proust's concept of time and indeed his novel has aspects of hypertext.

Memory, another key ingredient of Proust's great novel is linked to time, for it is through memory that we have a sense of the passing of time and it is memory that gives *la durée pure* direction. Bergson clearly delineates two forms of memory to which the adjectives 'voluntary' and 'involuntary' have been (confusingly) attached. Proust also describes two forms of memory to which these adjectives can also (equally confusingly) be attached. But as we have seen, the two forms of Proustian memory are not the same as those so clearly described by Bergson. Proust's *mémoire involontaire* is a rare occurrence that requires the congruence of some external cue, some chance occurrence with a similar element engraved and stored in the banks of spontaneous memory. If and when that chance congruence occurs, there is resonance and the recreation of the past happens in a shattering reminiscence that Gilles Deleuze likens to *l'image instantanée de l'éternité*.

The duality of self (*les deux aspects du Moi*), the superficial and the profound being, described by Bergson also take form in the Proustian text as the pensive, solitary hero searching for the essence of reality on the one hand and the snobbish socialite who frequents matinées and soirées with the titled elite of Paris. Bergson describes another dual form of being, the "I" who is reflected in the mirror of memory, the *actual* and the *virtual* self. This duality pervades the entire Proustian text as the duality between, "I" the hero and, "I" the narrator. This doubling of being is reflected in the duality of thought, for I am what I think, I am my memory, and as I think and remember so I create myself.

These elements, of Bergson's philosophy that also occur in Proust's great text, are often in altered form so that it might appear that if Proust did indeed read Bergson's texts, he did so through the deforming, and distorting magnifying glass that Proust himself describes: ". . . comme dans le verre grossissant de ces porte-plume qu'on achète aux bains de mer" (I 382).

Notes

1   Gilles Deleuze, *Le bergsonisme* (Paris: PUF, 1994) 45.

2   IV 467–468.

3   *Introduction à la métaphysique* is reproduced as chapter VI of *La pensée et le mouvant*.

4   t = time; a = acceleration; s = distance; u = initial velocity; d/dt = the differential.

5   Where x,y,and z represent the three dimensions of space, c is the velocity of light, i, the square root of (-1). According to special relativity, these four quantities may be treated mathematically in an identical manner as coordinates or dimensions. Thus, 't' or more correctly 'ict' may be considered the fourth dimension of spacetime. See Albert Einstein, *The Meaning of Relativity* (London: Methuen, 1950).

6   Symbols may have both a positive and negative connotation. Here the implication is negative in that there can be no accurate symbol of pure duration. Later the term is used with a more positive connotation.

7   Chapter 6, contains a fuller discussion of Bergson's use of imagery to communicate the notion of pure time.

8   Bertrand Russell, *A History of Western Philosophy* (New York: Simon & Schuster, 1972) 796.

9   Deleuze, *Bergsonisme* 45.

10 Deleuze, *Bergsonisme* 16.

11 In *Durée et simultanéité* (1922, Paris: PUF, 1992) 107 & 166, Bergson (1859–1941) cites Eddington's (1882–1944) *Space, Time and Gravitation* (Cambridge: CUP, 1920). This was Eddington's first book and it is possibly unlikely that Eddington's thought had any influence on Bergson's philosophy.

12 Arthur S. Eddington, *The Nature of the Physical World* (1928; Cambridge: Cambridge UP, 1942) 36.

13 Georges Poulet, *L'Espace proustien* (Paris: Gallilmard, 1982) 136.

14 Marcel Proust, *Choix de lettres,* ed. Philip Kolb (Paris: Plon, 1965) 277.

15 Lawrence Sklar, *Philosophy and Spacetime Physics* (Berkeley: U of California P, 1985).

16 John Ruskin, *Sesame and Lilies* (London: George Allen, 1913) 1–2.

17 Landow, George P. *Hypertext: The convergence of contemporary critical theory and technology* (Baltimore: Johns Hopkins UP, 1992) 4.

18   Landow 114.

19   This quotation is relegated to a *variante* in the 1989 Pléiade edition of *À la recherche*. It appears on page III, 696 of the text proper of the 1954 Pléiade edition.

20   *There is, of course, an extensive literature on the contemporary neurophysiology and psychology of memory.* Daniel L. Schacter, *Searching for Memory (New York: Basic Books, 1996), gives an up-to-date, authoritative and concise summary and includes a very comprehensive bibliography.*

21   It may, indeed, record events of which we are not conscious, and in that sense resembles the 'implicit memory' described by Schacter and Tulving. See Schacter, 161.

22   *The notion that the mind contains more than a single memory system is confirmed by contemporary neuroscience, [E. Tulving, 'Episodic and Semantic Memory,' E. Tulving & W. Donaldson, eds.* Organization of Memory *(New York: Academic Press, 1972) 381–403.] that delineates 'semantic' and 'episodic' memory which seem very similar, to Bergson's 'intentional' and 'spontaneous' memories. See also; Schacter, 169–171.* Semantic memory is the intricate network of concepts, associations, and facts that constitute our general knowledge of the world, while *episodic memory is the system that allows us to recollect specific incidents from the past. Amnesia and brain damage can result in selective impairment of one of these memory systems. It would be interesting, but clearly beyond the scope of this study, to compare in detail Bergson's memory systems with those of contemporary neurophysiology and psychology. I am not aware of this having been done.*

23   Bergson repeatedly uses the image of a painting to depict the analogic, a technique that is also used by Montaigne.

24   Draft entitled "Le Souvenir involontaire/chambres."

25   This quotation is very similar to that which I reproduce immediately before. The first is a draft whilst the second is the final text. The former perhaps gives additional insight into Proust's notion of voluntary memory, for he says: ". . . cette mémoire volontaire qui ne nous rend nullement notre passé, car elle le peint tout entier d'une couleur uniforme et faussée qu'elle emprunte au présent."

26   Gilles Deleuze, *Proust et les signes* (Paris: PUF, 1993) 72.

27   Marcel Proust, *Choix de lettres*, ed. Philip Kolb (Paris: Plon, 1965) 287.

28   Actually, 269 times.

29   Anthony E. Pilkington, *Bergson and his Influence: A Reassessment* (Cambridge UP, 1976) 146.

30   Françoise Fabre-Luce de Gruson, "Bergson et Proust," *Entretiens sur Marcel Proust,* eds. Georges Cattaui and Philip Kolb (Paris: Mouton, 1966) 236.

31   Pilkington, 150.

32   Deleuze, *Proust 78.*

33   Much has been written on Proust's choice of the name 'Madeleine' and with the importance of proper names in Proust's text; its selection was unlikely to have been fortuitous for Madeleine has a number of associations with the Proustian world. Madeleine Blanchet is the heroine of Georges Sand's *François le champi*, a text much loved by Proust and his hero. Proust's unpublished early novel *L'indifférent* contains a young man enamored of a Madeleine de Gouvres; there is an association between the biblical Mary Madeleine and Rachel *quand du Seigneur*, and the église de la Madeleine in Paris must have been a familiar sight to Proust on his walks. See e.g. Serge Doubrovsky, *La place de la madeleine* (Paris: Mercure de France, 1974); and Julia Kristeva, *Proust and the Sense of Time* (New York: Columbia UP, 1993) 38–43.

34   Helen Keller, *The Story of my Life* (New York: Doubleday, 1954) 36.

35   Deleuze, *Proust 79.*

36   Royston M. Roberts, *Serendipity: Accidental Discoveries in Science* (New York: John Wiley, 1989) 65.

37   Viscount Samuel, *The Physical Basis of Mind* ed. Peter Laslet (Oxford: Blackwell, 1950) 69.

38   *Profond* in both the sense of profound, difficult to comprehend and understand as well as deep and beneath spatially.

39   In his work on the narrative voices in *À la recherche,* Marcel Muller, [*Les Voix Narratives dans la recherche du Temps Perdu*, (Genève: Droz, 1983).] distinguishes nine separate voices: Le Héros, Le Narrateur, Le Sujet Intermédiaire, Le Protagoniste, le Romancier, L'Écrivain, L'Auteur, l'Homme and Le Signataire.

40   Marcel Proust, *Contre Sainte-Beuve* (Paris: Gallimard, 1954) 137.

41   Marcel Muller, *Les voix narratives dans la recherche du temps perdu* (Genève: Droz, 1983) 73.

42   Serge Doubrovsky, *La place de la madeleine* (Paris: Mercure de Fance, 1974) 191.

43   Emile Benveniste, *Problèmes de linguistique générale* (Paris: Gallimard, 1966) 252.

44   Or, "sujet de l'énonciation".

45   Doubrovsky 194.

46   Julia Kristeva. *Proust and the Sense of Time.* Trans. Stephen Bann (New York: Columbia UP, 1993) 54.

47   Muller 79.

48 Étienne Gilson, *La philosophie au moyen âge* (Paris: Payot, 1947) 525–550.

49 Blaise Pascal, *Oeuvres complètes* (Paris: Seuil, 1963) 512: fragment 110.

50 Michel de Montaigne, "Au lecteur," *Essais*, vol. I (Paris: Gallimard, 1965) 49.

51 Michel de Montaigne, *Essais*, vol. II (Paris: Gallimard, 1965) 426.

52 Himself also includes herself. Him includes her.

53 In physiology and pharmacology, a 'receptor' is a three dimensional structure, usually a protein, into which a molecule (for example, a hormone, neurotransmitter or drug) fits, rather like a key fitting into a lock and when the fit is perfect, there is activation of the receptor and a physiological or pharmacological response occurs. In the same manner, if the external text fits into the internal, endogenous, textual receptor,—there will be a response, the reader will recognize the text as being true.

54 There is another scientific—literary image here, which relates to the telescope and a text. The image of a star seen through a telescope is not a picture of the star, but rather the diffraction pattern of the objective of the telescope produced by the star acting as a point source, (this is why the image of the star seen through a telescope is *smaller* than that seen by the naked eye). Thus the image gives information about *both* the star (the object being observed) and the telescope (the instrument performing the observation), and different instruments will produce different images. The image of a literary text (the star) in our mind is interpreted by our senses (the telescope), and modified by our memory & experience, and different readers (instruments) will produce different readings (images). A literary text is 'interpreted' or 'read' by the reader. There is not necessarily an 'absolute reality' in literature, any more than the image of a star is that of 'absolute reality'—only that which the reader together with the text create in the reader's mind. Proust describes a rather different telescope when he says:

> . . . mon livre . . . est sorti tout entier de l'application d'un sens spécial . . . celle d'un télescope qui serait braqué sur le temps, car le **télescope** fait apparaître des étoiles qui sont invisibles à l'oeil nu, et j'ai tâché . . . de faire apparaître à la conscience des phénomènes inconscients qui, complètement oubliés, sont quelquefois situés très loin dans le passé . . . Lettre à Camille Vettard de juin 1922. (Proust, *Lettres* 277)

Proust's telescope is looking backwards in the time of memory, an astronomical telescope is seeing objects many light-years away and thus is also looking back in time.

55 ". . . je n'ai pas plus fait mon livre que mon livre m'a fait. . . ." See note 51.

56 Part of a lecture given by Bergson at Oxford University in May, 1911. A slightly different version of this text is published in ML, 893.

57   There is an interesting parallel between the notion of 'the endogenous text' described here and that of the endogenous opiate receptor in the brain, which is perhaps insufficiently relevant to the present study to be described in detail here. Briefly however, the opiates (e.g. morphine and related substances) are derived from a plant exogenous to the human body, yet there exist in the brain stereo-specific receptors to which the 'exogenous' opiates bind, as well as molecules endogenously present in the brain; the enkephalins and endorphins; which are the endogenous ligands for those opiate receptors. Thus the notion of a text, exogenous to the brain and written by an author which somehow interacts with an 'endogenous textual receptor' is paralleled by human physiology and pharmacology. See e.g. Andres Goth, *Medical Pharmacology* 10th ed., (St Louis: C.V. Mosby, 1981) 343.

58   Pascal, 588, fragment 652.

59   This is discussed in detail in Chapter 8.

Chapter 6

Language

Manier savamment une langue c'est pratiquer une espèce de sorcellerie évocatoire.

Baudelaire.[1]

La métaphore, c'est à dire sur le plan stylistique l'équivalence ontologique du qualitatif, se présente donc comme la voie royale d'une esthétique de l'Identité.

Henry.[2]

Language is a code of social conventions, and its use is an activity and function, not only of communication and self-expression, but occasionally an act of artistic creation. "In any natural history of the human species," says Steven Pinker,[3] "language would stand out as the preeminent trait . . . [it] is so tightly woven into human experience that it is scarcely possible to imagine life without it." In this chapter, I will analyze and compare the function and use of language by Henri Bergson and Marcel Proust, and will argue that the purpose of language in Bergson and Proust has an important difference. As an oversimplification and generalization one might say that Bergson uses language primarily to teach and communicate, whereas Proust uses it predominantly to suggest and evoke. A consideration of the function of language in literature and leads into an examination of the differences between scientific and literary language and the writings of Barthes, Paulson and Serres. Whereas the function of scientific language is to communicate as unambiguously as possible, information, theory and thought, this is not the case with literary writing, where ambiguity, suggestiveness and freedom in interpretation are important. However ambiguity does not, in any way, imply carelessness or negligence in the use of language. Proust's careful and poetic writing is rich in suggestive and evocative properties often linked to images and metaphor. Bergson also makes extensive use of imagery, some very similar to those of Proust, but the function of these images is somewhat distinct from those of Proust. It would be an erroneous simplification to equate the language of Bergson and Proust to the scientific and literary poles expounded by Barthes and others, and indeed some literary language may be 'scientific' in a certain way. Bergson's language is essentially scientific in that he is using it to teach and transmit what he considers to be a truth, which like all truths pre-exists his words, but his language nevertheless has a literary overlay of imagery.

The Language of Bergson and Proust

Language and its Functions

In relation to the general purpose of language, I will discuss two points. First that language has at least three different although related functions. One is to communicate pre-existing information, theory or truths. A second property is to improve and sharpen thought by the continuous feed-back of language onto thinking, the dialectic between language and thought. A third function of language, is its ability, through the poetic and somewhat ambiguous use of words, to suggest and evoke images and ideas which being modulated by the memory, culture and experience of the reader or listener are unique for each, and is what I call the *creative* function of language. Bergson and Proust differ in the emphasis they place on each of these functions.

The second point to be discussed is the difficulty in distinguishing whether thought precedes language or is constructed by the word, that is whether the word precedes the thought, whether there is a reality which precedes the word and whether there is thought before words.

Bergson, Language and Thought[4]

One of the basic principles of Bergsonian philosophy is the distinction between the quantitative and the qualitative. The external material world consists of objects which have mass, which occupy space and obey physical laws, and these are the elements for and about which language originally developed. They are quantitative, discontinuous, contiguous and essentially homogenous, and can be counted by lining them up in imaginary space and are coded digital. There is another realm of 'things' that are not quantitative, but qualitative, which do not occupy space, have no mass, and do not obey physical laws. Amongst these qualitative elements, which are coded analogic, are thoughts, emotions, aspirations and some elements of perception. Although language, whether spoken or written, is reasonably effective at transmitting and communicating commands, requests and descriptions concerning the content of our external quantitative, discontinuous and material or digital environment, it is not so successful at communicating and interpreting the contents of the subjective qualitative, and non-material or analogic world, at transmitting to others our inner thoughts, feelings and emotions and in representing duration. This, says Bergson, is because words like objects are quantitative and contiguous. In the opening lines of the preface to his first major work, *Essai sur les donnees immediates de la conscience*, Bergson gives the essence of an idea that is a recurring theme in his writings:

> Nous nous exprimons nécessairement par des mots, et nous pensons le plus souvent dans l'espace. En d'autres termes, le langage exige que nous établissions entre nos idées les mêmes distinctions nettes et précises, la même discontinuité qu'entre les objets matériels. (DI vii)

Material objects are essentially digital and quantitative, they can be arranged in a linear fashion in imaginary space and language can readily express information concerning material objects in space. But, whereas some thoughts lend themselves readily to this treatment, others involving sensations, emotions and aspirations do not, for they are qualitative not quantitative. Bergson writes at length about the detrimental influence of language on thought and conversely about the difficulty of faithfully expressing thoughts involving emotions and deeper feelings through language. His ideas on language may be summarized in five major points.

1. Language cannot communicate emotions, images and some thoughts without distorting them, for they are non-verbal, and analogic in nature, whilst words are digital. Perceptions, sensations, emotions and some ideas, says Bergson, remain inexpressible because language cannot seize and represent the notion without altering it (DI 95), this is because fluid and analogic thought is incommensurable with digital language:

> Mais de même qu'on pourra intercaler indéfiniment des points entre deux positions d'un mobile sans jamais combler l'espace parcouru, ainsi, par cela seul que nous parlons, par cela seul que nous associons des idées les unes aux autres et que ces idées se juxtaposent au lieu de se pénétrer nous échouons

à traduire entièrement ce que notre âme ressent: **la pensée demeure in-commensurable avec le langage**. (DI 124) (my emphasis)

As discussed in Chapter 3 and 5, perceptions, sensations and ideas exist, according to Bergson, in two forms, and in addition there are two aspects of self (*les deux aspects du Moi*). Bergson uses the spatial metaphor of uppermost to designate that aspect of being which relates immediately to the external material world. The second aspect of self or being which is beneath the first is deeper or more profound[5] and experiences thoughts which are diffuse, nebulous, non-verbal and highly personal. The uniqueness of the thoughts of this second aspect of being is not accurately expressible by language, and when one focuses attention on non-verbal thought in order to express it, the thought changes and solidifies into the generic, digital, verbal concept. This notion of Bergson's that attention to intuitive thought or our inner being results in its transformation is discussed in more detail later in this chapter.

2. Words crush thought. Not only are words and language incapable of expressing thought but language is brutal and mangles the uniqueness and delicate quality of personal impressions:

> Bref, le mot aux contours bien arrêtés, le mot **brutal**, qui **emmagasine** ce qu'il y a de stable, de commun et par conséquent d'impersonnel dans les impressions de l'humanité, **écrase** ou tout au moins recouvre les impression délicates et fugitives de notre conscience individuelle. (DI 98) (my emphasis)

3. If we are not careful, we tend to use clichés and commonplace expressions which not only fail to express accurately our thoughts but modify them and our manner of thinking. Our thought thus becomes modified and in part dictated by generic language, socially acceptable phrases and notions for which set expressions already exist:

> Il ne faut donc pas s'étonner si celles-là seules de nos idées qui nous appartiennent le moins sont adéquatement exprimables par des mots: . . . Mais si, creusant au-dessous de la surface de contact entre le moi et les choses extérieures, nous pénétrons dans les profondeurs de l'intelligence organisée et vivantes, nous assisterons à la superposition ou plutôt à la fusion intime de bien des idées (DI 101).

In *L'évolution créatrice* he expresses a similar idea, that socially correct phrases make it possible for one to express thoughts easily, although these expressions will not faithfully reproduce the original idea:

L'homme . . . doit à la vie sociale, qui emmagasine et conserve les efforts
comme le langage emmagasine la pensée, fixe par là un niveau moyen où les
individu devront se hausser d'emblée, et, par cette excitation initiale, empêche
les médiocre de s'endormir. (EC, 265)

Ultimately, we thus express an idea which is somewhat different from
the unique thought originally conceived and express concepts that are
not inherently our own but which we use merely because words are
readily available to express something similar.

    4. When we use words we think in space, for words like objects are
spatial and in using words we tend to spatialize our thought and think
verbally and logically rather than allow non-verbal intuitive thought to
guide us. If we think in space we are probably less original, less individual than if we think in the dimension of intuition:

. . . à mesure que nous nous éloignons des couches **profondes** du moi, nos
états de conscience tendent de plus en plus à prendre la forme d'une multiplicité
numérique et à se déployer dans un espace homogène . . . une forme de plus
en plus impersonnelle. (DI 101)

    5. Words are generic, they generalize and loose the uniqueness and
individuality of thought and being:

L'individualité des choses et des êtres nous échappe toutes les fois qu'il ne
nous est pas matériellement utile de l'apercevoir . . . nous ne voyons pas les
choses mêmes; nous nous bornons à lire des étiquettes collées sur elles . . .
Car **les mots désignent des genres** . . . Nous nous mouvons parmi des
généralités et des symboles, (RI 116, 117, 118)

Language, like the frantic gestures of Jean Paulhan's ship-wrecked
survivor attempting to signal a passing ship, is deficient and inad-
equate at expressing personal thoughts and emotions: "Le naufragé
sur son radeau, qui agite un chiffon de linge, traduit fort mal sa faim,
sa soif, son angoisse."[6]

Jean Paulhan's *Les fleurs de Tarbes*
In 1941, Paulhan published *Les fleurs de Tarbes*, which discusses at
some length the paradoxical inter-relationship between thought and
language, words and literature, and whether language creates and
shapes thought or merely communicates it. Paulhan's book, whose
arguments are relevant to the present discussion, was initially claimed
by Maurice Blanchot to be: "one of the most important works of contemporary literary criticism."[7] Paulhan's text is somewhat enigmatic

and laden with ambiguity, and paradox, perhaps making it an exemplary illustration of one of the messages that he was attempting to communicate, namely the difficulty of clearly separating thought from language as well as the important role of ambiguity in literary writing.

Paulhan felt that the literature of pre-world war II France (the book was first published in 1941) could be divided into two opposing camps which he calls *La Terreur* and *La Rhétorique*. The Terrorists, exemplified by Maurras, Valéry, Gide, Rimbaud, Apollinaire, Bergson and others, considered that thought should take precedence over language, and they supported a literature that rejects all literary commonplace phrases, conventions and clichés in an attempt to reach faultless and genuine linguistic expression of thought. In his recent book, *Paulhan le juste*, Frédéric Badré says in reference to the terror:

> Car les erreurs de la critique tiennent à certaines illusions du langage, sur lesquelles se fondent aussi bien les doctrines terroristes, opposées à l'usage des clichés, lieux communs et banalités, que les doctrines qui défendent la vieille rhétorique. La principale illusion terroriste, . . . est celle des "grands mots," en général ceux qu'utilisent les hommes politiques. . . . La Terreur, quête du langage originel, du "langage de Paradis," doit insuffler sa sève à la vieille rhétorique.[8]

It was because of Bergson's clear statements on the detrimental effect of language on thought as well as the inability of language to express thought faithfully that Paulhan considered him as the philosopher representative of his 'Terrorist' movement. Many of Paulhan's statements echo the essence of Bergson's view on language summarized above. When referring to the deleterious effect of commonplace phrases on language and thought, and that when one uses set phrases, one tends to do so without thinking, Paulhan writes: "Le langage et la littérature . . . on les compare au miel, que les abeilles font, paraît-il, sans y réfléchir"(38), and emphasizing the lack of intelligence in many conversations, he states: "Voyez des gens causer dans la rue . . . Rien ne passe sur leurs visages des mots qu'ils disent. C'est qu'ils ne pensent pas, qu'ils ne pensent jamais, qu'ils se servent de phrases toutes faites" (55). However, although commonplace expressions and clichés are detrimental to thought, they have the positive attribute of making writing 'reader-friendly,' for Paulhan says: ". . . le cliché est en toute oeuvre, ce que le lecteur retient le plus aisément" (118). The importance of removing commonplaces and clichés from literature is that these are examples of the word preceding and directing thought, rather than letting the thought generate the word.

Paulhan gradually adopts the view that expressing thoughts in clear language is nevertheless useful even with clichés and commonplaces. When it comes to the everyday practicalities of life, thinking through clichés and expressions is valuable, for in case of problems and difficulties, it enables us to simplify the obscure and helps us to think and reason clearly and effectively. The use of commonplaces and clichés in an emergency, for example, is valuable in that it ensures immediate comprehension and understanding. Evoking the notion of the dialectic between word and thought, that words help us think clearly, Paulhan says that words enable us to dissect a problem (76). Following these ideas, Paulhan expresses a change of heart: "Ainsi l'observation, sur quoi Bergson et les Terroristes fondent leur doctrine, nous est apparue *en tout cas* chimérique et fausse" (100), and therein lies the paradox both of his text and the question of the primacy of thought over language that it poses. Nevertheless, there is a certain degree of ambiguity involved in the use of clichés which he would like to see removed: "Les clichés pourront retrouver droit de cité dans les Lettres, du jour où ils seront enfin privés de leur ambiguïté, de leur confusion" (143). By allowing the use of clichés and set phrases, the Terrorist is freed from this constant preoccupation by recognizing that commonplace phrases are legitimate words and language. Thus, towards the end of his text, Paulhan confesses: "Comment ne pas faire ici l'aveu que j'étais, au fond, terroriste? C'est une situation singulière que de découvrir au prix de tant d'effort ce que tout le monde a su" (150), but that subsequenty, the separation between the Terrorists and the Rhetoricians has become blurred in his mind.

This paradoxical reversal of his position seems to occur by the process of writing his book "au prix de tant d'effort." Thus a major interest of Paulhan's text appears to be, not so much its content, but perhaps that the process of writing out his case for the Terrorists in clear and logical language has led him to reverse his position and to realize that the need for *La Terreur* is an illusion, that clichés and commonplaces, do indeed, have a place in language. *Les fleurs de Tarbes* is thus an excellent example of the feed-back of language on thought, of language influencing ideas beneficially, and not, as Bergson would say, to their detriment.

Maurice Blanchot also discusses the interrelationship between thought and language and compares this alliance to a sort of modified Copernican revolution whereby thought revolves around language and simultaneously language around thought:[9]

. . . sa révolution copernicienne consiste à ne plus faire tourner uniquement le
langage autour de la pensée, mais à imaginer un autre mécanisme très subtil
et très complexe où il arrive que la pensée, pour retrouver sa nature
authentique, tourne autour du langage.[10]

This implies a mutual interdependence of language on thought and
thought on language. The question of the primacy of thought over
language or language over thought remains unanswered and perhaps
unanswerable.

Paradox in Bergson

Paulhan's text fails to answer clearly the question of whether language
faithfully communicates thought or indeed whether that is its main
function, but does suggest that the two are interdependent and at
times that language improves thought. At first sight this appears contrary to Bergson's dogma summarized earlier that states that language
has a strongly detrimental influence on thought, but the paradox and
contradiction seen in Paulhan's text is also present in Bergson's, for
Bergson also states that language assists thought and that without
language thought will not be clear and precise and cannot be useful:

Une pensée laissée à elle-même, offre une implication réciproque d'éléments
. . . d'une continuité, et dans toute continuité il y a de la confusion. Pour que
la pensée devienne distincte, il faut bien qu'elle s'éparpille en mots:
nous ne nous rendons bien compte de ce qui nous avons dans l'esprit que
lorsque nous avons pris une feuille de papier, et aligné les uns à côté des
autres des termes qui s'entrepénétraient. Ainsi la matière distingue, sépare,
résout en individualités et finalement en personnalités des tendances jadis
confondues dans l'élan originel de la vie. (ES 22)[11] (my emphasis)

The translation of thought into language may be difficult but it is important and valuable and its difficulty is in contrast to the ease of
thinking, for whereas it may be relatively easy to think, it is far more
difficult to express that thought clearly and unambiguously in words.
Remembering that thoughts are essentially analogic in nature whilst
words ('le signifiant') are clearly digital, Bergson is emphasizing the
importance of digitalizing the analogic concept, in order to clarify it.
Thus, there develops a dialectic between thought and language, a continual and mutual exchange between language and thought, and
Bergson clearly states (EC 239) that the dialectic between intuitive
thought and language is necessary both for the clarification of thought
as well as for the transmission of thought to others. It is this exchange,

the continuous positive feed-back between intuitive thought and digital language that clarifies thought and assures us that our words are indeed correctly expressing our thought and at the same time allowing the evolution and growth of the original idea. By the continuous feed-back, the dialectic between thought and language, a notion may be greatly improved and sharpened, so that language becomes more than a mechanism in translating and communicating thought, it evolves into a tool essential in the process and development of clear thinking.

Ambiguity in Science and Literature

Neither Paulhan nor Bergson appear to perceive any value in ambiguity, an element so important in Proust, and in literature in general. A discussion of the role of ambiguity in literature takes us into the distinction between scientific and literary language. In 1967, Roland Barthes published an essay entitled "Science versus Literature" in which he discusses the difference in the function of language in scientific and literary writing, and in which he says:

> As far as science is concerned language is simply an instrument, which it profits it to make as transparent and neutral as possible: it is subordinate to the matter of science which exists outside language and precedes it. On the one hand and *first* there is the content of the scientific message which is everything; on the other hand and *next*, the verbal form responsible for expressing that content, which is nothing.[12]

The scientist experiments in a laboratory, collects data and makes observations with the expectation and requirement that data must be precise and reproducible by others. Thus lack of ambiguity in communicating that theory or data is crucial and the language of science aims to be as exact and unambiguous as possible. Furthermore the language is clearly secondary to observation, measurement or theory, and the reality the scientist is attempting to describe precedes the words used to express, as precisely as possible, the concept or data. Another basic tenet of science, usually not enunciated, is that reality should be describable in linear logical terms that is, through the medium of language, both verbal and mathematical. Images and metaphor, so important to the creativity of the literary writer are often viewed by the scientific writer as deviant and parasitic,[13] and are perceived as unnecessary, 'unscientific' frills. Modern science should shun 'the traditional seductions of writing, the rhetorical powers of language.'[14] Barthes agrees with this and says that science uses language as a tool for communicating the contents of the scientific message. For science, there is a reality, a truth that precedes the word. To summarize; Barthes states, that in science the word has secondary importance to the antecedent reality. In literature, however, a reality is suggested and created by words, there is no prior meaning outside and preceding the word.

In science, therefore, it is essential that the message received be the same as the message emitted. As pointed out by Paulson, this is one of the essential differences between the scientific and literary uses of language, and *les parasites* of Michel Serres,[15] the noise of literary culture, are not acceptable in normal scientific discourse, for ambiguity is non-scientific. On the other hand, the presence of noise, or ambiguity in discourse is an essential element in the literary use of language and a clear difference between the literary and scientific use of words. Barthes goes on to say:

> Although science has a certain need of language it is not, like literature *in* language . . . For literature, on the other hand . . . language can no longer be the convenient instrument or the superfluous backcloth of a social, emotional or poetic reality which pre-exists it and which it is languages' subsidiary responsibility to express. Language is literature's Being, its very world, the whole of literature is contained in the act of writing.[16]

In a later essay on "Reflections on a Manual," Barthes goes a step further and considers that not only is "language is literature's Being", but that literature is not something absolute that exists of itself: "The teaching of literature is almost tautological. Literature is what is taught, period. It is an object of teaching."[17] By this he means that the term and concept of 'a canon of literature' has no real existence outside of the teaching process. What constitutes literature and how it is perceived is not an absolute, but is dependent on the social climate and teaching curriculum of the day. This is a very different concept from the 'teaching of science,' where 'science' is considered to be absolute, irrespective of its teaching. Paulson emphasis the differences between scientific and literary language outlined above, and introduces another important one:

> The **artistic text exists in and for itself, not as the communicative instrument** of some project outside of it, though it may communicate as well. The commonplace analogy of literary text to organism arises from this insistence on autonomy: the literary work is opposed to the utilitarian use of language as the living creature is opposed to the machine or artifact. (Paulson, 80.) (my emphasis)

The metaphoric image of a literary text as a living organism is important, for like a living organism a literary text grows, changes and takes
different forms from various perspectives and diversified social cultures, and, in a sense, the words of a text resemble the cells of a
biological organism, for in isolation they are insignificant, it is only
when part of a whole that their real importance appears. Noam
Chomsky refers to the ambiguity in language in a somewhat different
manner when referring to words as signs he says:

> These common thoughts are expressed in a shared public language, consist-
> ing of shared signs. A sign has two aspects. First, it designates an object in
> the world, its referent; in a "logically perfect language," that will be true for
> every "well constructed" expression. Second, a sign has a "sense" that fixes
> the reference and is "grasped by everybody" who knows the language; to
> understand an expression is to know its sense in the shared public language.
> In addition, each person may have an **individual mental image** connected
> with the objective sense.[18]

The nature of this 'individual mental image' will depend on memory,
experience and culture. In addition, great literature like great art has
the property that its interpretation will evolve and grow as cultural
standards and ideas change and develop. The image of literature is
that of a growing and evolving organism and its perception changes
with the epoch and the cultural heredity of the reader. This is similar
to Barthes' view on literature as something which is not absolute, but
which evolves and changes with the culture of the teaching process.

In L'oeuvre ouverte, Umberto Eco[19] also emphasizes that a work
of art is fundamentally ambiguous, there being a plurality of signification, of images, of nuances, a range of interpretations that coexist
within one signifier, one text. A literary text should thus be an 'open
work', open to a variety of interpretations. A text, he says, is esthetically valid in proportion to the number of perspectives and points-of-
view by which it can be viewed, and it should provide for the possibility for numerous resonances according to the cultural heritage, and
memory of the reader whilst never ceasing to be uniquely itself. In a
literary text, the reader's recollections, experience and culture become
an integral part of the text, which thus becomes unique for each reader.
In contrast, a scientific text should be transparent and identical to all
readers. To use Eco's terminology, if a literary text is an 'open work',
then, scientific writing, like a patent specification or a legal brief, should
be devoid of ambiguity and be a 'closed text.'

Interestingly, Proust indirectly refers to a similar difference between the scientific and literary use of language when he writes:

> Seule l'impression, si chétive qu'en semble la matière, si insaisissable la trace, est un critérium de vérité, et à cause de cela mérite seule d'être appréhendée par l'esprit, . . . L'impression est pour l'écrivain ce qu'est l'expérimentation pour le savant, avec cette différence que chez le savant le travail de l'intelligence précède et chez l'écrivain vient après. (IV 458)

This is a somewhat Bergsonian thought, and Proust is saying that '*l'impression*' which is intuitive thought or inspiration, is that evanescent and almost unattainable property that contains truth, and it is the only object that merits attention by the mind. Intuitive thought or inspiration is for the writer what an experiment is for the scientist. For experimentation, according to Proust, is a contact with reality and is what artistic inspiration is for the writer. For the scientist, the hard work comes from conceiving, planning and carrying out the experiment which is the contact with reality. The writing and communicating of the results is clearly secondary to the experimentation. For the writer, on the other hand, the hard work comes from turning passive artistic inspiration (*l' impression*) into a digital text, a point that is emphasized by Bergson (ES 22).

Ambiguity and the Ordered Disorder of Marcel Proust

If some degree of ambiguity is a necessary prerequisite of an 'open' and literary text, this is not to imply that literature is carelessly and haphazardly constructed, on the contrary, it probably requires more care and precision than scientific writing and this is stated and exemplified in Proust's writing.

Whilst the Proustian hero is traveling with his grandmother to Balbec for the first time, she hands him a copy of the Letters of Madame de Sévigné through which he browses and later says:

> Mme de Sévigné est une grande artiste de la même famille qu'un peintre que j'allais rencontrer à Balbec et qui eut une influence si profonde sur ma vision des choses, Elstir. Je me rendis compte à Balbec que c'est de la même façon que lui qu'elle nous présente les choses, dans l'ordre de nos perceptions, au lieu de les expliquer d'abord par leur cause. (II 14)

and hundreds of pages later, when the hero is discussion art with Albertine, he makes a similar statement:

Il est arrivé que Mme de Sévigné, comme Elstir, comme Dostoïevsky, au lieu
de présenter les choses dans l'ordre logique, c'est-à-dire en commençant par
la cause, nous montre d'abord l'effet, l'illusion qui nous frappe. (III 880)

If the letters of Madame de Sévigné appear somewhat disordered at
times, it is no accident, because it is a contrived disorder, for as she
admits: ". . . ainsi mes lettres sont fort négligées; mais c'est mon style
et peut-être qu'il fera autant d'effet qu'un autre."[20] Thus, the seeming
disorder of Mme de Sévigné's correspondence was probably very deliberate art and in keeping with her aristocratic nonchalance.

Proust creates ambiguity and disorder to leave space for the imagination of his reader, and he does this with a flow of images, metaphors and memories which are not random or accidental, but rather
like the letters of Madame de Sévigné, which the Proustian narrator
and his author admired, and like the brush marks of an Impressionist
painter, they are very deliberate. Referring to the studied disorder
of Proust's imagery, Muller uses vivid imagery of his own when he
writes:

Loin de se lancer dans le courant du récit pour s'y dissoudre, le Narrateur
(comme l'auteur qu'il représente) est un éclusier qui domine le fleuve du souvenir et par un jeu de savantes manoeuvres permet tantôt à tel canal, tantôt
à tel autre de déverser des eaux destinées à alimenter la navigation . . .[21]

and using different imagery he continues:

. . . un peu comme Françoise nous aurait permis de visiter sa cuisine, mais
après y avoir mis un semblant d'ordre. Il n'y a pas là comédie, mais art. Ayant
à l'esprit ces intérieurs bourgeois où un Vermeer nous autorise à pénétrer
sans être annoncés, mais où le balai, le panier à linges, les ustensiles de
ménage ont été disposés en beau désordre . . . Proust est le Vermeer du
monologue intérieur.

The flow of Proustian imagery is very deliberate: the purposeful ambiguity and sometimes apparent disorder of memories and reflections
are part of Proust's studied art that enables us to create in our own
minds with the aid of memories and imagination the interiors of
Combray and Guermantes and the personages who occupy them.

To what extent, can one equate the use of language by Bergson on
the one hand and Proust on the other, with the extreme poles of
'scientific' and 'literary' writing? This can partially be answered by
comparing use of imagery the two authors.

Images in Bergson and Proust

Why Bergson Uses Imagery

Imagery is important in Bergson's writing since he is attempting to teach and communicate notions which are infered intuitively and which are non-spatial and non-verbal and therefore inherently difficult, if not impossible, to express in the linear discourse of words. "Nous n'avons que deux moyens d'expression, le concept et l'image," says Bergson (PM 131), and by *concept* Bergson means a linear logical, scientific and analytical description. He is stating that we have two manners of expression, the digital (*le concept*) and the analogic (*l'image*). Excellent examples of the use of images by Bergson occur in both the *Essai* and in *La pensée et le mouvant* when Bergson is describing and transmitting his concept of time, of 'la durée vraie'.

The knowledge of pure duration is, he says, something one possesses intuitively not logically, for we have an internal perception of "l'écoulement de moi-même," of the flow of myself within time and the flow of time within one's self. It is an abstraction that cannot be expressed in the linear, logical language of *l'esprit de géométrie*. But says Bergson: "A celui qui ne serait pas capable de se donner à lui-même l'intuition de la durée constitutive de son être, rien ne la donnerait jamais, pas plus les concepts que les images" (PM 185). Although no single image can communicate the concept of pure duration, perhaps a succession of widely differing images can approach asymptotically to that intuitive notion:

> Nulle image ne remplacera l'intuition de la durée, mais beaucoup d'images diverses, empruntées à des ordres de choses très différents, pourront, par la convergence de leur action, diriger la conscience sur le point précis où il y a une certaine intuition à saisir. (PM 185)

As well as communicating by and through images, a purpose of the philosopher's discourse, he says, is to teach his readers and listeners a correct method of thinking, to place obstacles in the path of simplistic and erroneous methods of thought. For example, the notion of time, is a concept that comes to us easily and habitually as an entity which is spatial in character, but this perception of time is incorrect.

There appears to be *three* types of images (PM 186 note), three stages of imagery through which Bergson's philosophy has to progress.[22] First, the intuitive thought itself, that is perhaps imagery of some form,[23] since it is non-verbal. Second, the images which

Bergson used to clarify the thought for himself, and which usually remain unexpressed. Third, there is the image that he uses to teach and transmit the notion to others. For the latter he apparently experimented with a series of images until he found one that was easily understood, yet reasonably close to the intuitive thought. Again, there develops a dialectic of imagery, a movement between successive images asymptotically approaching a reality that is never fully attained nor, perhaps, attainable.

In addition, it is important to use widely differing images in order to avoid the tendency of one image (for example, the image of time as that of a flowing stream) to replace the true intuitive concept, and furthermore to shun the use of an image which is too simplistic and which may become a symbol which replaces the intuitive element it is meant to represent. Images or symbols have other or secondary properties not possessed by the intuitive idea, and although an image may be used expressly for its multivalent character, it is often used to represent only a single property of an intuitive notion, but in using that image, that intuitive property tends to become generic with a host of other common objects with which the intuitive concept has possibly no relation. Bergson lists some properties of the ideal image when he says: ". . . je veux dire des représentations souples, mobiles, presque fluides, toujours prêtes à se mouler sur les formes fuyantes de l'intuition" (PM 188). A representation of a Bergsonian image might be that of a sort of *cire perdue*, a lost-wax sculpture through which one attempts to capture the flowing and continually changing picture of an intuitive thought. In order to form the figure in a stable and solid form, one perforce melts away and loses the original and changing waxen image.

A Bergsonian Image Should Disappear

Bergson wished to use images that conveyed a concept, but in such a manner that once the concept had been communicated, the image melted away, disappeared, leaving only the abstract idea. He gives a precise example of this when describing the concept of numbers as items existing in space:

> On verra que nous avons commencé par imaginer une rangée de boules, par exemple, puis que ces boules sont devenues des points, puis enfin que cette image elle-même s'est évanouie pour ne plus laisser derrière elle, disons-nous, que le nombre abstrait. (DI 58)

and he expands on his use of imagery in a letter to Floris Delattre in December 1935:

> Dans un livre comme *L'Évolution Créatrice* ou *Les Deux Sources*, l'image intervient le plus souvent parce qu'elle est indispensable, aucun des concepts existant ne pouvant exprimer la pensée de l'auteur, et l'auteur étant obligé alors de la suggérer. Cette suggestion ne pourra se faire que par une image.[24]

Bergson does not use imagery to give his language a literary flavor, but he uses images as the only manner of communicating his intuitive, non-verbal ideas. According to Adolphe,[25] if the reader of Bergson is interpreting the text correctly, it is not only the Bergsonian image that he sees in his mind, but he perceives something more profound that lies beyond, a glimpse of the image that Bergson was keeping for himself. Although Bergson's intention was to use images purely to teach and communicate his intuitive philosophy, his use of imagery gives his text, possibly inadvertently, a metaphoric and literary quality.

The Image of the Uncertainty Principle

Bergson employs a variety of images to communicate the idea of duration and another series of images when discussing the separation between logical, verbal and intuitive thought, and the demarcation between our superficial and inner self, and when describing the dual nature of consciousness, he introduces another notion:

> La vie consciente se présente sous un double aspect, selon qu'on l'aperçoit directement ou par réfraction à travers l'espace. Considérés en eux-mêmes, les états de conscience profonds n'ont aucun rapport avec la quantité; ils sont qualité pure; ils se mêlent de telle manière qu'on ne saurait dire s'ils sont un ou plusieurs, **ni mêmes les examiner à ce point de vue sans les dénaturer aussitôt**. (DI 102) (my emphasis)

One form of consciousness, the spatial and digital, is readily observable, but when we attempt to examine and focus our attention on the qualitative, non-verbal form of our dual consciousness, it fades away to be replaced by a quantitative and spatial symbol:

> C'est le même moi qui aperçoit des états distincts, et qui, fixant ensuite davantage son attention, verra ces états se fondre entre eux comme des aiguilles de neige au contact prolongé de la main. (DI 103).

Thus the more we attempt to fix our attention on that true inner self, the more rapidly it melts away under our burning gaze. Or again, in a different manner, he says:

Dès qu'on cherchera à se rendre compte d'un état de conscience, à l'analyser, cet état éminemment personnel se résoudra en éléments impersonnels, extérieurs les uns aux autres, dont chacun évoque l'idée d'un genre et s'exprime par un mot. (DI 123).

The above three examples, illustrate the imagery that Bergson utilizes and his somewhat round-about manner of expressing a difficult concept by using a variety of approaches and images. But more importantly, he is expressing the fact that we cannot focus on highly personal and non-verbal intuitive thoughts without changing them into generic ideas that are commonplace and thus expressible by words.

Proust expresses a similar notion, that using logic and analysis to focus on intuitive inspirational thought, makes those analogic images faint away and disappear, for such concepts are not available to the cold eye of scientific logical analysis, but only to intuitive contemplation: "Des impressions telles que celles que je cherchais à fixer ne pouvaient que s'évanouir au contact d'une jouissance directe qui a été impuissante à les faire naître" (IV 456). Again, when discussing the difference between the *roman d'introspection* (a term which he prefers to the *roman d'analyse*) and the *roman d'aventures*, and the writer's desire to use intelligence to explore and analyze the deeper regions of the self without disturbing it, he uses his own imagery when he states:

Pour dire un dernier mot du roman dit d'analyse, ce ne doit être nullement un roman de l'intelligence pure, selon moi. Il s'agit de tirer hors de l'inconscient, pour le faire entrer dans le domaine de l'intelligence, mais en tâchant de lui garder sa vie, de [ne pas] la mutiler, de lui faire subir le moins de déperdition possible, une **réalité que la seule lumière de l'intelligence suffirait à détruire**, semble-t-il. Pour réussir ce travail de sauvetage, toutes les forces de l'esprit, et même du corps, ne sont pas de trop. C'est un peu le même genre d'effort prudent, docile, hardi, nécessaire à quelqu'un qui, dormant encore, voudrait examiner son sommeil avec l'intelligence, sans que cette intervention amenât le réveil.[26] (my emphasis)

These passages from Bergson and Proust are essentially similar and reiterate that focusing closely on one parameter, such as the *moi profond*, will disturb it, changing the object being examined, so that it is no longer what was being investigated. This idea that close examination of an object will inevitably alter it has a distinct similarity to the uncertainty principle (sometimes called the indeterminacy principle) of quantum mechanics enunciated by Heisenberg[27]. Furthermore, one can find the clear expression of the philosophical equivalent of the uncertainty principle in both Bergson's and Proust's writings well before Heisenberg's publication of the equivalent in quantum mechanics. Bergson's ideas were first published in 1889 in the *Essai*, and the first of the above quotations from Proust occurs in *Le Temps retrouvé*, whilst the second was written in 1922 in response to an inquiry from a journalist. The equivalent statement in quantum mechanics by Heisenberg did not appear until 1927, almost forty years after Bergson and five years after Proust. The ways in which some of Bergson's work seems to have preceded or been a prefiguration, in philosophical terms, of the equivalent thoughts in the physical sciences is beyond the scope of this study but is discussed by Papanicolaou and Gunter.[28]

Images Common to Bergson and Proust

Bergson and Proust's writing contain a number of similar images, but these images, although comparable, are used in subtly different ways and illustrate the inherent difference in their styles. I will discuss three of these images.

A Nearby Clock Striking the Hour

In this passage, Bergson is attempting to communicate the notion of pure duration *la durée pure*, as indicated earlier in this chapter, he (PM 185) considers that no single image can successfully communicate the notion of pure duration, but perhaps a succession of images of different nature can guide the mind to the intuitive concept:

> Au moment où j'écris ces lignes, l'heure sonne[29] à une horloge voisine; mais mon oreille distraite ne s'en aperçoit que lorsque plusieurs coups se sont déjà fait entendre; je ne les ai donc pas comptés. Et néanmoins, il me suffit d'un effort d'attention rétrospective pour faire la somme des quatre coups déjà sonnés, et les ajouter à ceux que j'entends. Si, rentrant en moi-même, je m'interroge alors soigneusement sur ce qui vient de se passer, je m'aperçois que les quatre premiers sons avaient frappé mon oreille et même ému ma conscience, mais que les sensations produites par chacun d'eux, au lieu de se juxtaposer, s'étaient fondues les unes dans les autres de manière à en faire une espèce de phrase musicale . . . Bref, le nombre des coups frappés a été perçu comme qualité, et non comme quantité; la durée se présente ainsi à la conscience immédiate, et elle conserve cette forme tant qu'elle ne cède pas la place à une représentation symbolique, tirée de l'étendu. (DI 94–95).

The number of strokes of the clock sounding the hour are not counted as such, they are perceived like the notes of a melody which flow into each other and form a continuity, a whole which cannot be dissected into separate notes without destroying the original melody. This image also serves to illustrate the analogic and digital comparison, for the sounds of the bell can be heard as an analogic, continuous and melodious entity, or alternatively, they can be dissected into its digital components, the individual notes or the distinct striking of the bell, so that by the process of analysis one loses the wholeness and melodic beauty of flowing reality. In the same way, true duration, *la durée vraie* is continuous and analogic, but often we dissect, digitalize it and loose its true continuous essence.

Bergson's intention in the use of this imagery is clearly to communicate a concept which he succeeds in doing brilliantly. But is that all he does? The image does not disappear leaving merely a concept of pure duration. By the use of flowing words and rippling imagery he has created something in addition to merely communicating, for Bergson was clearly poet as well as philosopher and there is distinctive literary quality and creative element in his writing whose poetically flowing character is not accidental.[30] Of the relationship between graceful beauty and the reality he wishes to describe, he writes:

> Ainsi, pour celui qui contemple l'univers avec des yeux d'artiste, c'est la grâce qui se lit à travers la beauté et c'est la bonté qui transparaît sous la grâce. Toute chose manifeste, dans le mouvement que sa forme enregistre, la générosité infinie d'un principe qui se donne. Et ce n'est pas à tort qu'on appelle du même nom le charme qu'on voit au mouvement et l'acte de libéralité qui est caractéristique de la bonté: (PM 280)

Grace and beauty are visible to he who contemplates the universe with the eyes of an artist, and Bergson attempts to make that beauty and grace visible through and in the words and style he uses to describe it. In relation to his technique of literary composition he said:

> Le côté musical du style, c'est peut-être l'essentiel. Dans la prose, le rythme est inventé pour chaque expression d'idées . . . dans un exposé philosophique, c'est le rythme qui est l'essentiel: la pensée n'a atteint une précision absolue que si elle a créé, d'une part la "proportion" dans laquelle chaque partie doit figurer dans le tout, et d'autre part les relations entre les différents "mouvements" que sont ces parties. Quand j'écris tel paragraphe, les points et les virgules sont placés avant le texte; la ponctuation précède la phrase et les mots. Un mouvement intérieur m'indique qu'à un certain moment doit venir, si c'est possible, des mots à consonances identiques qui se suivent.[31]

If one studies the above quotation (DI 95) of the hour being rung by a church bell, one sees elements of his literary technique. The first half of the quotation is the image, whilst the second is the philosophical deduction and analysis from the image. He commences the passage by setting the scene and putting his reader in a quiet and contemplative frame of mind by: "au moment où j'écris ces lignes". Then he creates the image of a nearby church slowly striking the hour in the still night air, and the sound of the first part of the peel is likened, not to a blacksmith striking an anvil, but to a musical melody drifting across the still air to the ears of a person at peace with himself and with the world. Like a poet, he is using the specific example to replace the global concept, the simple sounds of a nearby clock striking the hour, to communicate the abstract philosophical notion of the ever-present and universal movement of time, so that the majestic importance of the continuity of time is replaced by the flowing lightness of simple expressions and imagery. We also hear in this quotation the rhythm evoked by the repetition of the consonants *s* and *c*, (in italics in the quotation of DI 95) and the poetic cadence of first two or three lines.

In *Combray*, Proust uses a similar image involving the sounds of a nearby church bell striking the time:

> . . . et quand une heure sonnait au clocher de Saint-Hilaire, de voir tomber morceau par morceau ce qui de l'après-midi était déjà consommé, jusqu'à ce que j'entendisse le dernier *c*oup qui me permettait de faire le *t*otal et après lequel le long silence qui le suivait semblait faire commencer, dans le ciel bleu, toute la partie qui m'était encore concédée pour lire jusqu'au bon dîner qu'apprêtait Françoise . . . (I 86)

The similarity between the two passages is interesting and striking. Both involve someone who, somewhat quietly and peacefully hears the mellow tolling of the time, and retrospectively counts the peals of the bell. In one sense, Proust's passage gives a clearer vision of pure duration for it is often in silence, "le long silence qui le suivait," the stillness that follows the peels of the bells that one can feel or almost hear the passage of pure time.

Nevertheless, the purpose and intent of the authors of the two passages is somewhat distinct, for in the Proustian passage there is no antecedent profound philosophical thought or abstract concept that its author is attempting to communicate. He is striving and succeeding in evoking and recreating in the minds of his readers the mood, feelings, emotions, and thoughts as well as the subtlety that his consciousness was experiencing on a sunny afternoon as he was reading in the garden under the shade of the chestnut tree. Part of this mood is clearly the sense of the quiet flow of that element, time, which is so important in *À la recherche*. In this example the sense of the flow of time is not only intermixed with sound as in Bergson but also with the sight of the blue dome of the heavens above and a feeling of well-being and quiet contentment as well as the pleasant anticipation of "le bon dîner qu'apprêtait Françoise." As with Bergson's passage there is a rhythm, here associated with the alliteration of *morceau* and the sound of similar consonants.

The similarity of this passage with Bergson's (DI 95) is that both authors are attempting to express the qualitative, the non-verbal, that essence of reality which is entirely subjective thus, not readily expressible by words. Bergson has a precise philosophical concept that he attempts to communicate using a variety of images, whilst Proust's purpose is somewhat different, for he is using language to suggest, evoke and create in the mind of the reader a mood, and feeling of well-being and contentment, and secondarily the notion of the continuous flow of time. He is eliciting something akin to, but not identical with, those memories which inspired the words. In that sense, Proust's language is purely 'literary', and in Barthes' terms, the language is everything, there is nothing explicit that precedes the language but a mixture of memories and emotions in the creative mind of its author. These two passages read in juxtaposition emphasize the poetic qualities in Bergson's writing.

A Chorus of Anvils and the Music of Summer

In yet another attempt to describe the concept of pure qualitative duration, Bergson refers to the sounds of someone hammering. The continuous sounds of the hammer, rather like the tolling of the bell, form a sort of melody, which is continuous thus analogic:

> Ainsi, quand nous entendons une série de coups de marteau, les sons forment une mélodie indivisible en tant que sensations pures . . . mais sachant que la même cause objective agit, nous découpons ce progrès en phases que nous considérons alors comme identiques; et cette multiplicité de termes identiques ne pouvant plus se concevoir que par déploiement dans l'espace, nous aboutissons encore nécessairement à l'idée d'un temps homogène, image symbolique de la durée réelle. . . (DI 93)

As in the previous passage (DI 95) involving the chiming of the clock, Bergson is emphasizing that when we focus our attention we analyze and resolve the continuous sound into discrete contiguous identical elements, which can be lined up in imaginary space and counted like the beeds of an abacus, thus again, Bergson's text and image successfully assists in transmitting the notion he is attempting to express.

Proust's uses a similar image, but again in his text, the sounds of the blows of a hammer create a quite different picture.

> Il faisait à peine assez clair pour lire, et la sensation de la splendeur de la lumière ne m'était donnée que par les coups frappés dans la rue de la Cure par Camus . . . contre des caisses poussiéreuses, mais qui, retentissant dans l'atmosphère sonore, spéciale aux temps chauds, semblaient faire voler au loin des astres écarlates; et aussi par les mouches qui exécutaient devant moi, dans leur petit concert, comme la musique de chambre de l'été . . . (I 82)

In this remarkable and often quoted passage, we have a melding together of at least four of our five senses. The sense of **sight**, of light and shade, of **touch** of the heat and of the dust emanating from the cases being hammered, of **sound** not only of the hammer but of the flies dancing in the room, and of imagined **fragrance.** There is one type of stimulus, reading and imagination together with images of sound and light, which evoke secondary subjective sensations of smell, mood and general emotion. A fusion of smells and sounds in a rather small, yet wonderfully congenial, room into which penetrates the breezes, smells, sounds and atmosphere of summer. Although there is no specific mention of taste or odors the figuration of the dusty cases, the closeness and warmth of the room on that summer afternoon creates in one's mind a unity of the senses, so that there is linguistically induced synesthesia. Again, Proust's words are less intent in communicating an abstract philosophical idea than in using the imagery to suggest and evoke the qualitative essence of the mood and feelings, the **affect**, associated with reading in a small room on a summery afternoon.

In part, this recreation illustrates some of the major signification of À la recherche, namely that time need not and does not always destroy, but that firstly through memory and then through words intermixed with memory these precious moments can be removed from the contingencies and ravages of time and attain some element of the eternal. Proust is not preaching the philosophy of what he is attempting, he teaches by example and by evoking analogic images in our minds which serve as an illustration of his thesis.

A Stroll in an Unknown Town
The third example of similar imagery involves the authors strolling through the streets of an unfamiliar town. In this passage, also from Essai, Bergson is beginning to discuss some properties of memory and perception:

> Quand je me promène pour la première fois, par exemple, dans une ville où je séjournerai, les choses qui m'entourent produisent en même temps sur moi

une impression qui est destinée à durer, et une impression qui se modifiera sans cesse. . . . Pourtant, si je me reporte, au bout d'un assez long temps, à l'impression que j'éprouvai pendant les premières années, je m'étonne du changement singulier, inexplicable et surtout inexprimable . . . Il semble que ces objets, continuellement perçus par moi et se peignant sans cesse dans mon esprit, aient fini par m'emprunter quelque chose de mon existence consciente . . . (DI 96–97)

This passage illustrates how a first impression is rarely the same as the image of the same scene seen later when the setting has become familiar. Here again, the images are successfully used as a tool to communicate the notion of memory influencing our perception of material objects. Our perception of the external physical world is to some extent molded by the previous experience laid down in our long-term, spontaneous memory which continuously influences perception and our experience of reality is modified by earlier experience. In this case, the imagery rapidly fades leaving the concept behind.

In a somewhat similar passage, Proust describes his hero or narrator walking through an unfamiliar part of Paris, or an unfamiliar provincial town:

. . . si, dans une grande ville de province ou dans un quartier de Paris que je connais mal, un passant qui m'a "mis dans mon chemin" me montre au loin, comme un point de repère, tel beffroi d'hôpital, tel clocher de couvent levant la pointe de son bonnet ecclésiastique au coin d'une rue que je dois prendre, pour peu que ma mémoire puisse obscurément lui trouver quelque trait de ressemblance avec la figure chère et disparue, le passant, s'il se retourne pour s'assurer que je ne m'égare pas, peut, a son étonnement, m'apercevoir qui, oublieux de la promenade entreprise ou de la course obligée, reste là devant le clocher, pendant des heures immobile, essayant de me souvenir, sentant au fond de moi des terres reconquises sur l'oubli qui s'assèchent et se rebâtissent . . . (I 66)

Not only does this passage involve walking through an unfamiliar town, but memory plays a part also. Again, there is not a precise philosophical concept being communicated, but Proust is using a series of images and invoking memory to create a feeling and impression, and evoking and suggesting similar events dormant in our own memory and imagination.

Bergson Teaches and Communicates, Proust Suggests and Evokes

Both Bergson and Proust are attempting to communicate something of the qualitative essence of reality, but there is an important difference in their conception of reality, and a subtle yet significant distinction in their use of language which is partly linked to their different intentions.

Bergson—Reality

Bergson was primarily a teacher, first at a number of secondary schools, then at the École Normale Supérieure and finally at the Collège de France. The principal purpose of Bergson's writing was to teach and to communicate his philosophy and the concept of reality that he constructed through his intuitive method. Whether one agrees with Bergsonism or not, it is would seem that Bergson must have considered that he was teaching, informing and communicating something of a qualitative, yet objective, reality that existed outside and before himself. He surely considered his notion of time, memory, self and language as being a reality, a truth, that existed beyond himself and that he wished to communicate and teach as clearly and as unambiguously as possible. The various images of pure duration, for example, that he uses are merely to transmit and to teach that concept of continuous duration of la *durée pure*, for he was attempting to convey information that he considered external to and preceding himself and an aspect of objective truth.[32]

Bergson—Language

It has been said that: "l'esprit de finesse rêve parfois de se donner les moyens de l'esprit de géométrie."[33] That goal, to express one's intuitive notions obtained through *l'esprit de finesse* with the clear and unambiguous precision of *l'esprit de géométrie* is one that Bergson strives to attain, but such a logical exactitude is not possible, and Bergson had to resort to various images in order to teach and enlighten his readers. As mentioned previously, he states (PM 131), that we only have two manners of transmitting and communicating information, one method is through clear logical statements of concepts and the other is through images, which in a written text are also expressed in linear series of digital words. But, are the images created in the minds of Bergson's readers the same as the ones which were in his own? Do his words accurately translate the image in his mind?

> Nous nous rapprocherons d'elle . . . fantôme qui nous hante pendant que nous tournons autour de la doctrine et auquel il faut s'adresser pour obtenir le signe décisif . . . L'image médiatrice qui se dessine dans l'esprit de l'interprète, au fur et à mesure qu'il avance dans l'étude de l'oeuvre, exista-t-elle jadis, telle quelle, dans la pensée du maître? (PM 130)

The image in the mind of the reader, Bergson continues, has probably the same relation to the original as two translations in different languages of an original text, not identical but an excellent approximation. The concept of translation is more than metaphor, for Bergson is attempting to translate intuitive concepts into linear digital language, that is, he is using language and images to communicate a reality that is antecedent to and outside himself, and he chooses words carefully in an attempt not to modify that antecedent thought in the process of communication. In order to approach, albeit asymptotically, the original concept, Bergson uses imagery which introduces ambiguity and a literary component in his discourse, and his style is thus 'scientific' with a literary overlay. One could perhaps summarize his use of language by paraphrasing Roland Barthes and stating:

> As far as Bergson's writing is concerned, language is simply an instrument, which it profits him to make as transparent and as neutral as possible: it is subordinate to the matter of reality which exists outside his words and precede them.[34]

Proust—Reality

For Proust, reality is not the material reality of the world external to himself, nor is it identical for everyone. Reality is not objective, nor a sort of ciné film of the world (IV 468), but something highly subjective and yet more real. It is an artistic reality and creation, a world perceived through the eyes and mind of an artist, and as original and different as is that artistic perception:

> Et voici que le monde (qui n'a pas été créé une fois, mais aussi souvent qu'un artiste original est survenu) nous apparaît entièrement différent de l'ancien, mais parfaitement clair . . . nous avons envie de nous promener dans la forêt pareille à celle que le premier jour nous semblait tout excepté une forêt . . . (II 623)

and again:

> Vous m'avez dit que vous aviez vu certains tableaux de Ver Meer, vous vous rendez bien compte que ce sont les fragments d'un même monde . . . la beauté neuve que Dostoïevski a apportée au monde, comme chez Ver Meer il y a création d'une certaine âme, d'une certaine couleur des étoffes et des lieux, il n'a pas seulement création d'êtres, mais de demeures . . . (III 879–880)

The qualitative essence of reality that Proust is attempting to communicate is different from Bergson's, it is not a description of a reality that precedes him and exists outside of himself. It is a reality that is constructed from memory and exists only in the mind, for it is the world of the subjective and qualitative, yet just as 'real' if not more so than the objective external 'reality.' Proust's vision of reality is formed through a link between present sensations and past memories and the evocation of past memories by present perceptions, including those of words. Reality, he says, is a relationship, that we perceive simultaneously, between present sensation and past memory (IV 467).[35] A moment in time is filled with feelings, aspirations, emotions, moods, smells and sounds all qualitative in nature and also filled with reminiscences. Artistic reality is the relationship between seemingly different objects that can be united with words, for words, images and metaphor are able to remove these enchanted moments from the destructive power of time. In a draft in one of his *Cahiers*, Proust discuses his artistic view of reality and the role of imagery and metaphor in literature:

> Comme la réalité artistique est un rapport, une loi réunissant des faits différents (par exemple des sensations différentes que la synthèse de l'impression pénètre) la réalité n'est posée que quand il y a eu style c'est-à-dire alliance de mots. C'est pourquoi il n'y a pas de sens à dire que le style aide à la durée des oeuvres d'art. L'oeuvre d'art ne commence à exister qu'au style. Jusqu'alors il n'y a qu'un écoulement sans fin de sensations séparées qui ne s'arrêtent pas de fuir. . . Dans la Préface de Sésame et les Lys je parle de certains gâteaux du dimanche, je parle de "leur odeur oisive et sucrée" . . . En disant odeur oisive et sucrée j'établis au-dessus de cet écoulement un rapport qui les assemble, les tient ensemble, les immobilise. Il y a réalité il y a style.[36]

Literary language, says Proust, is attempting to make a synthesis of various feelings and sensations that the mind perceives, and the purpose of literary language is to create or evoke a certain aspect of reality which only occurs when a bridge or link (Chapter 4) is formed joining different impressions, thus immobilizing them, and removing them from the 'contingencies of time.' Jean Milly states: "C'est pour luter contre la fragilité des apparences, l'instabilité de la vie psychologique, l'érosion de temps, que Proust élabore un art dont le fondement est la stabilité."[37] Reality for Proust, is this unison of the present qualitative essence with past memories so that the enchanted present moment can be removed from the destructive power of time, made eternal and timeless by linking first with memory and then by evoking memory with words and literature, for Proust, like Bergson, was concerned with Time.

For Bergson, time was a quality of external reality to be studied and described, but for Proust, time was a perpetual concern and cause of anxiety: "si l'oeuvre de Proust exprime une angoisse évident, c'est celle de la perte vertigineuse du temps, du changement perpétuel de la désagréation du monde et de tous les êtres."[38] This is clearly illustrated by the feeling of dismay and hopelessness experienced by the hero when he attends the matinée Guermantes, *le Bal de têtes*, and sees the disintegrating ravages of Time:

> Des poupées, mais qui pour les identifier à celui qu'on avait connu, il fallait lire sur plusieurs plans à la fois . . . quand on avait devant soi ces vieillards fantoches, car on était obligé de les regarder en même temps qu'avec les yeux avec la mémoire, des poupées baignant dans les couleurs immatérielles des années, des poupées extériorisant le Temps, le Temps qui d'habitude n'est pas visible . . . Alors moi qui depuis mon enfance, vivant au jour le jour et ayant reçu d'ailleurs de moi-même et des autres une impression définitive, je m'aperçus pour la première fois, d'après les métamorphoses qui s'étaient produites dans tous ces gens, du temps qui avait passé pour eux, ce qui me bouleversa par la révélation qu'il avait passé aussi pour moi . . . leur vieillesse me désolait en m'avertissant des approches de la mienne. (IV 503 & 505).

À la recherche is a quest which succeeds in finding *le Temps retrouvé*, a quest for that essence of reality that will not be dissipated by time. Is not a major theme of Proust's great work this, almost desperate attempt to remove some of the qualitative essence of reality from the continuous, irrepressible, inexorable, relentless and destructive flow of time:

> . . . le geste, l'acte le plus simple reste enfermé comme dans mille vases clos dont chacun serait rempli de choses d'une couleur, d'une odeur, d'une température absolument différentes; sans compter que ces vases, disposés sur toute la hauteur de nos années pendant lesquelles nous n'avons cessé de changer . . . sont situés à des altitudes bien diverses, et nous donnent la sensation d'atmosphères singulièrement variées. Il est vrai que ces changements, nous les avons accomplis insensiblement; mais entre le souvenir qui revient brusquement et notre état actuel, de même qu'entre deux souvenirs d'années, de lieux, d'heures différentes, la distance est telle que cela suffirait en dehors même d'une originalité spécifique, à les rendre incomparables les uns aux autres. (IV 448)

For Proust, time past, intermixed with emotions, feelings, scents and images is locked away in small packages of memories, but there seems to be an unbridgeable gulf between the present instant and those precious moments in the past and it is this discontinuity and destructive essence of time that he is seeking to overcome. As discussed earlier in this study, Proust achieves this encapsulation of the qualitative essence of reality with words and bridges and above all with metaphor which are both words and bridges, by the art of suggestion and evocation but not by photographic reproduction.

Proust—Language

In discussing the power of poetic language, Baudelaire said: "Manier savamment une langue c'est pratiquer une espèce de sorcellerie évocatoire"[39] Proust certainly knew how to manipulate words and language, and it is by combining words, their associations, and imagery that Proust evokes, suggests, creates and finally encapsulates. His words and text are less an explicit and detailed description, than an evocation, a suggestion that is both specific enough to stimulate the imagination and memory of his readers yet sufficiently general and ambiguous to let the reader create his own images by combining Proust's words with his or her own store of experience, culture and memory.

The reader of Proust is like the Proustian hero whose imagination is stimulated by the presence of the duchesse de Guermantes and who sees in the *eyes of his imagination* the medieval duchess with all her pomp and ceremony as well as the sculptures on the portals of the cathedral. The Proustian reality, like those of the protagonist, is more in the eyes of the mind than in those of the body:

> Tous les châteaux des terres dont elle était duchesse, princesse, vicomtesse, cette dame en fourrure bravant le mauvais temps me semblait les porter avec elle, comme les personnages sculptés au linteau d'un portail tiennent dans leur main la cathédrale qu'ils ont construite ou la cité qu'ils ont défendue. Mais ces châteaux, ces forêts, **les yeux de mon esprit** seuls pouvait les voir dans la main gantée de la dame en fourrures, cousine du roi. **Ceux de mon corps** n'y distinguaient, les jours où le temps menaçait, qu'un parapluie dont la duchesse ne craignait pas de s'armer. (III 540)

The mind of the Proustian reader, like that of the Proustian hero, is stimulated by suggestive imagery to combine present images with past memory and thus create a world unique to himself yet similar to those of its author. At times, the hero sees a sort of optical illusion or distortion that evokes in his mind other associations and images, and by so doing causes the reader to think like the hero and recall to mind similar images in his experience:

... mais ce que j'avais pris pour la fente illuminée de la porte, qui au contraire
était fermée, n'était que le reflet blanc de ma serviette dans une glace posée
le long du mur ... je repensais à tous les mirages que j'avais ainsi découverts
dans notre appartement et qui n'étaient pas qu'optiques. (II 685)

Proust's descriptions are not meticulous and detailed, for these would
be like a photographic reproduction, which he says are not reality. His
words often describe a mixture of sensations, sounds, smells and visions which call up ideas, feelings and memories and suggest, arouse
and create. The Proustian art of suggestion sometimes involves choos-
ing words and setting together a series of brief images each evocative
in itself which have rich and multitudinous associations. Along the
same line, the following quotation has a minimum of descriptive elements, but just enough to evoke memories of similar scenes so that
the reader creates sensations and images analogue to those of the
slightly elated hero who is reminiscing:

... ce parfum d'aubépine qui butine le long de la haie où les églantiers le
replaceront bientôt, un bruit de pas sans écho sur le gravier d'une allée, une
bulle formée contre une plante aquatique par l'eau de la rivière et qui crève
aussitôt, mon exaltation les a portés et a réussi à leur faire traverser tant
d'années successives ... (I 181)

On rare occasions Proust's images are fairly detailed, as in the following example, but then it is not the detailed image that is the most
important, but the association of ideas, the emotions that the view of
various women generates, the desire not only for women but to enter
their realm, to explore and discover, the street, the town and the world:

... j'allais écarter un instant le rideau de ma fenêtre ... c'était aussi pour
apercevoir quelque blanchisseuse portant son panier à linge, une boulangère
à tablier bleu, une laitière en bavette et manches de toile blanche tenant le
crochet où sont suspendues les carafes de lait, quelque fière jeune fille blonde
... et sans la vision de laquelle j'aurais appauvri la journée des buts qu'elle
pouvait proposer à mes désirs de bonheur. (III 537)

The purpose is not so much the image, but the mood, feelings and
emotions created by the view in the mind of the hero and subsequently
in the mind and imagination of the reader.

In the same way, we the reader become the Proustian hero when
we imagine, or see with the eyes of our mind the images elicited and
evoked by Proust's language, but these images are unique to each of
us and dependent on our own culture, experience and memories:

Comment la littérature de notations aurait-elle une valeur quelconque, puisque c'est sous de petites choses comme celle qu'elle note que la réalité est contenue (la grandeur dans le bruit lointain d'un aéroplane, dans la ligne du clocher de Saint-Hilaire, le passé dans la saveur d'une madeleine, etc.) et qu'elles sont sans signification par elles-mêmes si on ne l'en dégage pas?

Peu à peu, **conservée par la mémoire, c'est la chaîne de toutes ces expressions** inexactes où ne reste rien de ce que nous avons réellement éprouvé, qui constitue pour nous notre pensée, notre vie, la réalité, et c'est ce mensonge-là que ne ferait que reproduire un art soi-disant "vécu". . . **La grandeur de l'art véritable . . . c'était de retrouver, de ressaisir, de nous faire connaître cette réalité** loin de laquelle nous vivons, de laquelle nous nous écartons de plus en plus au fur et à mesure que prend plus d'épaisseur et d'imperméabilité la connaissance conventionnelle que nous lui substituons, cette réalité que nous risquerions fort de mourir sans l'avoir connue, et qui est tout simplement notre vie. (IV 473) (my emphasis)

I have quoted this long passage almost in its entirely for it is important and clearly states Proust's view that literature should not attempt to reproduce exact images, but rather to liberate and redeem moments in the past which are encapsulated and held captive in our memory. Literature can secure elements of past reality, but the mind with the help of literature has to liberate, release and redeem these elements which are entrapped in our memory. False art (*un art soi-disant "vécu"*) will attempt to make an exact reproduction and image of these past moments, but the function of true art and true literature, is not to reproduce dead images of the past but rather to enable us to find, grasp and allow us to know that reality entrapped in our own memory, to evoke moments which are now distant from the present. As time progresses layer upon layer of conventional thoughts and feelings cover and are substituted[40] for genuine reality, that without the help of authentic literature, we may never experience. The art of Proust lies in the use of suggestion to help the reader evoke and create his personal images by unlocking those images and remembrances in the reader's own mind, images that are unique to each and everyone. True literature has the power of *Sesame*, the ability to unlock those memories just as much as "la saveur d'une madeleine."

For Bergson there is a *reality* which pre-exists the word and which he is attempting to describe in language, but not for Marcel Proust. Proust uses language to suggest and elicit and thus to create in the minds of the reader *l'essence des choses*, the essence of reality, the world of Combray, of Balbec and Guermantes. His purpose is through the art of suggestion and evocation to induce his reader to create a comparable, but not identical, universe in his own mind. Proust the artist, only succeeds if and when the reader combines Proust's words and language with his own repository of memories, recollections, culture and imagination. Then, if there is resonance, the miracle of art will take place and a new universe will originate in the mind of the reader. But a universe that is personal and unique to the reader. For Combray is not Illiers and visiting Illiers may be of interest to the literary historian but of little appeal to the reader, for just as Illiers is not identical to the Combray of Proust, so the Combray of Proust is not identical to the Combray of the Proustian reader, and imagining Combray is incomparably superior to visiting Illiers.

Although the use of images by Proust is usually very different from that of Bergson, even though the same or a similar image is used, Jean Mouton considers that there is, on rare occasions, a resemblance in their use of imagery:

> Souvent, pour traduire des phénomènes psychologiques particulièrement subtils, Proust a recours à des comparaisons d'une telle délicatesse qu'elles provoquent presque toujours . . . un ébranlement poétique . . . Ces évocations . . . c'est la marque même des comparaisons bergsoniennes.[41]

As Megay[42] points out there is an abyss between the images and metaphors of Proust and those of Bergson. Proust wishes us to remain contemplating the metaphoric image which provides a bridge and a certain quality of the eternal to his style, but the function of the Bergsonian image is to serve a purpose, to communicate and then disappear.

Bergson deplores the fact that language cannot communicate that subjective and highly personal aspect of the internal world, for language, he says repeatedly, tends to destroy that world whilst attempting to communicate it. In contrast the sophisticated artistry of Proust consists in not attempting to communicate accurately or reproduce identically that analogic reality in his mind, for that would be the false art of the "soi-disant vécu." Through suggestive images and ambiguity he is allowing the reader to create in his mind that highly personal and subjective world which Bergson says is incommunicable.

In order to create the universe of À la recherche, Proust is using language as the fictitious Elstir uses paint, to create images with ambiguity, images that elicit memories and imagination, images which blur the separation and remove the barriers between 'real' and 'unreal'. Reflections in which the normal order of time is altered, and events no longer appear in the linear sequence of their occurrence, but emerge, as in memory, in a somewhat random order dependent on the stimulation of sensation, perception and recognition. Bergson wishes to avoid ambiguity, but for Proust ambiguity, images and impressions are a necessary part of his art of suggestion. He does not wish to recreate a photographic image of the external world, for that would be a digital world devoid of feelings, emotions and imagination. In order to recreate *l'essence des choses* in the minds of the reader he needs to use ambiguity, noise, *les parasites*. Then and only then are the *vases clos* opened and the entrapped essence of reality liberated by and for the reader.

In the first part of *Combray*, the Proustian narrator ponders on the old Celtic legend of souls imprisoned in natural objects:

> Je trouve très raisonnable la croyance celtique que les âmes de ceux que nous avons perdus sont captives dans quelque être inférieur, dans une bête, un végétal, une chose inanimée, perdues en effet pour nous jusqu'au jour, qui pour beaucoup ne vient jamais, où nous nous trouvons passer près de l'arbre, entrer en possession de l'objet qui est leur prison. Alors elles tressaillent, nous appellent, et sitôt que nous les avons reconnues, l'enchantement est brisé. Délivrées par nous, elles ont vaincu la mort et reviennent vivre avec nous. (I 43)

With *Sesame* the *vases clos* are opened and the reader with Proust emancipates the thoughts, the analogic and imaginary kingdom entrapped in Proust's mind, the images which would die with him. By recreating them in the mind of his reader Proust removes them from *les contingences du temps*. They become immortalized in his readers: "délivrées par nous elles ont vaincu la mort et reviennent vivre avec nous."

Conclusion

Both Bergson and Proust are attempting to use language to communicate a qualitative essence of reality, but the function and use of language by the two authors is different. Bergson faces a real dilemma, for he is attempting to communicate ideas which are to him intuitive and non-verbal, and as he repeatedly states, words crush and distort ideas. Yet his mode of communication is not music or paint, but words, and he thus has to translate intuitive, non-verbal ideas into a text, so he makes extensive use of imagery, for himself and his reader. He is careful not to place too much emphasis on any one image in case it were to become a symbol and replace the non-spatial intuitive thought.

He thus uses a succession of images which perhaps transmits the idea he is attempting to convey, but he wishes the image to disappear once the concept had been transmitted. But words are tainted, they are contaminated by their prior use, and they carry with them traces of their previous application and former meaning, which can distort and tarnish an original pristine intuitive idea. An important quality of Bergson's style is thus simplicity, moreover as far as possible he avoids abstract, 'philosophical' language, and shuns clichés and common-places so decried by Paulhan, so that his writing is simple, 'reader-friendly,' and replete with ingenious imagery. As Michel Serres succinctly puts it, Bergson's writing is an ingenious assembly of common words.[43]

Bergson's language is 'scientific' in concept, for there is an idea for which and about which he is using language, furthermore the concept precedes the word, although to some extent the original idea is perhaps modified by the word. Yet by the use of imagery, Bergson, inadvertently perhaps, introduces a literary flavor in his writing. His language is not purely at the 'scientific' pole of the Barthes opposition, yet it is closer to the 'scientific' than to the purely 'literary.'

Proust's use of language is literary and his concept of reality is quite different from Bergson's. Like the philosopher however, Proust also has an analogic image of reality that he is attempting to communicate, but his refined skill lies in not attempting to communicate the incommunicable, or an exact reproduction. Rather, Proust suggests and elicits, and uses words, images, metaphors to evoke, with the assistance of the imagination, memory of his readers, that world of qualitative emotions, aspirations, memories, and images which cannot be accurately communicated. By the use of words and imagery he finds resonance in the mind of his readers, and thus elicits, creates, resurrects and brings to life images, thoughts, emotions which perhaps were merely nascent or almost forgotten. His words evoke feelings and images which like the images of Vermeer are beyond the ravages of time. The likeness is not only to Vermeer, but also to the Impressionist painters[44] who were Proust's contemporaries. Proust decried photographic reproduction and precise description which leave no room for the imagination and creativity or the involvement of the reader's memory, for explicit portrayal does not resurrect the reality of times past. Ambiguity leaves room for imagination and suggestion, and ambiguity constructed with care and precision is a characteristic of the Impressionist painters and also of Proust's writing.

Bergson teaches and communicates whilst Proust suggests and evokes, and the Proustian quest for lost time is successful, through the words which suggest, stimulate and evoke, like "la saveur d'une madeleine," both memory and the imagination and form a link between present moment and past memory. The present word can unlock past reminiscence, so that the wonder of the evanescent past which was encapsulated, placed in the *vases clos* of memory are liberated by suggestion and by *Sesame*, by the reader uncovering the charmed jars of Ali-Baba, by the reader opening the book of literature.

Notes

1   Charles Baudelaire, *Oeuvres complètes* (Paris: Seuil, 1968) 464.

2   Anne Henry, *Marcel Proust: théories pour une esthétique* (Paris: Klincksieck, 1981) 267.

3   Steven Pinker, *The Language Instinct* (New York: William Morrow, 1994) 16–17.

4   Chapter 3, 'Mentalese,' of Steven Pinker's book, cited above, provides an excellent discussion of the internelationship between thought and language.

5   Bergson sometimes uses the word *profond* to express the location of this self. *Profond* means both profound in the sense of difficult to apprehend and comprehend as well as deep spatially.

6   Jean Paulhan, *Les fleurs de Tarbes or la terreur dans les lettres* (Paris: Gallimard, 1990) 83.

7   Michael Syrotinski, "How is Literature Possible?" *A New History of French Literature*, ed. David Hollier (Cambridge: Harvard UP, 1989) 953–958.

8   Frédéric Badré, *Paulhan le juste* (Paris: Grasset, 1996) 187–188.

9   Another model of this inter-relationship is provided by the exchange theory of nuclear forces (Yukawa force). According to this theory the proton and neutron in the atomic nucleus are held together by the exchange of a messenger (meson) which continually transforms each into the other, a process made possible under the Heisenberg uncertainty principle. Neutron and proton are thus continually exchanging identity with each other, and it is meaningless to consider which is which. This exchange results in the very powerful nuclear binding of neutron to proton. A similar situation can be said to exist between thought and language, each continually changing into, and not separable or distinguishable from, the other. Perhaps like the meson oscillating between proton and neutron, 'thought-language' is reverberating across the *corpus callosum* between left and right hemispheres. See e.g. Sybil P Parker, ed. McGraw-Hill Encyclopedia of Physics, (New York: McGraw-Hill, 1983) 898. This scientific image clearly echoes Bergson's writings.

10   Maurice Blanchot, *Comment la littérature est-elle possible?* (Paris: José Corti, 1942) 25.

11   This passage is again discussed in Chapter 7.

12   Roland Barthes, "Science versus Literature," *Introduction to Structuralism*, ed. Michael Lane (New York: Basic Books, 1970) 411. The essay was originally published in *The Times Literary Supplement* of September 28, 1967.

13   Andrew Ortony, "Metaphor, Language and Thought," *Metaphor and Thought*, ed. Andrew Ortony (Cambridge: Cambridge UP, 1993).

14   William R. Paulson, *The Noise of Culture* (Ithaca: Cornell UP, 1988) 12.

15   Michel Serres, *Le parasite* (Paris: Grasset, 1980).

16   Barthes *Science versus Literature* 411.

17   Roland Barthes, "Reflections on a Manual," trans. Sandy Petrey *PMLA* Jan (1997): 69–75.

18   Noam Chomsky, *Language and Thought* (Wakefield: Bell, 1995) 17.

19   Umberto Eco, *L'oeuvre ouverte* trans. Chantal Roux de Bézieux (Paris: Seuil, 1965).

20   Madame de Sévigné, *Lettres* vol. I (Paris: Gallimard, Bibliothèque de la Pléiade 1953–57) 393.

21   Marcel Muller, *Les voix narratives dans la recherche du temps perdu* (Genève: Droz, 1983) 57.

22   Lydie Adolphe, *La dialectique des images chez Bergson* (Paris: PUF, 1951) 11.

23   Steven Pinker (55) refers to this type of non-verbal thought as 'mentalese.'

24   Adolphe 11.

25   Adolphe 14.

26   Marcel Proust, *Contre Sainte-Beuve* (Paris: Gallimard, 1971) 640–641. I am grateful to Marcel Muller for drawing this passage to my attention.

27   In quantum mechanics the uncertainty principle (W. Heisenberg, 1927) states that accurate measurement of an observable quantity (e.g. position) of an elementary particle, necessarily produces uncertainty in one's knowledge of the values of other related observables (e.g. velocity). For a discussion on the uncertainty principle, see for example Parker, 1211–1212.

28   Andrew C Papanicolaou and Pete A.Y. Gunter, eds. *Bergson and Modern Thought: Towards a Unified Science* (London: Harwood, 1987).

29   The consonants *s* and *c* are italisized to illustrate the poetic cadence as discussed later.

30   This is reflected in the citation to Bergson's Nobel Prize in literature in 1928 which states: "En reconnaissance de la richesse et la fécondité de ses idées et de l'art remarquable avec laquelle elles ont été exprimées." Michel Dansel, *Les Nobel Français de littérature.* (Paris: André Bonne, 1967) 107.

31   Adolphe 199.

32   The notion of "le mouvement rétrograde du vrai." Bergson, PM, 1–23.

33 Georges Auclair, "Roland Barthes: S/Z," *La nouvelle revue française* (Paris: Nouvelle Revue Française, 1970) 786.

34 The original statement is in Barthes *Science versus Literature* 411.

35 The full quotation is given in Chapter 3, and at the beginning of Chapter 5.

36 Marcel Proust, "Cahiers d'ébauches, No XXVIII," Jean Milly, *Proust et le style* (Genève: Slatkine, 1991) 89.

37 Jean Milly, *Proust et le style* (Genève: Slatkine, 1991) 90.

38 Milly 91.

39 Baudelaire 464.

40 This echoes Bergson's view on the layers of conventional thought that cover the true *moi*.

41 Jean Mouton, *Le style de Marcel Proust* (Paris: Nizet, 1969) 71–76.

42 Joyce N. Megay, *Bergson et Proust: Essai de mise au point de la question de l'influence de Bergson sur Proust* (Paris: J. Vrin, 1976) 144.

43 Michel Serres, *Éloge de la philosophie en langue française* (Paris: Fayard, 1995) 195.

44 This is discussed more fully in Chapter 8.

Chapter 7

Esthetics and Artistic Creation

Ce que l'art nous fait retrouver, c'est le temps tel qu'il est enroulé dans l'essence.

Deleuze.[1]

Ainsi, toujours poussés vers de nouveaux rivages,
Dans la nuit éternelle emportés sans retour,
Ne pourrons-nous jamais sur l'océan des âges
Jeter l'ancre un seul jour?

These opening lines of one of Lamartine's most evocative poems[2] provides a remarkable image of the notion of Bergson's *durée pure,* of the continuity and ever-flowing qualitative multiplicity that is pure duration, as well as an illustration of the power of poetic language. In addition, it furnishes us with a representation of Proust's view of Art that we shall discuss in this chapter, for retaining Lamartine's metaphor, one might say that for Proust, true Art lowers the anchor of perception and consciousness into the ocean of pure duration, so that time's perpetual progression is halted, as for one brief moment we enter the eternal present.

* * *

Through the communicative and evocative properties of language both Henri Bergson and Marcel Proust cleanse the windows of perception and open the *vases clos* to a universe of the qualitative. As we have seen in the previous chapter, the use of language by both writers is similar yet subtlety and importantly different. In this chapter, I will discuss the conception of art and its function as expressed by Henri Bergson and Marcel Proust, as well as the process of artistic creation.

I will suggest that Bergson's and Proust's notion of art and its purpose are similar, although Proust has a very exalted and exacting view
of the function and duty of the artist. An important difference between the two writers relates to the role of time and the prominence
of memory, particularly, spontaneous or involuntary memory in Proust's
conception of art. For Bergson art and philosophy are similar, both
being a perception of, and discourse on, reality. Proust's conception
of art involves the process of 'thinking backwards' and thus has a
resonance with Bergson's philosophical method. Although Bergson
does not use the digital-analogic taxonomy, his description of *l'analyse*
and *l'intuition* are very similar to the notion of the digital and the
analogic.

Having compared the views of Bergson and Proust on art, I will
discuss the process of artistic creation. The passage of *Les clochers
de Martinville* in the Proustian text can be read as an illustration of
the process of artistic creation. Bergson's description of the genera-
tion of a work of art as the organization of a sea of chaotic thoughts
and ideas has similarities to *Maxwell's demon* reversing the second
law of thermodynamics. Finally, I will suggest that in the language of
the digital-analogic taxonomy, artistic creation can be depicted as the
fusion of analogic inspiration with digital materiality.

The Function of Art

Both Henri Bergson and Marcel Proust had a very clear and precise
conception of art and its function, which are similar but with an interesting difference. In order to emphasize this similarity I have juxta-
posed below some statements written by each author. Most of Bergson's
view on esthetics are to be found towards the end of *Le rire*, but in
addition, there are not infrequent references to esthetics throughout
his works. In *Le rire*, Bergson asks:

> Quel est l'objet de l'art? Si la réalité venait frapper directement nos sens et
> notre conscience, si nous pouvions entrer en communication immédiate avec
> les choses et avec nous-mêmes, je crois bien que l'art serait inutile, ou plutôt
> nous serions tous artistes . . . (RI 115)

But we are not all artists and usually our sense of perception is so
altered by habit, social conventions and the necessities of everyday
life that we do not see reality clearly. Art is a perception of that reality,
a transcription or translation of *a* reality which is qualitative, continu-

ous, often intuitive and not necessarily logical, and this reality, which perhaps is felt intuitively rather than clearly seen or understood analytically, is a perception which one can describe as 'analogic' as opposed to 'digital,' and art is a transposition of that reality into terms that we can all see and understand. One of the reasons we cannot normally see reality or perceive the true essence of things is that our mind is conditioned by years of habituation and indoctrination, by generic ideas, and by socially acceptable conventions:

> Entre la nature et nous . . . entre nous et notre propre conscience, un voile s'interpose, voile épais pour le commun des hommes, voile léger, presque transparent, pour l'artiste et le poète. (RI 115)

and furthermore:

> . . . qu'il soit peinture, sculpture, poésie ou musique, l'art n'a d'autre objet que d'écarter les symboles pratiquement utiles, les généralités conventionnellement et socialement acceptées, enfin tout ce qui nous masque la réalité pour nous mettre face à face avec la réalité même. (RI 120)

In the same manner that normal generic language masks true thought (Chapter 5), so social conventions and perceptions obscure our view of reality and truth, cloud our window of perception, and the function of art is to draw aside that shroud of obscurity, even if only for a short period.

The Proustian narrator is stating something similar, albeit in perhaps more poetic language, when, referring to the paintings of Elstir, he says that we only see nature, that is reality, as it actually exists, when we see a work of art, such as one of Elstir's paintings:

> Mais les rares moments où l'on voit la nature telle qu'elle est, poétiquement, c'était de ceux-là qu'était faite l'oeuvre d'Elstir. Une de ses métaphores les plus fréquentes dans les marines . . . était justement celle qui comparant la terre à la mer, supprimait entre elles toutes démarcations. C'était cette comparaison, tacitement et inlassablement répétée dans une même toile qui y introduisait cette multiforme et puissante unité . . . (II 192)

Elstir's land- and seascapes emphasize the analogic qualities of reality, the unity and continuity, the absence of demarcation and separation between things which we normally separate. For Bergson, art, like intuitive thought, is a view of reality that comes to our awareness directly through *les données immédiates de la conscience*. In a sense, children are perhaps closer to reality than adults, for that veil of habit, convention and training has not yet obstructed the perception of reality which is thus clearer. It is perhaps partly for this reason that so much of the Proustian novel appears to be a yearning for, and an attempted return to, the pure essence of reality that the narrator experienced in his childhood. As we mature and learn 'social graces', we tend to loose that perception of reality's true essence. For Proust, art is a perception of that reality, and an eternity that is beyond and outside time and which thus is a form of truth. The music of M. Vinteuil was, for the Proustian hero, a glimpse of that truth:

> . . . les questions de la réalité de l'Art, de la Réalité, de l'Éternité de l'âme: c'est un choix qu'il faut faire entre elles; et pour la musique de M Vinteuil, ce choix se représentait à tout moment sous bien des formes. Par exemple, cette musique me semblait quelque chose de plus vrai que tous les livres connus. (III 876)

In a lecture: "La perception du changement" given at Oxford in 1911 (ML 888), Bergson juxtaposes and compares the objects of philosophy with those of art and raises the same question as raised in *Le rire*.[3] How can we see more deeply, perceive more clearly the nature of reality?

> Supposez que nous insérions *en elle* notre volonté, et que cette volonté, se dilatant, dilate notre vision des choses. . .
> On dira que cet élargissement est impossible. Comment demander aux yeux du corps, ou à ceux de l'esprit, de voir plus qu'ils ne voient? L'attention peut préciser, éclairer, intensifier: elle ne fait pas surgir, dans le champ de la perception, ce qui ne s'y trouvait pas d'abord . . . Il y a en effet, depuis des siècles, des hommes dont la fonction est *précisément* de voir et de nous faire voir ce que *naturellement, nous n'apercevrions pas*. Ce sont les artistes. (ML 893) (Bergson's emphasis)

His answer is again that artists have that clear vision of reality, they possess the gift of enabling us to draw back the obscuring film that hangs between us and reality and thus have the ability to make us see the world more clearly. By *l'attention*, Bergson is referring to our intelligence and power of intellectual concentration, our logic and power to dissect and analyze, but digitalization is not the way to improve our perception of reality. He continues by raising a related question:

> A quoi vise l'art, sinon à nous *faire découvrir*, dans la nature et dans l'esprit hors de nous et en nous, *une foule de* chose qui ne frappaient pas explicitement nos sens et notre conscience? Le poète et le romancier qui expriment un état d'âme ne le créent certes pas de toutes pièces: ils ne seraient pas compris de

nous si nous *n'éprouvions pas nous-mêmes, au moins à l'état naissant, tout ce qu'ils nous décrivent.* (ML 893) (Bergson's emphasis)

In an earlier version of this text, quoted in the discussion of 'The Endogenous Text' in Chapter 5, he expresses himself differently, and introduces an interesting image:

> Au fur et à mesure qu'ils (le poète et le romancier) nous parlent, des nuances d'émotion et de pensée nous apparaissent qui pouvaient être représentées en nous depuis longtemps, mais qui demeuraient invisible: telle l'image photographique qui n'a pas encore été plongée dans le bain d'où elle se révélera, le poète est ce révélateur. (PM 149–150)

As the artist describes impressions of ideas and feelings, we realize that these emotions were already present, perhaps dormant, within ourselves, although we had perhaps never directly recognized or experienced them. They were within us, but not discernible or understandable, like the latent image on a photographic plate that requires a developer to reveal itself to us.

The notion that the artist reveals truths which, although present in us, remain unknown until uncovered and revealed by the artist is also clearly expressed by Proust, who uses a metaphor similar to that of Bergson, that of the artists who develops a photographic plate and reveals a latent image, and in a soliloquy on the importance of art, the narrator says:

> La grandeur de l'art véritable . . . c'était de retrouver, de ressaisir, de nous faire connaître cette réalité loin de laquelle nous vivons, de laquelle nous nous écartons de plus en plus au fur et à mesure que prend plus d'épaisseur et d'imperméabilité la connaissance conventionnelle que nous lui substituons . . .
>
> La vraie vie, la vie enfin découverte et éclaircie, la seule vie par conséquent pleinement vécue, c'est la littérature. Cette vie qui, en un sens, habite à chaque instant chez tous les hommes aussi bien que chez l'artiste. Mais ils ne la voient pas, parce qu'ils ne cherchent pas à l'éclaircir. Et ainsi leur passé est encombré d'innombrables **clichés** qui restent inutiles parce que l'intelligence ne les a pas "**développés.**" Notre vie . . . Il est la **révélation**, qui serait impossible par des moyens directs et conscients, de la différence qualitative qu'il y a dans la façon dont nous apparaît le monde, différence qui, s'il n'y avait pas l'art, resterait le secret éternel de chacun. (IV 474)[4] (my emphasis)

The artist develops images, thoughts and desires, perhaps latent in ourselves and which reveal that internal reality to both observer and reader; the artist thus reveals to us the 'endogenous text' discussed in Chapter 5. The poet and artist is the being who develops these latent thoughts within us, and we, the reader, listener or observer are an essential element of the work of art. Shakespeare 'created' *Hamlet*, and Proust *À la recherche*, but many of the qualities of the Prince of Denmark and the essence of the Proustian hero were already within each of us and awaiting liberation by an artist of genius. In that sense perhaps, literature like science, is *discovering* that which already exists, rather than *creating* something new. Restating this notion in another manner, Proust says: "Le devoir et la tâche d'un écrivain sont ceux d'un traducteur" (IV 469),[5] the writer is one who renders into language the notions and thoughts already present in each of us.

It would be an unfortunate error to read *À la recherche* as merely a rearranged autobiography, or the communication of a piece of embellished personal history, for as suggested in Chapters 4, 5 and 6, memory, the remembrance and imagination of the reader play an essential part in the creation of the Proustian text:

> Le vrai Combray, le vrai Balbec, la véritable Albertine, engloutis dans les cavernes de la mémoire cachées dans les coffres de l'inconscient, vont resurgir, trouver miraculeusement le visage qu'ils n'ont jamais eu pour le narrateur mais que le lecteur leur a toujours vu.[6]

The real towns and villages of *À la recherche* and the authentic characters of the Proustian novel are not necessarily those that were in Proust's imagination, but those that the reader of Proust creates by a combination of the Proustian text with the images in his or her memory. These are images which were latent, perhaps, but which are resurrected by Proust's text and which come to life in the reader's mind. Proust resuscitates and develops those latent images to which Bergson also refers, for as discussed in Chapter 6, the art of Proustian language is less to communicate a message or idea, than to suggest, to evoke, revive and create a new world in the mind of the reader.

Once the reader has participated in the process of artistic creation, he is no longer a simple individual, he has partaken of something wider and deeper than himself.[7] There is identity, says Anne Henry, of the reader, and writer, with pure duration and the qualitative essence of reality:

> . . . la manifestation téléologique qui constitue l'acte du génie, la révélation qui s'accomplit grâce à lui de l'identité (temps pur, essence qualitative du monde), révélation qui devra se compléter nécessairement de sa fixation dans l'œuvre d'art. (Henry, 263)

The concept that a successful work of art must find a chord, a resonance within the mind of the perceiver for it to be appreciated is one which interestingly parallels the sentiment of Umberto Eco who in *L'œuvre ouverte*[8] tells us that a work of art is esthetically true only to the extent that it has multiple perspctives and can activate resonance in a wide audience. By the same token, a work of art should contain ambiguity for in that manner, the readers, listeners or observers will find elements in the work with which they find congruence and resonance. An artistic creation should therefore suggest and evoke rather than dictate a unilateral message, and an artistic work should find an equivalence, an idea, memory or emotion, albeit dormant yet living, within the minds of the reader or perceiver.

The function of art is thus to enable us to see and perceive not only the external world but also the internal universe within ourselves. For Proust, it is only through authentic art that we can travel beyond ourselves, and it is only through the medium of artistic creation that we can see as others worlds, and perceive nature and the universe as it is: "Par l'art seulement nous pouvons sortir de nous, savoir ce que voit un autre de cet univers qui n'est pas le même que le nôtre et dont les paysages nous seraient restés aussi inconnus que ceux qu'il peut y avoir dans la lune" (IV 474). Indeed how could we ever see, know and understand the worlds of Combray or Guermantes but through the artistry of Marcel Proust?

For convenience of communication and understanding, and also by force of habit, the mind tends to replace elements of qualitative reality by symbols. Bergson tells us that: ". . . la conscience . . . n'aperçoit la réalité qu'à travers le symbole." (DI 96). Symbols[9] occupy space and replace the qualitative, non-spatial by the quantitative and spatial and in time we may overlook that the element is merely a symbol that masks the qualitative concept, but art helps us remove that symbolic spatial character so that we become aware of the true qualitative essence that is reality.

Proust expresses a somewhat similar thought, and when visiting the studio of Elstir, from whom the Proustian hero learned much about esthetics and art, the protagonist contemplates some works which he likens to the images created by a magic lantern, whose images often stimulated his imagination. He wishes to rely on what some would dismiss as "illusions" or artificial symbols, in the belief that these are in fact the path of a true contact with reality. Thus, Proust endeavors to obtain, through art, not only a vision of the world, but to experience and encapsulate the true essence of existence even if only for an evanescent and fleeting instant: "Dès lors n'est-il pas logique, non par artifice de symbolisme mais par retour sincère à la racine même de l'impression, de représenter une chose par cette autre que dans l'éclair d'une illusion première nous avons prise pour elle?" (II 712). Moreover, although during his solitary walks through the countryside of Combray and Méséglise in his youth, the protagonist obtained fleeting glimpses of reality, it is not until many years later that he realizes that the true function of art and literature is the recapturing and preservation of those ephemeral glimpses of reality to remove them from 'the contingencies of time'.

For Proust, Art is Linked to Memory and Time

Although there are similarities between Bergson's and Proust's theories on art, there is also an important difference linked to time and memory. For Proust memory is an integral part of art, but memory does not seem to be an important ingredient in Bergson's conception of the artistic. For Proust, art, linked to memory, enables one to glide back in pure duration to the reality that was once perceived but later destroyed by time; hence a major function of art is to immobilize time, or to enable one to move entirely outside time:

> C'est parce que je croyais aux choses, aux êtres, tandis que je les parcourais, que les choses, les êtres qu'ils m'ont fait connaître, sont les seuls que je prenne encore au sérieux et qui me donnent encore de la joie. Soit que la foi qui crée soit tarie en moi, **soit que la réalité ne se forme que dans la mémoire**, les fleurs qu'on me montre aujourd'hui pour la première fois ne me semblent pas de vraies fleurs. (I 182) (my emphasis)

For the Proustian hero reality is partially in the past and is linked and perceived through memory, and associated with the things he saw and the people he knew, and above all the intermingling of sight, smell, sound, touch and memory in one magnificent experience. Often it seems that the hero's memories of childhood seem more real to him than present experience, and he wishes to immobilize that past so that, in a sense, he can stroll through those past memories that art has resurrected and made motionless:

> Dans plus d'une autre, l'immense paysage . . . est rendu, des sommets à la mer, avec une exactitude qui donne plus que l'heure, jusqu'à la minute qu'il est, grâce au degré précis du décline du soleil, à la fidélité fugitive des ombres. Par là l'artiste donne, en l'instantanéisant, une sorte de réalité historique vécue au symbole de la fable, le peint et la relate au passé défini. (II 715)

This conception of an art that stops the flow of time is clearly manifest in many impressionist paintings which Proust loved and admired,
and which are also glimpses of a world which are not photographic
representations. Literature, like painting, uses metaphor, (Chapter 6)
which changes the perception of things and discloses their transcen-
dental essence and the layers of meaning and signification:

> . . . le charme de chacune consistait en une sorte de **métamorphose des**
> **choses représentées, analogue à celle qu'en poésie on nomme**
> **métaphore** et que si Dieu le Père avait créé les choses en les nommant, c'est
> en leur ôtant leur nom, ou en leur en donnant un autre qu'Esltir les recréait.
> (II 191) (my emphasis)

There is in the above passage an echo of Bergson's views on language
and the generic properties of words, as discussed in previous chapters.

For Gilles Deleuze the importance of memory in Proust's conception of art is at a lower level than that of art itself. Although *l'essence*
des choses may be incarcerated in involuntary memory, the quality of
this is somehow inferior to what we can perceive in true art:

> Mais l'essence se réalise dans le souvenir involontaire à un degré plus bas que
> dans l'art, elle s'incarne dans une matière plus opaque . . . L'essence artiste
> nous révèle un temps originel, qui surmonte ses séries et ses dimensions.
> C'est un temps "compliqué" dans l'essence elle-même, identique à l'éternité.[10]

He considers that *l'essence* as viewed through memory is different
from that viewed in art: "Une essence s'incarne dans le souvenir
involontaire, mais elle y trouve des matières beaucoup moins
spiritualisées, des milieux moins 'dématérialisés' que dans l'art."[11]
Memory is individual whereas art is universal, thus art is a superior
source of *l'essence des choses* than involuntary memory, for art is
more generalized yet retaining the uniqueness of *l'essence*.

The Purpose of Art is Not to Generate a Photographic Reproduction

Before the hero realizes himself, and before the narrator reveals to his
readers the true function and power of art and literature, the narrator
takes his reader through the process of considering what is **not** true
literature. The hero, at Tansonville, reflecting on the disappointing
qualities of fashionable literature as exemplified by the "journal des
Goncourt," concludes that he has no gift for writing, and in addition

that literature itself does not fill his expectation of an art which reveals truth and reality. His negative opinion of his own qualities and abilities are closely allied with these pessimistic views of literature itself:

> . . . mon absence de dispositions pour les lettres, pressentie jadis du côté de Guermantes, confirmée durant ce séjour dont c'était le dernier soir . . . me parut quelque chose de moins regrettable, comme si la **littérature ne révélait pas de vérité profonde**; et en même temps il me semblait triste que la littérature ne fût pas ce que j'avais cru. (IV 287)

These same views of both his lack of ability as a writer and the failure of literature itself to communicate or create anything of value, recur a number of times with increasing force. All his life the hero has been in search of his vocation and for that qualitative essence of reality perceived in his youth, seeking a way of preserving or recreating that essence of reality, but in his mature years he becomes increasingly despondent of his vocation and of the merit of literature:

> . . . la pensée de mon absence de dons littéraires, que j'avais cru découvrir jadis du côté de Guermantes, que j'avais reconnue avec plus de tristesses encore dans mes promenades quotidiennes avec Gilberte avant de rentrer dîner, fort avant dans la nuit, à Tansonville, et qu'à la veille de quitter cette propriété j'avais à peu près identifiée, en lisant quelques pages du journal des Goncourt, à la vanité, au mensonge de la littérature, cette pensée, moins douloureuse peut-être, plus morne encore, si je lui donnais comme objet non une infirmité à moi particulière, mais l'inexistence de l'idéal auquel j'avais cru . . . (IV 433)

As his increasingly depressive analysis of his literary abilities and the quality of true literature continues, the hero comes to the conclusion that literature is nothing more than a rendition of mundane expressions and phrases that totally fail to reproduce the qualitative feelings, that literature cannot duplicate or accurately express real feelings and emotions, and the multiple layers of original experience:

> . . . j'avais maintenant la preuve que je n'étais plus bon à rien, que la littérature ne pouvait plus me causer aucune joie, soit par ma faute, étant trop peu doué, soit par la sienne, si **elle était en effet moins chargée de réalité** que je n'avais cru. (IV 444) (my emphasis)

The hero fears that literature is not true art, but merely like photographs which, although they reproduce the exact physical *quantitative* appearances and backdrop, fail completely to express and evoke those *qualitative* feelings, emotions and sensations associated with experience, perception and reality, which he knows, from his madeleine experience, are enshrined in memory . He is dismayed that literature may perhaps only be *ennuyeuse comme une exposition de photographies.*

The True Function of Art and Literature

However, following this succession of depressive statements on literature and his own artistic abilities, the hero, attends the *matinée des Guermantes*, at which a series of extraordinary reminiscences reveal to him, not only his vocation but also the enchanting and miraculous power of literary art. The protagonist discovers simultaneously both that he has a vocation for writing and that real literature can, through words that suggest and evoke memories, recreate the essence, the truth and reality of the past that lies entrapped, dormant in the mind:

> On peut faire se succéder indéfiniment dans une description les objets qui figuraient dans le lieu décrit, la vérité ne commencera qu'au moment où l'écrivain prendra deux objets différents, posera leur rapport, analogue dans le monde de **l'art**, à celui qu'est le rapport unique de la loi causale dans le monde de la science, et les enfermera dans les anneaux nécessaires d'un beau style. (IV 468)

A detailed literary description, like a photographic reproduction is insufficient; it is not art, but by linking the present moment with past memory, one brings past memory into the present, one moves past memory out of time and into the eternal present.

For Proust, the true function of art is, through memory and the evocative power of language, images or music, to evoke and recreate reality with all the miraculous essence of the senses. It is to reconstitute the wonder of living in the present instant, a reality that is not merely a mental picture, but a vision which has associated with it, sound, smell and touch so that art resurrects, in its entirety, those images hidden in the *vases clos* of our inner memory where, but for the power of true art, they may forever remain. By the miraculous and evocative powers of *Sesame*, the poetic word, Proust considers that the true artist is able through his art to reconstruct reality, and thus having removed it from the destructive effect of time, bring it into the eternal present, to enable the reader, viewer or listeners to move a parcel of experience outside of time. Memory is a series of layers of names and images each continuous with, and forming part of another reminiscence which is not a separate or distinct memory; for there is not a contiguous sequence, rather an intermingling and continuous quality, reminiscent perhaps of the brush strokes of an Impressionist painting, each continuous with and forming part of the previous:[12]

> Ainsi les espaces de ma mémoire se couvraient peu à peu de noms qui, en s'ordonnant, en se composant les uns relativement aux autres, en nouant entre eux des rapports de plus en plus nombreux, imitaient ces œuvres d'art achevées où il n'y a pas une seule touche qui soit isolée où chaque partie tour à tour reçoit des autres sa raison d'être comme elle leur impose la sienne. (II 826)

The unity of art and the layers of human experience that Proust perceives in the paintings of the Impressionists and that he is endeavoring to capture in words is the unity that in this study we have termed the analogic. The function of all the arts, whether musical, painting or literary, is the same, and Proust's view on literary art are revealed throughout À la recherche by his statements on both the paintings of Elstir discussed in Chapter 4 and the music of Vinteuil. Not only is the function of art to resurrect past reality, but it is also to evoke and reveal the multiple layers of human personality and experience. It is to give a voice to that which Bergson says is inexpressible in words, to reveal the diverse strata, qualities and meanings of existence, to give utterance to the many universes in which humankind exists, the qualitative as well as the quantitative, and the various strata of human character that Bergson terms *les aspects du Moi*.

The final revelation occurs in the library of the Prince de Guermantes, where the hero, become narrator, finally understands both his own vocation and the wonderful power and the nature of literary art:

> Or la recréation par le mémoire, d'impressions qu'il fallait ensuite approfondir, éclairer, transformer en équivalents d'intelligence, n'était-elle pas une des conditions, presque l'essence même de l'oeuvre d'art telle que je l'avais conçue tout à l'heure dans la bibliothèque? (IV 621)

Proust here delineates, in terms that can readily be translated into the digital–analogic taxonomy, not only the purpose of art but also the two major stages of artistic creation. First, the process of inspiration, the perception often through the medium of memory, of qualitative and analogic impressions of reality which the artist has to contemplate and clarify. Secondly, these qualitative and analogic impressions have to be transformed, translated into logical digital terms, *transformer en équivalent d'intelligence*. This is a restatement, in simple verbal terms, of the content of '*les clochers de Martinville*', to be discussed below.

He is also stating that true art and real literature is the evocation and liberation of images and remembrances locked in the mind which are then further elaborated by words. For words, like *Sesame* and *la saveur d'une madeleine* are able to unlock and liberate the past memories entombed in the mind, and by moving reminiscences into the eternal present, liberate them from the ravages of time:

> Peu à peu, conservée par la mémoire, c'est la chaîne de toutes ces expressions inexactes où ne reste rien de ce que nous avons réellement éprouvé, qui constitue pour nous notre pensée, notre vie, la réalité, et c'est ce mensonge-là que ne ferait que reproduire un art soi-disant "vécu" . . . **La grandeur de l'art véritable . . . c'était de retrouver, de ressaisir, de nous faire connaître cette réalité** loin de laquelle nous vivons, de laquelle nous nous écartons de plus en plus au fur et à mesure que prend plus d'épaisseur et d'imperméabilité la connaissance conventionnelle que nous lui substituons, cette réalité que nous risquerions fort de mourir sans avoir connue, (IV 473) (my emphasis)

Literature and art are not those photographic images of the past, not the clichés and expressions that fail entirely to recreate former events. The true function of art and literature is to uncover, to resurrect that reality entombed in our memories, to liberate them and bring them again into the present, so that, through true art, time past comes into the eternal present, so that *le temps perdu* becomes *le Temps retrouvé*.

Art and Philosophy

Is not the removal of the veil of intellect, the shroud of obscurity, that lies between our senses and reality which both Bergson and Proust state as the purpose of art also the function of philosophy as expounded by Henri Bergson? Indeed Proust the poet and writer and Bergson philosopher and writer have much in common, for they are attempting to achieve the same thing with different tools and a different medium. Indeed, Bergson clearly states this:

> C'est donc bien une vision plus directe de la réalité que nous trouvons dans les différents arts . . . Eh bien, ce que la nature fait de loin en loin, par distraction, pour quelques privilégiés, la philosophie, en pareille matière, ne

pourrait-elle pas le tenter, dans un autre sens et d'une autre manière, pour tout le monde? Le rôle de la philosophie ne serait-il pas ici de nous amener à une perception plus complète de la réalité par un certain déplacement de notre attention? (PM 153)

For Proust, art is also to provide a new and direct vision of reality:

Et voici que le monde (qui n'a pas été créé une fois, mais aussi souvent qu'un artiste original est survenu) nous apparaît entièrement différent de l'ancien, mais parfaitement clair . . . nous avons envie de nous promener dans la forêt pareille à celle que le premier jour nous semblait tout excepté une forêt . . . (II 623)

For Bergson, the role and function of the philosopher is the same as that of the artist, to enable us to perceive the world with a fresh vision, and Proust's concept of art and Bergson's of philosophy are indeed very similar. In *Le Temps retrouvé* the mature hero begins to understand what he was seeking in his solitary walks through the countryside of Combray and Méséglise in his youth, and says to himself:

Ce travail de l'artiste, de chercher à apercevoir sous la matière, sous l'expérience, sous des mots quelque chose de différent c'est exactement **le travail inverse** de celui que, à chaque minute quand nous vivons détourné de nous-même, l'amour-propre, la passion, l'intelligence, et l'habitude aussi accomplissent en nous, quand elles amassent au-dessus de no impressions vraies, pour nous les cacher entièrement, les nomenclatures, les buts pratiques que nous appelons faussement la vie . . . Ce travail qu'avaient fait notre amour-propre, notre passion, notre esprit d'imitation, notre intelligence abstraite, nos habitudes, **c'est ce travail que l'art défera, c'est la marche en sens contraire, le retour aux profondeurs** où ce qui a existé réellement gît inconnu de nous, qu'il nous fera suivre. (IV 474 & 475) [my emphasis]

This seems very much like Bergson's writing, stating that the artist attempts to perceive reality beneath the veils of experience, beneath ordinary words, that the function of art is to work backwards, to **reverse normal habit and thought**. The notion of reversal, of working backwards, of thinking backwards is striking and there is similarity, indeed almost identity, of Proust concept of art with Bergson's notion of philosophy:

. . . la métaphysique . . . ne peut être qu'un effort pour *remonter la pente naturelle* du travail de la pensée, pour se placer tout de suite, par une dilatation de l'esprit, dans la chose qu'on étudie, (PM 206) [compare with Proust's line 1,2, & 9 above]

Il faut pour cela qu'il se violente, qu'il **renverse le sens de l'opération** par laquelle il pense habituellement, qu'il retourne ou plutôt refonde sans cesse ses catégories. (PM 213) [Compare with Proust's lines 7–9]
Philosopher consiste à invertir la direction habituelle du travail de la pensée. (PM 214) (Bergson's emphasis) [compare with Proust's line 1–3]

Thus not only does Bergson say that the function of philosophy is similar to that of art, but the description by Proust of the purpose of art is almost identical to Bergson's description of philosophy.

The Digital and the Analogic of Art: (*L'analyse et l'intuition*)

As discussed in Chapter 2, the terms 'digital' and 'analogic' did not exist in Bergson's days, but his term '*intuitive*' is similar although not identical with 'analogic,' for whilst the intuitive is analogic not all things analogic are necessarily intuitive, and Bergson opposes the term '*analyse*' to '*intuition.*' Intuition, says Bergson, is the process of transporting oneself into the interior, into the essence of an object in order to understand it (PM 181). There is something very Proustian in the concept of transporting one's mind into the interior of an object to coincide with it, to experience *l'essence des choses.* Thus both art and philosophy consist of expressing '*l'intuition,*' of traveling within the essence of objects and attempting to express their qualitative nature which in normal words is inexpressible:

C'est dire que **l'analyse** opère sur l'immobile, tandis que **l'intuition** se place dans la mobilité ou, ce qui revient au même, dans la durée. Là est la ligne de démarcation bien nette entre **l'intuition** et **l'analyse**. (PM 202) (my emphasis)

It is of note that in the above excerpt Bergson is stating that intuition is fluidity (*la mobilité*) and is in *la durée*, that is intuition is within or part of real time, of pure duration which is non-spatial and non-digital:

On reconnaît le réel, le vécu, le concret à ce qu'il est la variabilité même. On reconnaît l'élément à ce qu'il est invariable. Et il est invariable par définition, étant un schéma, une reconstruction simplifiée, souvent un simple symbole, en tout cas une vue prise sur la réalité qui s'écoule.
Mais l'erreur est de croire qu'avec ces schémas on recomposerait le réel. Nous ne saurions trop le répéter: de l'intuition on peut passer à l'analyse, mais non pas de l'analyse à l'intuition. (PM 202)

L'analyse is thus a static representation of the continuity and ever-changing mobility of analogic reality. The sea is a symbol of Bergson's *mobilité,* the ever changing, continuous, flowing quality of moving waves, in addition the sea is symbolic of 'la durée vraie,' indivisible, ever-changing yet continuous. The symbolic importance of flowing water in the Proustian novel, both La Vivonne and the sea at Balbec have already been discussed in Chapters 4 and 5, and are illustrative of the analogic in Proust. Although in both Proust and Bergson the continuous and qualitative elements are the dominant, both the analogic and the digital may be viewed as complementary representations, for intuition needs logic and scientific logic gains much from the intuitive. As Pilkington says: "The faculty of intuition bears only upon phenomena which exist in real time or 'la durée'; since these phenomena alone, that is, the facts of consciousness are distorted by being explained as if they were extended in space."[13]

Art Reverses the Effects of Intelligence

Proust considered that true art can reverse the destructive effects of logic and intelligence. Inspiration,[14] and a vision of the essence of reality comes from pondering and reflecting on the nature of simple things of nature: ". . . un nuage, un triangle, un clocher, une fleur, un caillou, en sentant qu'il y avait peut-être sous ces signes quelque chose de tout autre que je devais tâcher de découvrir . . ." (IV 457). In contrast, information, data, knowledge that logical intelligence obtains from a direct analysis of things are less profound than those glimpses of eternity and reality that spontaneously enter our intellect and from which we can distill the essence of reality. The intuitive, inspirational vision of nature is different from, and superior to logical analysis. Poetic inspiration which perceives the essence of reality and which is born when analogic thought is linked with memory is often destroyed by the cold unimaginative gaze of logical analysis and intelligence:

> Il languit dans l'observation du présent où les sens ne peuvent la lui apporter, dans la considération d'un passé que l'intelligence lui dessèche, dans l'attente d'un avenir que la volonté construit avec des fragments du présent et du passé auxquels elle retire encore de leur réalité en ne conservant d'eux que ce qui convient à la fin utilitaire, étroitement humain, qu'elle leur assigne. (IV 451)

For Proust, then, intelligence and logic reverse and inhibit the process by which inspiration leads to the creation of a work of art.

The Process of Artistic Creation

There are two distinct ways of communicating a complex idea. One is by direct detailed description of the principles involved in a form of philosophical or scientific discourse. Another, and often more effective manner of communication, is by giving an example or recounting a story. Marcel Proust uses both these methods to communicate his conception of art and artistic creation. More especially, he uses a special form of the second, for the entire text of À la recherche, may be read as a discourse on esthetics, the search for art, reality and its ultimate discovery. As Anne Henry writes: "Proust a en tête non l'exposé d'une esthétique mais celui d'une véritable philosophie de l'art" (259).

Les clochers de Martinville

There are two important passages in À la recherche which can be read as a commentary on art and more precisely as a discourse on the process of artistic creation. These are the passage often referred to as Les clochers de Martinville, and Les trois arbres d'Hudimesnil. Inspiration, or artistic enlightenment may be a perception of the essence of reality, and artistic creation is the process of transforming that illumination or view of analogic reality into words, into a literary, musical or artistic, and thus digital, creation.[15] In view of its relevance to these arguments, this passage will be analyzed in some detail. Numbers in brackets have been inserted in the quotation to assist in referring to portions of the passage:

(P1). Au tournant d'un chemin j'éprouvai tout à coup ce plaisir spécial qui ne ressemblait à aucun autre, à apercevoir les deux clochers de Martinville, sur lesquels donnait le soleil couchant et que le mouvement de notre voiture et les lacets du chemin avaient l'air de faire changer de place . . . je sentais que je n'allais pas (P2). au bout de mon impression, que quelque chose était derrière ce mouvement, derrière cette clarté, quelque chose qu'ils semblaient contenir et dérober à la fois

(P3). Je ne savais pas la raison du plaisir que j'avais eu à les apercevoir à l'horizon et l'obligation de chercher à découvrir cette raison me semblait bien pénible. (P4) J'avais envie de garder en réserve dans ma tête ces lignes remuantes au soleil et de n'y plus penser maintenant . . . force me fut, faute d'autre compagnie, de me rabattre sur celle de moi-même et d'essayer de me rappeler mes clochers.

(P5) un peu de ce qui m'était caché en elles m'apparut, j'eus une pensée qui n'existait pas pour moi l'instant avant, qui se formula en mots dans ma tête, et le plaisir que m'avait fait tout à l'heure éprouver leur vue s'en trouva tellement accru que, pris d'une sorte d'ivresse je ne pus plus penser à autre chose.

Sans me dire que ce qui était caché derrière les clochers de Martinville devait être quelque chose d'analogue à une jolie phrase, puisque c'était sous la forme de mots qui me faisaient plaisir, que cela m'était apparu, demandant un crayon et du papier au docteur je composai . . .le petit morceau suivant . . . (I 177 to 179)

(P6) Je me trouvai si heureux, je sentais quelle m'avait si parfaitement débarrassé de ces clochers . . .comme si je venais de pondre un œuf, je me mis à chanter à tue-tête. (I 180)

The first phase (P1) is that of a feeling of pleasure or happiness resembling no other known to the narrator. This is rapidly followed by (P2) the feeling that there is something, an important truth perhaps, hidden or contained within the view of *les clochers de Martinville*. This feeling or effusive emotion is perhaps that of *la réalité pressentie*, that essence of reality which is behind and within all things, but that we so often do not perceive.

In a third phase (P3), the hero recognizes that he does not understand the reason for this feeling of profound happiness which remains unknown to him. At the same time, the hero realizes that he should attempt to understand its significance, although this may be hard work. In the fourth phase (P4) the hero attempts to retain and conserve that feeling evoked by the view of the steeples by preserving the analogic image in a text. In the fifth (P5) and perhaps most important phase, the hero translates, in his mind, the inspiration provided by the analogic images of the spires into digital words and experiences great joy at this act. Subsequently he asks for a piece of paper and composes a literary text. The sixth and final phase (P6) is the realization that it was this transformation of the analogic image into linear digital words, this process of artistic creation, that produced the emotion of stillness, joy and happiness. The narrator has been transformed from a passive observer into an active creator, and has experienced the joy of creation: ". . .comme si j'avais été moi-même une poule et si je venais de pondre un oeuf, je me mis à chanter à tue-tête."

The joy experienced by the hero when he has written the text is the same as the joy he encounters following the madeleine experience, and the three major reminiscences at the matinée des Guermantes. They are the joy of creation, the joy of perceiving reality, as well as the peace and calm enchantment associated with identify of self with pure time and the qualitative essence of reality.

Les trois arbres d'Hudimesnil

There is a second and somewhat similar passage slightly later *in À la recherche*, which occurs when the hero is riding in a car with Mme. de Villeparisis on the outskirts of Hudimesnil near Balbec. The protagonist has a very similar experience to that of *les clochers de*

Martinville when he sees three trees (*les trois arbres d'Hudimesnil*)
on the horizon:

> . . . tout d'un coup je fus rempli de ce bonheur profond que je n'avais pas
> souvent ressenti depuis Combray, un bonheur analogue à celui que m'avaient
> donné, entre autres, les clochers de Martinville. Mais cette fois il resta
> incomplet. Je venais d'apercevoir, en retrait de la route . . . trois arbres . . .
> que je ne voyais pas pour la première fois . . . mais je sentais qu'il m'avait été
> familier autrefois; de sort que mon esprit ayant trébuché entre quelque année
> lointaine et le moment présent, les environs de Balbec vacillèrent et je me
> demandais si toute cette promenade n'était pas une fiction, Balbec un endroit
> où j'étais jamais allé que par l'imagination . . . et les trois arbres la réalité
> qu'on retrouve en levant les yeux de dessus le livre qu'on était en train de lire
> . . .
>
> Je regardais les trois arbres, je les voyais bien, mais mon esprit sentait
> qu'ils recouvraient quelque chose sur quoi il n'avait pas prise . . . Mais pour
> que mon esprit pût ainsi se rassembler, prendre son élan, il m'eût fallu être
> seul. . . . Je reconnaissais ce genre de plaisir qui requiert, il est vrai, un
> certain travail de la pensée sur elle-même . . . Ce plaisir, dont l'objet n'était
> que pressenti, que j'avais à créer moi-même je ne l'éprouvais que de rares
> fois, mais à chacune d'elles il me semblait . . . qu'en m'attachant à sa seule
> réalité je pourrais commencer enfin une vraie vie . . . Je sentis de nouveau
> derrière eux le même objet connu mais vague et que je ne pus ramener à moi
> . . . Ou bien ne les avais-je jamais vus et cachaient-ils derrière eux comme tels
> arbres, telle touffe d'herbe . . . un sens d'un passé lointain de sorte que,
> sollicité par eux d'approfondir une pensée, je croyais avoir à reconnaître un
> souvenir? . . . Cependant ils venaient vers moi; peut-être apparition mythique
> . . . des fantômes du passé, de chers compagnons de mon enfance, des amis
> disparus . . .. Comme des ombres ils semblaient me demander de les emmener
> avec moi, de les rendre à la vie . . . Elle m'entraînât loin de ce que je croyais
> seul vrai, de ce qui m'eut rendu vraiment heureux, elle ressemblait à ma vie.
> . . . j'étais triste comme si je venais de perdre un ami, de mourir à moi-
> même, (II 76 to II 79)

I wish to contrast the experience of '*Martinville*' with that of
'*Hudimesnil*,' which the Proustian hero realizes are very similar. First,
and most obviously, both episodes occur when the hero is taking a
drive in the country. The drive allows for the movement, in relation to
the observer, of objects forming part of the scenery. In both cases the
objects of the hero's attention are new to him, although in the case of
Hudimesnil there is a feeling of *déjà-vu*, that he is not seeing the
trees for the first time. In both cases the principal objects are three,
tall, thin elements (steeples and trees) which are silhouetted against
the light and whose apparent and relative positions change with the
movement of the car, and at the end of the second episode, the three

objects take on the form of three personages. Let us compare the main stages of the *Hudimesnil* passage with that of *Martinville*.

The *Hudimesnil* experience starts with a feeling of joy and profound happiness which the narrator realizes is similar to the feeling he experienced at Martinville. The second stage of the *Hudimesnil* experience resembles the second stage of *Martinville*. At Martinville, the special emotion of joy was followed by a notion that there must be something special behind the movement. At Hudimesnil, the experience of happiness is followed by the notion that the objects must have been familiar in the past and the hero recognizes that he is probably not seeing them for the first time. This feeling is similar to that of imagination, or to the impression of *déjà-vu*.

The third stages in the two passages are also very similar to each other. In the *Martinville* experience, the hero realizes that he is unaware of the reason for his feeling of joy, and that in order to discover the reality behind the impression, a considerable effort will be necessary and that to accomplish this he must be alone. In the case of *Hudimesnil* the hero recognizes the feeling of happiness but that the impression is only nascent and that he should create something. (". . . que j'avais à créer moi-même,") The hero thinks he has recognized something in memory, again perhaps an evocation of *déjà-vu*.

The fourth and fifth stages of *Martinville* do not exist in the *Hudimesnil* experience since the hero does not succeed in being alone nor in enlarging the impressions behind the scene. At the sixth stage at the end of the *Martinville* passage, the hero has become writer and creator. He has transformed those ephemeral and evanescent analogic images into a permanent digital text and is joyful and pleased:

> Sans me dire que ce qui était caché derrière les clochers de *Martinville* devait être quelque chose d'analogue à une jolie phrase, puisque c'était sous la forme de mots qui me faisaient plaisir, que cela m'était apparu, demandant un crayon et du papier au docteur je composai . . . le petit morceau suivant . . . (I 179)

The hero is telling us that behind or within the images of the three steeples, there was something non-material, something in the form of phrases of words which might be transformed into a literary text. In the case of *Martinville*, inspiration is rapidly followed by the moment of artistic creation, the transformation of the analogic image into a digital text. The 'jolie phrase' to which the hero refers, is, of course metaphor, the only manner by which an analogic vision can be transposed into a digital text. Thus artistic creation is the transformation of those evanescent analogic impressions into a permanent linear and digital text. The hero accepts the inspiration and recognizes that this illumination must be followed by work, that concentration and solitude is necessary, as is the opportunity for introspection.

In the case of *Hudimesnil*, however, creation does not taken place. The hero does not manage to be alone and apparently does not realize that he should translate the fleeting analogic image into a permanent and digital text. He does not transform the intuitive inspiration into artistic creation, and he experiences sadness akin to grief. He has failed, and he laments the loss of the inspiration, the lost opportunity, "triste comme si je venais de perdre un ami, de mourir à moi-même." This last phrase is, of course, in contrast to the last phrase of the *Martinville* episode: "je me mis à chanter à tue-tête."

Both passages (*Martinville* and *Hudimesnil*) may be read as allegories of artistic inspiration, but it is only in the case of *Martinville* that we have a description of the successful transformation of artistic illumination, that brief ephemeral sight of reality, into a permanent work of art, in this case a short literary text. Inspiration[16] is that essence behind and within: "la chose derrière ce mouvement, derrière cette clarté quelque chose qu'ils semblaient contenir et dérober." Artistic enlightenment is also that special impression of incipient, germinating joy, and in both passages that moment of illumination arrives like a breath of fresh air on a hot, sunny day, analogous to a summer breeze: "qui d'aele passagere par le monde volez, et d'un sifflant murmure l'ombrageuse verdure doulcement esbranlez:"[17]

> . . . comme si nos plus belles idées étaient comme des airs de musique qui nous reviendraient sans que nous les eussions jamais entendus, et que nous nous efforcerions d'écouter, de transcrire. (IV 456)

For the essence of artistic creation comes to us like a melody carried on the breeze, one that we feel we have heard before although we never have. We hear, we listen and we attempt to transcribe. Artistic illumination is something that is offered and that we have the freedom of accepting or rejecting. Although inspiration is passive it is followed by the necessity of hard work if the moments of enlightenment are to be transformed into an artistic creation. Often, as in both these cases, the metamorphosis of inspiration into artistic creation necessitates solitude.

In the *Martinville* episode in which esthetic illumination is followed by artistic creation, there is a view, a vision of something new, unique and subjective, valuable yet evanescent and its subsequent metamorphosis into an enduring, digital text.[18] The inspiration is clearly analogic with an intuitive quality; it is continuous, non-verbal and qualitative, and although the scenery is spatial, the artistic enlightenment induced is not spatial, and if one wished to ascribe a dimension to the inspiration, it would be the qualitative dimension of pure duration. The qualitative inspiration is then transformed into an entity which is quantitative, spatial and (temporarily at least) beyond the 'contingencies of time.' But perhaps even more interesting is the fact that Proust has not given us a logical scientific and intellectual description of the process of artistic creation, but rather presented an example or illustrative story of the process of the transformation and fusion of the analogic with the digital.

The example is itself a text and the description of the transformation of analogic enlightenment into digital work of art is carried out entirely digitally, textually. Thus we have two descriptions, in linear digital text, of the *Martinville* episode. The first (I 177–178) is the experience, the vision, the artistic illumination evoked by the apparent movement of the three steeples. The second description (I 179) is the linear digital text that the adolescent hero, becoming writer, transcribes onto paper. The first is the text of the mature writer at the height of his literary achievement, whilst the second is that of a young man beginning to experiment with his nascent literary skills, so that the first text is more poetic whereas the second is more 'linear' and perhaps more logical.

In the case of *Les clochers de Martinville*, the narrator has become a writer, and has transformed the essence or reality revealed to him by inspiration into words, into a linear and digital text, he has taken part in artistic creation that has given him the extraordinary feeling of happiness resulting from that activity. In the case of *Hudimesnil*, however, the hero's receives a similar artistic enlightenment, has a comparable vision of the essence of reality, but the process is aborted, he never transforms that inspirational illumination into a work of art and the would-be creator is sterile and mournful.

The passage *Les clochers de Martinville* can perhaps be read as a prefiguration of the entire Proustian novel, as an allegory of the long and winding path to be followed towards the goal of artistic creation. The reader of Ruskin's lecture "Of Kings' Treasuries" is told that he or she may understand the full message of the talk until the end: ". . . until we unexpectedly reach the best point of view by winding paths."[19]

In the same manner, the full purpose of the (Proustian) text is not revealed until the end of the reader's journey along the text, until the reader has followed the winding path of the novel up to its ending. Artistic creation is the process of fusion, and hence of preservation, of the inspirational analogic vision of reality with the digital written word that is the text. In another sense the *Martinville* passage can be read as an account of the life of the hero, of the youth with the inspirational visions, who, at the end of the long and winding path of life's journey, eventually achieves his vocation and becomes a writer.

If *Les clochers de Martinville* can be read as an example or pre-figuration[20] of the life of hero become writer-creator, *Les trois arbres d'Hudimesnil* can perhaps be read as an illustration of the life of one of the other major character in the novel, Charles Swann. There are, of course, many similarities between the narrator and Swann, suffice to say that Swann is a failure, for he has talent, moments of artistic enlightenment, and has ample opportunity to become a creator, but he becomes distracted by the snobbish life of high Parisian society and does not possess the energy and self-discipline to undertake the hard (*pénible*) work of completing a literary work. Swann is, of course, the person that the narrator-hero might have become had he not understood that inspiration, ideas, dreams and memories, however noble and unique are for nothing if they are not transformed, through "l'effort pénible, mais précieux," into a literary text or comparable work of art. Inspiration has to be fused with and transformed into the digital, else it is lost.

In *Le temps retrouvé*, the narrator realizes and verbalizes the fact that Swann probably experienced artistic inspiration, but never had the self-mastery and energy to transform inspiration into a text, into a work of art: "Était-ce cela, ce bonheur proposé par la petite phrase de la sonate à Swann qui s'était trompé en l'assimilant au plaisir de l'amour et n'avait pas su le trouver dans la création artistique," (IV 456). Thus the inspiration of Vinteuil's sonata, which was misinterpreted and misconstrued by Swann, could not transform him into the writer and artist that he lacked the will power and self-discipline to become.

Bergson and Artistic Creation. *L'ombre de nous-même*

There are two descriptions of the process of artistic creation in Bergson's writings that one may compare with the allegory of *Les clochers de Martinville*. The first is from the *Essai* and the second from *L'énergie spirituelle*.

In the *Essai*, Bergson spends time and space discussing our attempts to translate thoughts, sentiments and emotions into words. This important passage will be quoted and analyzed in detail, for not only does it reinforce Bergson's views on language, discussed in the previous chapter, but it also describes the translation of ideas into words, the process of literary creation. The passage refers to Bergson's often stated assertion that language is unable to translate accurately and communicate emotions and thought, and begins by emphasizing that words (*le mot brutal*) crush or cover all delicate subjective impressions and thoughts of our inner selves, changing them into the non-personal and generic. He goes on:

> Nulle part cet écrasement de la conscience immédiate n'est aussi frappant que dans les phénomènes de sentiment . . . **ce sont mille éléments divers qui se fondent, qui se pénètrent,** sans contours précis, sans la moindre tendance à s'extérioriser les uns par rapport aux autres; leur originalité est à ce prix. Déjà ils se déforment quand nous démêlons dans leur masse confuse une multiplicité numérique: que sera-ce quand nous les déploierons, isolés les uns des autres, dans ce milieu homogène qu'on appellera . . . temps ou espace? Tout à l'heure chacun d'eux empruntait une indéfinissable coloration au milieu où il était placé: le voici décoloré, et tout prêt à recevoir un nom. Le sentiment lui-même est un être qui vit, qui se développe, qui change par conséquent sans cesse; . . . Mais il vit parce que la durée où il se développe est une durée dont les moments se pénètrent: en séparant ces moments les uns des autres, en déroulant le temps dans l'espace nous avons fait perdre à ce sentiment son animation et sa couleur. Nous voici donc en présence de l'ombre de nous-mêmes: nous croyons avoir analysé notre sentiment, nous lui avons substitué en réalité une juxtaposition d'états inertes, **traduisibles en mots**, et qui constituent chacun l'élément commun, le résidu par conséquent impersonnel, des impressions ressenties dans un cas donné par la société entière. (DI 98–99) [my emphasis]

Bergson refers to *mille éléments divers qui se fondent*, the sea of ideas, emotions and feelings each interpenetrating and not separate one from the other. This is similar to the 'confusion of the continuity of ideas' referred to in the passage quoted on page 214 from *L'énergie sprituelle*. But as soon as one begins to unravel this interwoven tapestry of thoughts, one begins to change them, and as one isolates one thought from another one moves them from the dimension of true time (*la durée vraie*) and one lines them up, like beads of an abacus, in imaginary space or spatial time, and their nature changes even more. One is moving the original qualitative thought from analogic reality of continuous time to the quantitative environment of space and spatial time. Whereas the thoughts had possessed a unique aspect, as one moves them to spatial time they loose those unique properties and become mundane, prosaic and are ready to receive a name. The original thought is like a living thing which is incessantly changing like the multitudinous analogic seas from which it originated. The thoughts are animated and exist in that real time (*la durée vraie*) in which all things and moments are continuous and interpenetrating. But as one transfers that thought from real duration to spatial time, one causes it to loose that uniqueness, that animation and coloration, so that one expresses but a mere outline of the original concept. We might consider that we have analyzed and expressed our innermost thoughts and emotions. But in fact, we have transformed them into structures and thoughts that are translatable into normal discourse made up of words, those generic elements that express notions common to all of society, and which, like the pictures hanging on a grade-school wall, have lost all individuality:

> Les mots nous présentent des choses une petite image claire et usuelle, comme celles que l'on suspend aux murs des écoles pour donner aux enfants l'exemple de ce qu'est un établi, un oiseau, une fourmilière, choses conçues comme pareilles à toutes celles de même sorte. (I 380)

Moreover, in the quotation from the *Essai* (DI 98–99) cited above, Bergson is again stating that the process of translating ideas and emotions into words leads to a loss of their unique qualities and renders them similar to the mundane thoughts of others. Bergson then considers the skills of the creative writer, who partially succeeds in translating those unique ideas into a literary text, and continues as follows:

> Que si maintenant quelque romancier hardi, **déchirant la toile habilement tissée** de notre moi conventionnel, nous montre sous cette logique apparente une absurdité fondamentale, sous cette juxtaposition d'états simples une pénétration infinie de mille impressions diverses qui ont déjà cessé d'être au **moment où on les nomme,** . . . et par cela même qu'il déroule notre sentiment dans un temps homogène et en exprime les éléments par **des mots**, il ne nous en présente **qu'une ombre à son tour**: seulement il a disposé cette ombre de manière à nous faire **soupçonner la nature extraordinaire** et illogique de l'objet qui la projette; il nous a invités à la réflexion en mettant dans l'expression extérieure quelque chose de cette contradiction, de cette pénétration mutuelle, qui constitue l'essence même des éléments exprimés. Encouragés par lui, **nous avons écarté pour un instant le voile** que nous interposions entre notre conscience et nous. Il nous a remis en présence de nous-mêmes. (DI 99–100) [my emphasis]

The creative writer or poet will necessarily use digital words to attempt to express these personal and qualitative feelings, and not only does he or she use digital and linear words but necessarily these are in spatial time, so that he translates subjective impressions into something objective and in so doing changes their essence. Nevertheless, if the writer is a creative artist he will have achieved something more important, he will have evoked a doubt, a suspicion, a feeling in the mind of the reader that there is perhaps something profound, yet to be discovered, behind and before the linear text of generic words. Although not specified by Bergson, it is clearly by the artful use of metaphor that the creative writer formulates the analogic in the mind of the reader, suggests to him and evokes in him, the reality that he is attempting to create. As discussed in Chapter 5 with Bergson's *deux aspects du Moi*, Proust also tells us that true literature is not produced by our everyday social and habitual being, but by a being, a self, that resides deep within us, and requires effort and work to evoke.

Bergson's Demon

The final passage dealing with artistic creation, that I should like to discuss, comes from *L'énergie spirituelle*, and here Bergson describes the process of literary creation as being comparable to the mind creating order from a chaotic sea of disorganized thoughts, a process, echoed by Proust's statement above:

> Une pensée laissée à elle-même, offre une implication réciproque d'éléments dont on ne peut dire qu'ils soient un ou plusieurs: c'est une continuité, et **dans toute continuité il y a de la confusion**. Pour que la pensée devienne distincte, il faut bien qu'elle s'éparpille en mots: nous ne nous rendons bien compte de ce qui nous avons dans l'esprit que lorsque nous **avons pris une feuille de papier**, et aligné les uns à côté des autres **des** termes qui s'entrepénétraient. Ainsi la matière distingue, sépare, résout en individualités et finalement en personnalités des tendances jadis confondues dans l'élan originel de la vie. D'autre part, **la matière provoque et rend possible l'effort**. La pensée qui n'est que pensée, l'oeuvre d'art qui n'est que conçu, le poème qui n'est que rêvé, ne coûtent pas encore de la peine; c'est la réalisation matérielle du poème en mots, de la conception artistique en statue ou tableau, qui demande un effort. **L'effort est pénible**, mais il est aussi précieux, plus précieux encore que l'oeuvre où il aboutit, parce que, grâce à lui, **on a tiré de soi plus qu'il n'y avait**, on s'est haussé au-dessus de soi-même. (ES 22)

Bergson is stating that the transference of a diffuse notion into a digital text is not only necessary to clarify one's thoughts, but is an essential part of literary creation. This passage has a certain similarity to the ideas expressed allegorically in *Les clochers de Martinville*, although, the character and method of Bergson is analytical and scientific, and distinct from Proust's literary style in *Les clochers.*

When Bergson writes "dans toute continuité il y a de la confusion," he is referring to ideas, thoughts, memories possibly inspirational images that come to one's mind. They are all interpenetrating, with no boundary or separation between one and the next, they are a continuous, qualitative multiplicity. In this continuity there is necessarily disorder, the confusion of a churning sea of analogic ideas, for our thoughts do not become clear to us until we take a sheet of paper and separate the confusion of ideas into discrete and separate notions, and we need to digitalize the analogic sea of ideas in order to clarify them in our mind. The similarity with the basic philosophical notion of *les clochers* becomes apparent.

There is also another image in this quotation from *L'énergie spirituelle*, that of 'Maxwell's demon' reversing the second law of thermodynamics, increasing negentropy, and creating order out of chaos.[21] The mind is selecting and placing in a logical sequence, organizing, increasing order and negentropy. Bergson is stating that the function of the mind in artistic, literary or philosophical creation is separating, making clear and distinct, of digitalizing those vague and interpenetrating ideas and images. The quantitative *matière* makes that effort possible, makes feasible the transposition of the qualitative into the quantitative. There thus has to be fusion or interaction of mind with matter. Work, ("l'effort est pénible") and energy have to be expended to reverse the second law of thermodynamics, and to overthrow the naturally ordained increase of entropy with time. But this hard work, although *pénible*, is rewarding, for one has drawn from oneself more than there previously was, and one has become a creator and produced something which formerly did not exist. In another passage, Bergson writes that the process of artistic or philosophical creation is similar to the joy of child-birth, reminiscent of the Proustian hero's desire at *Martinville*, to crow like a hen who had laid an egg.

In this passages (ES 22), that from the *Essai*, (DI 99–100) as well as the text of *les clochers de Martinville,* both Bergson and Proust state that the purpose of art and philosophy is the removal of obstacles that obstruct our view of the essence of reality. Bergson considers that a true translation, an exact reproduction of inspiration and emotions into linear digital language is not possible, for such a process necessarily destroys the unique analogic quality. But in the realm of literature, words and language are the medium of expression and whilst a perfect reproduction of the original concept is not possible, the creative writer can perhaps, by the artful use of metaphor, stimulate the imagination and evoke memory of the reader so that he or she may become aware of that original essence.

Conclusion

The views of Henri Bergson and Marcel Proust on art and esthetics are almost identical, and for both writers art is a vision of reality that is expressed in terms that can be communicated to others, that is in the digital medium of the painter, musician, or writer. Art is the process of lifting the veil that clouds our window of perception and that is interposed by, learning, habit and social conventions between our senses and the absolute. There is throughout Bergson's writings an important esthetic property intermingled with his philosophy. The reason for this is that the sort of vision of reality which Bergson maintained that the philosopher ought to cultivate, is precisely the vision with which the artist is by nature endowed.[22] The Proustian hero is also seeking a vision of reality, of nature, of l'essence des choses, and he ultimately understands the nature of that vision and the esthetics of inspiration and art. Proust's view of art and artistic creation involves stepping backwards and entering into the essence of simple objects. This is also Bergson notion of philosophy, which consists of reversing the normal direction of thought and placing one's self within the subject being studied. The similarity if not identify between the two concepts is remarkable.

An important difference between these two views of art relates to the prominence of memory and time in Proust's conception of art. Artistic inspiration is that brief glimpse of reality that comes uninvited and unexpected like a summer's breeze, the taste of a madeleine, or the aroma of a waxed floor. Art is a bridge between present sensation and past perception linked through memory, and existing outside of time in the eternal present. For Bergson, inspiration is an ocean of intuitive ideas and thoughts which are perhaps: "toujours poussés vers de nouveaux rivages." For both Bergson and Proust, hard digital work is required to untangle those multitudinous seas of interpenetrating ideas, to drop the anchor into the waters of pure duration, and thus immobilize beyond time that brief vision of reality. Artistic creation is the amalgamation of analogic inspiration with hard digital work, the union of the abacus with the rainbow.

Notes

1   Gilles Deleuze, *Proust et les signes* (Paris: PUF, 1993) 59.

2   Alphonse de Lamartine, "Le Lac," *Méditations poétiques* (Paris: Hachette, 1915) 133.

3   *Le rire* is essentially three essays originally published in *Revue de Paris* in 1899.

4   The similarity of this passage with the statements of Bergson is also pointed out by: Francoise Fabre-Luce de Gruson, "Bergson et Proust," *Entretiens sur Marcel Proust*, eds. Georges Cattaui and Philip Kolb (Paris: Mouton, 1966) 244.

5   The full quotation is in Chapter 6.

6   Anne Henry, *Marcel Proust: Théories pour une esthétique* (Paris: Klincksieck, 1981).

7   "For he on honey-dew hath fed, And drunk the milk of Pardise." Samuel Taylor Coleridge, "Kubla Khan," *Coleridge: Select Poems*, ed. S.G. Dunn (London: Oxford UP, 1918) 94.

8   Umberto Eco, *L'oeuvre ouverte*, trans. Chantal Roux de Bézieux (Paris: Seuil, 1962). 17.

9   "Un symbole est un objet ou fait naturel de caractère imagé qui évoque, par sa forme ou sa nature, une association d'idées "naturelles", un objet ou image ayant une valeur évocatrice, et mystique. C'est un élément ou énoncé descriptif ou narratif qui est susceptible d'une double interprétation sur le plan réaliste et sur le plan des idées" *Le Petit Robert* (Paris: Le Robert, 1990) 1903. In contrast: Allégorie is: "Suite d'éléments descriptifs ou narratifs dont chacun correspond aux divers détails de l'idée qu'ils prétendent exprimer. 'De l'allégorie au symbole, il y a la différence du mécanisme au vivant, et de la symétrie à la souplesse' (Thibaudet)". (*Le Petit Robert* 50)
        I might also add that whilst allegory is essentially digital, a symbol is, or replaces, the analogic.

10 Deleuze 77.

11 Deleuze 79.

12 The continuous and interweaving nature of (spontaneous) memory is an example of that which Bergson calls a qualitative multiplicity, see Chapter 1 and 3.

13 Anthony E. Pilkington, *Bergson and his Influence: a Reassessment* (Cambridge: Cambridge UP, 1976) 15.

14 Proust does not use the word 'inspiration', but his phrases; "la foi qui crée" (I, 182); "nos plus belles idées" (IV, 456); and "l'appel rouge et mystérieux" (IV, 456) refer to artistic enlightenment and illumination.

15 The text is necessarily digital, since it consists of words and letters, but by the use of metaphor, a text can, and and in this case does, convey, represent and contain, the analogic.

16 The word *inspiration* means both: "a breathing in, a drawing of air into the lungs," as wells as: "a stimulus to creative thought or action," and the two meanings are clearly metaphorically related. In addition inspiration can have a theological connotation.

17 Joachim Du Bellay, "D'un vanneur de blé, aux vents," *Divers jeux rustiques* ed. V.-L Saulnier, (Genève: Droz, 1965) 16–17. This poem may be read as the breeze of poetic inspiration. Louis MacKenzie, *French Forum, 20,* 133, 1995.

18 The text is necessarily digital. It is an enduring work of art if it encapsulates the analogic, in the case of literature, by the use of metaphor.

19 The full quotation is given in Chapter 8.

20 Marcel Muller, *Préfiguration et structure romanesque dans À la recherche du temps perdu* (Lexington: French Forum, 1979).

21 James Clerk Maxwell introduced the notion of this 'demon' in his text *Theory of Heat* (1871). He says: "Now let us suppose that such a vessel [containing the molecules of a gas] is divided into two portions, A and B, by a division in which there is a small hole, and that a being, who can see the individual molecules, opens and closes this hole, so as to allow only the swifter molecules to pass from A to B, and only the slower ones to pass from B to A. He will thus, without expenditure of work, raise the temperature of B and lower that of A, in contradiction to the second law of thermodynamics." The notion of the demon also shows that consciousness or intelligence can reverse the second law, creating order out of chaos. The second law is one of probability, it is highly unlikely that the above process would take place spontaneously, but it is, of course, not impossible.
    W. Ehrenberg. "Maxwell's Demon," *Scientific American* November 1967: 103.

22 Pilkington 14.

Chapter 8

The Origins of the Common Themes

Plus tard on croira découvrir partout son influence sur notre époque, simplement parce que lui-même est de son époque et qu'il cède sans cesse au mouvement. D'où son importance représentative.

André Gide[1]

Mais j'ai assez lu de Bergson, et la parabole de sa pensée étant déjà assez décrivable après une seule génération pour que quelque Évolution créatrice qui ait suivi, je ne puisse quand vous dites Bergson, savoir ce que vous voulez dire. . .

Marcel Proust[2]

We are all, to a greater extent than perhaps we care to admit, the product of the age in which we live. Each age and each epoch often appears to have a spokesperson who seems to be representative of that period, and the words and thoughts of this person are in part a reflection, echo and articulation of the general current of thought characteristic of that age and period in time. This was the situation in France towards the end of the 19th century when Henri Bergson began to expound his philosophy of intuition against materialistic and deterministic science. As Victor Hugo put it: "nothing is so powerful as an idea whose time has come," and in the latter part of the nineteenth century, the time for the revolt against materialism had come, and Floris Delattre said: "C'est le cri de révolte poussé contre la philosophie matérialiste qui régnait alors presque sans conteste, selon laquelle la réalité, bornée aux phénomènes, était entièrement connaissable, et par les seules facultés rationnelles."[3]

The unifying themes of this study are the common elements running through the philosophical works of Henri Bergson and the great novel of Marcel Proust, in spite of their very different styles, methodology and purpose. This final chapter will examine some possible reasons for this similarity and suggest possibly explanations. These reasons or conjectures are certainly incomplete, and there are very probably other likely explanations that we have either under-estimated or not thought of. The first of these possible reasons is the direct and conscious influence of Bergson's work on Proust which has been explored and rejected by Megay. Second, there is the possibility that both writers were influence by a common third person, which we shall explore below. A third reason is what may be termed the *Zeitgeist* hypothesis according to which both Bergson and Proust were part of that curious, independent and parallel convergence of philosophical and artistic ideas that pervaded France and probably Europe of that period, and that the similarity is entirely due to this autonomous convergence. A fourth reason relates to Thibaudet's[4] notion that Bergson's philosophy was replete with *idées-mères*, seeds of thought which grew and bore fruit in the minds of others. A final reason, is somewhat a composite, and relates to the extreme popularity and vogue of Bergson's lectures and books in France in the period just preceding the first World War, and the publicity and notoriety given to Bergson by the conflict with the Sorbonne, such that his philosophical notions, in addition to being part of the *Zeitgeist*, were as Proust himself indicates in *À la recherche*, probably the subject matter of conversations in some of the social circles frequented by Proust. However, as suggested and illustrated in the previous chapters, the similarities and differences between Bergson and Proust are complex, and it would seem unlikely that this was the result of a simple or single factor.

Possible Direct Incorporation of Bergsonian Philosophy by Proust

The possible direct influence of Bergson's books or lectures on Proust is the subject matter of Joyce Megay's thorough study summarized in Chapter 1. I have accepted the essence of her arguments, nevertheless it should perhaps be emphasized that although there may be but few references to Bergson's work in Proust's notes this does not necessarily imply a corresponding lack of influence. In addition Proust's not infrequent denials of any Bergsonian influence were perhaps to distance his novel from the suggestion of influence and thus claim greater originality for himself. One of these denials occurs during the well-known interview with Élie-Joseph Bois and published in *Le temps* of November 13, 1913 and also quoted in Chapter 1:

A ce point de vue, mon livre serait peut-être comme un essai d'une suite de "Romans de l'Inconscient": je n'aurais aucune honte à dire de "romans bergsoniens," si je le croyais, car à toute époque il arrive que la littérature a tâché de se rattacher—après coup, naturellement—à la philosophie régnante. Mais ce ne serait pas exact, car mon oeuvre est dominée par la distinction entre la mémoire involontaire et la mémoire volontaire, distinction qui non seulement ne figure pas dans la philosophie de M. Bergson, mais est même contredit par elle.[5]

The reference to ". . . la distinction entre la mémoire involontaire et la mémoire volontaire, distinction qui non seulement ne figure pas dans la philosophie de M. Bergson, mais est même contredit par elle," is only partially correct, as previously discussed, yet indicates a familiarity, albeit incomplete, with Bergson's work. Another denial is quoted by Megay and occurs in Proust's *Cahier LIX* in which he writes:

Un grand philosophe qui, depuis que ces pages ont été écrites, a beaucoup pensé sur le rêve et sur la mémoire (l'homme de génie qui a nom Bergson) est en opposition flagrante avec moi sur ces deux sujets . . . Par exemple M. Bergson prétend que les bruits que nous entendons en rêve, conversations de personnages, etc., sont seulement les bruits entendus dans la chambre et avec lesquels nous nourrissons les conversations, sans cela silencieuses, de nos interlocuteurs.[6]

It is interesting that Proust should take the trouble to make such a denial in his personal notes, moreover to make this refutation, he clearly had to be quite familiar with Bergson's notions of memory and dreams, or at least with what he considered to be Bergson's theories.

The Possible Influence of John Ruskin

The second explanation mentioned above for the common themes in the writings of Bergson and Proust might be that both authors were influenced by the same third party, and amongst these, the name of John Ruskin immediately comes to mind since both writers were very familiar with his work and his intuitive esthetics seems to resemble somewhat Bergson's intuitive metaphysics. In addition, Proust was a commentator and translator of Ruskin's writing.

Ruskin and Proust
In his youth, Proust was clearly a devotee of Ruskin's esthetics, translated two of Ruskin's works,[7] and wrote short articles on Ruskin in 1900, the year of his death.[8] His extensive introduction, *Sur la lec-*

ture,[9] to his translation of *Sesame and Lilies* attests to the time he spent reading and studying Ruskin's essays, and ultimately to the possible influence of that text on his thinking, but in notes to this Introduction, he states: "En exposant mes idées, je me trouve involontairement les opposer d'avance aux siennes."[10] Proust also translated and annotated Ruskin's *Bible of Amiens* which Henri Bergson presented to *L'Académie des Sciences Morales et Politiques* (ML 629) in May 1904 with his own flattering introduction. Ruskin is also mentioned by Proust in an interestingly autobiographical manner in *À la recherche,* for example, during the Proustian narrator's stay in Venice he mentions: ". . . je prendrais des notes relatives à un travail que je faisais sur Ruskin," (IV 224)[11] and later makes reference to a translation (without specifying the translator) of *Sesame and Lilies* when in conversation with Jupien the narrator (and author) makes the parenthetical statement: "il [Jupien] faisait allusion à une traduction de *Sésame et les lys* de Ruskin que j'avais envoyée à M. de Charlus" (IV 411).

The possibility that the overall structure of *À la recherche* was inspired, to some extent, by the winding path leading to an unsuspected view mentioned in Ruskin's essay "Sesame: of Kings' Treasuries" has been referred to previous in this study:

> I had even intended to ask your attention for a little while on trust, and (as sometimes one contrives, in taking a friend to see a favourite piece of scenery) to hide what I wanted most to show, with such imperfect cunning as I might, until we unexpectedly reached the best point of view by winding paths.[12]

In addition, Proust makes ample use of the metaphorical implications of Sesame in notes to his translation of *Sesame and Lilies.* Another direct indication of the possible, although minor, influence of Ruskin's essay on Proust's novel is possibly indicated towards the end of the essay, "Lilies: of Queen's Gardens," the companion to "Sesame: of Kings' Treasuries," in which Ruskin quotes the familiar Tennyson poem "Come into the garden, Maud," and replaces Maud with the biblical Mary Magdalene (*Madeleine*) when he writes:

> Who is it, think you, who stands at the gate of this sweeter garden, alone, waiting for you? Did you ever hear, not of a Maud, but a Madeleine, who went down to her garden in the dawn and found One waiting at the gate, whom she supposed to be the gardener ?[13]

Ruskin thus replaces the simple ordinary Maud with the prostitute become saint, Mary Magdalene. Proust elaborates and expands on this exchange of personages and that things are not always as they first appear, for memory and imagination can modify perception, and initial perceptions can sometimes be deceptive. The passage which seems to reflect Ruskin's text occurs in an episode of À la recherche that takes place appropriately just before Easter, when the hero joins Robert de Saint-Loup in the Parisian suburbs to meets Robert's beloved mistress and, perhaps soon to be, fiancée. Robert's beloved turns out to be none other than 'Rachel-quand-du Seigneur,' a common prostitute professionally known to the hero:

> Ce n'était pas "Rachel quand du Seigneur" qui me semblait peu de chose, c'était la puissance de l'imagination humaine, l'illusion sur laquelle reposaient les douleurs de l'amour que je trouvais grandes. . . . Ces arbustes que j'avais vus dans le jardin, en les prenant pour des dieux étrangers, ne m'étais-je pas trompé comme Madeleine quand, dans un autre jardin, un jour dont l'anniversaire allait bientôt venir, elle vit une forme humaine et "crut que c'était le jardinier"? (II 458)

Is Rachel the prostitute to become, like Mary Magdalene, a saint? Whether Proust's excerpt is inspired, in part, by Ruskin's passage seems likely, but can only be a conjecture. Proust's admiration for Ruskin's work is clearly stated in a letter he wrote to Marie Nordlinger (who helped him with the translation of Sesame and Lilies) in January 1900, at the occasion of Ruskin's death:

> Mais quand j'ai appris la mort de Ruskin, j'ai voulu exprimer à vous, plutôt qu'à tout autre, ma tristesse, tristesse saine, d'ailleurs, et bien pleine de consolation, car je sais combien c'est peu que la mort en voyant combien vit avec force ce mort, combien je l'admire, l'écoute, cherche à le comprendre et lui obéir plus qu'à bien des vivants.[14]

and:

> Ruskin n'a jamais lu les guides que pour omettre tout ce qu'ils signent et signaler tout ce qu'ils omettent. La moitié au moins des peintres, des architectes que nous admirons ont été découvertes par lui.[15]

There is perhaps a little of John Ruskin in Charles Swann the devotee of art and architecture. Although Proust was clearly a follower of Ruskin in his youth, he later changes somewhat his point of view, for in July 1906, he writes of Ruskin: "Mais si ses jugements sont souvent faux, et dans leurs considérants presque toujours "à côté" ils ne sont nullement hasardés dans le sens où tu le dis."[16] Thus, it seems likely that Ruskin's writings and thought did influence Proust, and Jean Autret concludes his lengthy study of the potential influence of Ruskin on the life, ideas, and work of Proust with the statement: "Nous pouvons donc conclure en affirmant que Ruskin a eu une grande influence sur Proust et sur sa vie, sur ses idées esthétiques et sa technique, enfin sur la matière de son oeuvre."[17]

Ruskin and Bergson

Ruskin (1819–1900) was born forty years before Bergson, and was at the beginning of the movement, the collective rebellion, against deterministic science. For both Ruskin and Bergson, intuitive insight rather than logic and reason was the path to reality and truth. Bergson was apparently very familiar with the works of Ruskin, whose philosophy and writings on esthetics were well-known in France and Europe in the late nineteenth century. One should also remember that Bergson's mother, Katherine Lewison, was English, that her knowledge of French was rather limited, such that Bergson learnt English from her and normally spoke to her in English. In his younger days, Bergson, who was presumably virtually bi-lingual, spent many vacations in England and had ample opportunity to become familiar with English literature and philosophy. In his lecture *Ruskin et Bergson*, Floris Delattre[18] emphasizes the similarity of many aspects of their philosophy: ". . . tous deux ont voulu substituer à l'intolérance de la raison dogmatique les aspirations spirituelles de l'individu, ce que Pascal avait appelé déjà la philosophie du coeur."[19] Delattre attests to Bergson's familiarity with Ruskin's writing by stating that Bergson lent Delattre (who was Bergson's nephew[20]) his copy of Ruskin's book *Modern Painters,* which was extensively annotated in the margins with Bergson's notes and comments.

According to Delattre, the esthetics of Ruskin were: "Fondée sur l'observation directe de la nature extérieure d'abord, puis sur une sympathie vibrante avec elle," while "l'interprétation artistique vise à atteindre, sous les apparences visibles, l'essence même des choses."[21] Thus Ruskin, like Bergson and Proust, was concerned with the discovery and exploration of *l'essence des choses*, the true essence of reality. For both Ruskin and Bergson, reality is hidden from everyday observation by a veil, thick for most people but thin for the artist, and Ruskin considered that the beauty of the world is revealed by a sudden apprehension and perception of those otherwise invisible aspects of nature, by penetrating with intuitive appreciation the protective crust to attain reality. The function of the artist is to penetrate this veil that separates perception from reality, to reproduce that vision in his or her art form, and to communicate that which is timeless in nature and the universe. There is thus a similarity between Ruskin's and Bergson's view of art, furthermore, the esthetic intuition of Ruskin, like that of Bergson, is not one of the intellect, but an intuition which is based on sensibility and creative imagination of nature such as reproduced in a great work of art.

Ruskin, like Bergson, emphasized the importance, indeed the dominance of intuition, of the immediate intuitive knowledge of self and reality, rather than logical analysis, and applied intuitive awareness to esthetics, to the beauty and joy of nature and the world. By contrast, Bergson appears to transpose this intuitive path to knowledge and reality to an intellectual level, to that of intuitive metaphysics. Thus, one of the differences between Ruskin's intuitive esthetics and Bergson's intuitive metaphysics is the importance of precision in thought and writing which Bergson attained through a dialectic between the intuitive and the verbal. In scientific matters, Ruskin always remained an amateur, a dilettante and a 'dabbler' who was neither a precise mathematician nor an experimental scientist. In contrast to Ruskin, Bergson was always very precise and even meticulous in his thought and methodology. "Ce qui a le plus manqué à la philosophie," he said, "c'est la précision. Les systèmes philosophiques ne sont pas taillés à la mesure de la réalité où nous vivons" (PM 1). The literary styles of Ruskin and Bergson are also very different. Ruskin was a master of ornate prose and liked to use flowery phrases and flamboyant language which was lacking in precision, and now seems archaic. In contrast, and as discussed in Chapter 6, Bergson avoided flowery 'literary' language and used simple words and phrases to describe with a minimum of ambiguity the philosophical notion he wished to communicate.

Thus, although there is a resemblance between the intuitive esthetics of Ruskin and the intuitive philosophy of Bergson, the similarity is only superficial, and Delattre concludes that he sees no evidence of direct influence of Ruskin's esthetics on Bergson's philosophy. In summary, although the writings and intuitive esthetics of John Ruskin were important in the artistic education of Marcel Proust, and were studied by Henri Bergson, it seems unlikely that the intrinsic similarity between the philosophy of Henri Bergson and that which is inherent in Proust's À la recherche is due to the common influence of John Ruskin.

The Convergence and Correspondence
of the Arts with Philosophy

An important, yet subtle reason for the inherent similarity between some aspects of Bergson's philosophy and aspects of Proust's ideas comes from the curious, independent yet parallel, convergence and correspondence between the arts and philosophy of the time. It is an example of what Marcel Raymond, writing about Bergson and late nineteenth century poetry, describes as: "La correspondance des arts et de la philosophie, en cette fin de siècle, la curieuse convergence de diverses manifestation de l'esprit. . . ."[22] In his recent biography on Bergson, Philippe Soulez invokes the *Zeitgeist*, the spirit of the age, when he writes: ". . . Bergson est en phase avec le Zeitgeist . . . Bergson, en France comme en Amérique, est perçu comme représentatif d'une époque. Ici prenne leur place les comparaisons de Bergson et de Proust. . . ."[23] But perhaps a clearer expression of Bergson's thought as being representative of his age is given by André Gide, who after reading Thibaudet's *Le bergsonisme* which was published in 1913 by Gide's La Nouvelle Revue Française, writes in his diary for March 1st 1914:

> Thibaudet sur le bergsonisme; après avoir pris grand intérêt à la préface (intérêt d'autant plus vif que je connais à peu près rien de Bergson), je perds contact.
> Ce qui me déplaît dans la doctrine de Bergson, c'est tout ce que je pense déjà sans qu'il le dise, et tout ce qu'elle a de flatteur, de caressant même, pour l'esprit. Plus tard on croira découvrir partout son influence sur notre époque, simplement parce que lui-même est de son époque et qu'il cède sans cesse au mouvement. D'où son importance représentative.[24]

This interesting phenomenon of the parallel, yet independent, convergence of ideas in the sciences and the arts seems to illustrates a point made many years later by Umberto Eco:

> L'art a pour fonction non de connaître le monde, mais de produire des compléments du monde: . . . a chaque époque, la manière dont se structurent **les diverses formes d'art révèle la manière dont la science ou la culture contemporaine voit la réalité.**[25] [my emphasis]

Furthermore, Eco sees an important place for the liberty and individuality of the interpreter, whether reader, listener, or viewer who takes part freely in the artistic process which is not dictated unilaterally by the artist. As we have previously noted, the absence of an observer as an integral part of reality is a characteristic of the Newtonian universe and its presence a property of Bergsonian philosophy of the continuous, of the unity of the self with the external world. Even the somewhat austere mathematical insight of Sir Arthur Eddington discerned, as discussed in Chapter 1, a parallel convergence between Impressionism in painting and the trends of physics in the reaction against microscopic analysis, reflected by the second law of thermodynamics and the movement towards viewing the entirety of a system rather than dissecting the independent, digital, parts. In addition the Bergsonian uncertainty or indeterminacy principle discussed in Chapter 6 is another clear example of the parallel yet independent convergence of ideas in philosophy and physics.

Discussing the relationship between French literary and philosophical writings and art, and evoking the image both of Elstir and Bergson, Michel Serres says:

> Si certains tableaux de peinture s'y rapprochent des schémas proposés par les sciences dites dure, et, les deux ensemble, des lieux de la terre et du ciel, les philosophes de langue française approchent au moyen de certains concepts ces mêmes sites-là. Passé la faille tragique de la guerre et la perversité de son retentissement dans le milieu du siècle, Gilles Deleuze . . . derrière Bergson qu'il suit et comprend mieux que personne, un monde à la Perrin et à la Poincaré, déjà fractal et chaotique. Ne va-t-il pas . . . jusqu'à tirer, en plein coeur de la philosophie, et pour en définir la nature et la référence, un plan d'immanence?[26]

And later evoking "le mouvement rétrograde du vrai" of *La pensée et le mouvant*, he writes: "Et voici que, par mouvement rétrograde du vrai, nous nous retrouvons, Gilles Deleuze, moi, et d'autres, plongés dans l'héritage de Poincaré, Monet, Debussy, Péguy, Ponge, Perec . . . tous enfants de Leibniz, Rousseau, Diderot et Bergson."[27] Thus for Serres, mathematician, painter, musician and philosopher are all part of one movement seeking and expressing truth with similar paradigms. Moreover, it is probably no accident that Bergson's philosophy should have flourished at the same time as one of the most sweeping revolutions in the history of art: Impressionism. Indeed the leader of that revolution, Claude Monet (1840–1926) was born only nineteen years before Bergson. With Cézanne, Degas, Manet, Pissarro, Renoir and Sisley, the principal goal of these artists was to register primary naive impressions.[28] Like Proust's Elstir, the Impressionists were not attempting to give a precise sentimentalized or photographic reproduction of a scene, but rather, to evoke in the mind, as well as in the eyes, of the viewer all the impressions associated with the scene depicted. The feeling of warmth in the sun shining through the still air, the gurgling of water flowing over the falls, the smell of the flowers in the garden, and above all, the intermixing, the synesthesia, of all those sensations, so that similarly to Elstir at Carquethuit there was no barrier between land, sea and sky, no separation between sight, sound and odor, and all are fused together in one sensuous and uninterrupted impression of reality. Clearly the esthetics of the Impressionists is one of fusion, and as such it is consonant with many of Bergson's ideas and Proust's own ideals. The images and the emotions associated with Impressionist paintings are related to the spontaneous memory of Bergson or the involuntary memory of Proust rather than to digitalized photographic reproduction. Monet, like Bergson, was concerned with time and its true representation:

> Monet used his unique understanding of the empty envelope as a vehicle to comment on the basic contingencies of all experience: space and time. Monet's Normandy coast paintings of the 1880's, which stress the manifest interactions of solar and tidal time, likewise transformed everyday Impressionist Realism into commentaries about the elemental verities of nature. . . . In his Rouen Cathedral paintings, Monet recorded the modern clock over the medieval structure's central portal as nothing more than a thick disk of color, suggesting the inadequacy of this device to assess the measureless majesty of time revealed in ever-changing individual perception.[29]

Is this not very similar to what Bergson is stating in his philosophy, the inadequacy of usual digital time to represent the reality of pure duration? The relationship between Monet's rendition of the sea and sky on the Normandy coast, and Proust's description of Elstir's paintings of Carquethuit is striking and not irrelevant to the arguments being made here. The name Elstir is said to be a composite of Helleu and Whistler whilst his paintings are clearly reminiscent of Turner and perhaps Hubert Robert as well as Monet:

> Au lieu de photographies de la cathédrale de Chartres, des Grandes Eaux de Saint-Cloud, du Vésuve, elle se renseignait auprès de Swann si quelque grand peintre ne les avait pas représentés, et préférait me donner des photographies de la cathédrale de Chartes par Corot, des Grandes Eaux de Saint-Cloud par Hubert Robert, du Vésuve par Turner, ce qui faisait un degré d'art de plus. (I 40)

Movement, which is an integral part of Bergsonism, is also an integral part of Impressionism, whether it be movement of water, clothing, or clouds. For Proust, the function of the artist is not only to provide an impression of reality in which continuity predominates, but also he reminds us that the artists enables the viewer to see reality in a new and perhaps different manner, so that the world seems fresh and altered thanks to the artist who enables us to see anew:

> Les gens de goût disent aujourd'hui que Renoir est un grand peintre du XVIIIᵉ siècle. Mais en disant cela ils oublient le Temps et qu'il en a fallu beaucoup, même en plein XIXᵉ, pour que Renoir fût salué grand artiste. Pour réussir à être ainsi reconnus, le peintre original, l'artiste original procèdent à la façon des oculistes. Le traitement par leur peinture, par leur prose, n'est pas toujours agréable. Quand il est terminé, le praticien nous dit: "Maintenant regardez." Et voici que le monde (qui n'a pas été créé une fois, mais aussi souvent qu'un artiste original est survenu) nous apparaît entièrement différent de l'ancien mais parfaitement claire. Des femmes passent dans la rue, différentes de celles d'autrefois, puisque ce sont des Renoir, ces Renoir où nous nous refusions jadis à voir des femmes. Les voitures aussi sont des Renoir, et l'eau, et le ciel: (II 623)

The movement and continuity of Bergsonian philosophy that is clearly discernible in Impressionism is also present in the sculpture of Auguste Rodin (1840–1917)[30] who successfully integrated a sense of motion in an otherwise static piece of marble or bronze. The motion and life of a Rodin bronze is not a jerking cinematographic motion, but a continuous flowing one that is conceived in the mind of the viewer together with the flow of time. For example, commenting on his statue of Ney, Rodin said:

> Il est aisé de remarquer que la statue du maréchal Ney unit deux attitudes: La main gauche et les jambes sont placées comme elles étaient au moment où le maréchal tirait son sabre; le torse, qui devait être incliné, se redresse au contraire en même temps que le bras droit élève l'arme en signe de commandement. De cette dualité résulte la vie de la figure.[31]

Baudelaire (1821–1867) in *Les fleurs du mal* invokes the superiority of the analogic whole rather than to the process of digitalization and analysis when, in his poem "Tout entière," he refers disparagingly to "l'impuisante analyse":

> Et l'harmonie est trop exquise,
> Qui gouverne tout son beau corps,
> Pour que l'impuissante analyse
> En note les nombreux accords.[32]

For Bergson, the art of poetry, like for Baudelaire, is the art of suggestion. It comes from a form of spiritual intuition that linear logical discourse fails to apprehend. This was the spirit of the age in which

Bergson and Proust flourished and in which continuity, movement and self were part of art, literature and philosophy. But is this sufficient to be the cause of the similarity in the themes common to Bergson and Proust? I think it is only a partial explanation.

Indirect Influence through Hearsay

The Controversy between *l'esprit de finesse* of Henri Bergson and *l'esprit de géométrie* of the Sorbonne

In the period between 1910 and 1914, Bergson became an international celebrity and perhaps the most discussed philosopher in the world. Furthermore, his philosophy and teaching became the center of a then famous controversy between the Sorbonne and the sister institution across the rue Saint-Jacques on the corner with rue des Écoles, the Collège de France, such that even if Marcel Proust neither read Bergson's books nor attended his famed and fashionable lectures, he could hardly have escaped being well aware of the essentials of his teachings. This Bergsonian controversy was part of the political and social scene in Paris during the pre-1914 years and probably part of the socially correct conversations in the more intellectual of the Parisian salons frequented by Proust in the period when he was writing À la recherche.

Part of this controversy was the rivalry that arose between Henri Bergson and Emile Durkheim (1858–1917), Professor of the Science of Education and Sociology at the Sorbonne. Durkheim was a powerful and authoritarian figure in the University community with strong socialist views, and although Bergson and Durkheim had both been students at the École Normale, whilst Bergson was in the true tradition of *un normalien*, Durkheim abhorred the literature and philosophy so characteristic of École Normale tradition and was critical of dilettante philosophers. Bergson and Durkheim were perhaps the two most popular academics of the day, but in many respects they were diametrically opposite in their thought and beliefs. Durkheim was an unadulterated rationalist who strongly believed in the scientific tradition, that all things were attainable through human reason, and furthermore that science and knowledge should lead to utility. The essence of Bergsonism was the power of intuition and the spiritual as opposed to the scientific, logical and rational. Furthermore, the utilitarian was not of major importance.[33] The rivalry and opposition between Bergson and Durkheim and their respective followers escalated into a conflict between the Sorbonne and the Collège de France. Grogin summarizes this situation as follows:

> There was a clear gulf separating the Sorbonne from its rival, the Collège de France. The Collège de France seemed more spontaneous and innovative (at least where philosophy was concerned). The Sorbonne faculty, particularly the Durkheimians, viewed the Collège de France as the source of much of the hostility towards rational philosophy, modern languages and sociology.[34]

Writing in 1941 long after the conflict between the Collège de France and the Sorbonne had subsided, Emmanuel Mounier recalls:

> Le péché mortel de la Sorbonne, c'est d'avoir, elle la gardienne éloignée du spirituel, constitué à l'encontre de sa mission la métaphysique et la technique de cette décadence: le déterminisme, qui veut nous faire croire "que l'homme et que la nature a dit son dernier mot," que le monde a tari pour toujours sa ressource;[35]

The Sorbonne was regarded by students of the day as the stronghold of reason where the cult of science was taken to an extreme; it was the home of arid intellectualism. Across the street at the Collège de France, the bastion of those opposed to Durkheim and his sociological doctrines, a brilliant and charismatic orator, Henri Bergson, was expounding a new and exciting philosophy of a modern age and a flowing time.

Péguy and Bergson

Charles Péguy (1873–1914) as editor of *Les cahiers de la quinzaine,* gave additional publicity to Bergson's writings and philosophy as well as supporting his ideas against those of the Sorbonne. Indeed, one of the most direct attacks on the Sorbonne and its faculty came from Péguy, a former pupil of Bergson's at the École Normale; a staunch supporter and faithful disciple, of whom Bergson said: "Il avait un don merveilleux pour franchir la matérialité des êtres, la dépasser et pénétrer jusqu'à l'âme. C'est ainsi qu'il a connu ma pensée la plus secrète, telle que je ne l'ai pas exprimée, telle que j'aurais voulu l'exprimer." The writings of Péguy (who was killed on the front in September 1914), like those of Bergson were part of the general intellectual and literary climate of pre-1914 France in which Proust was immersed. Péguy said he was, like Bergson, not opposed to science itself, but was opposed to the cult and reverence that scientific belief generated. According to Péguy, Bergsonism was not a quarrel against reason, logic and intelligence nor was it a move to dethrone reason and to crown instinct and intuition. It was a parallel operation that existed within reason, a revolution against the artificial, a revolt of the authentic against the superficial. Bergsonism was not a philosophy of irrationalism, but its was a form of rationalism which was, because of its method of questioning intuition, more demanding than the rationalism which it opposed. According to Péguy: "Le bergsonisme ne consiste pas à s'interdire les opérations de la pensée. Il consiste à les modeler constamment sur la réalité dont il s'agit chaque fois."[36] Péguy and his *Les cahiers de la quinzaine,* gave publicity and support to Bergson's writings and philosophy, and for example, in February 1903 wrote:

> La Revue de Métaphysique et de Morale, dans son numéro de janvier, publiait de M. Henri Bergson: "Introduction à la métaphysique," un article dont il ne suffit pas de dire, ce que je ne dis presque jamais, qu'il est très admirable, mais dont on peut dire, je crois, qu'il est capital . . .
>   Il est indispensable que les travaux de ce véritable philosophe parviennent à un public plus large; le public tous les jours plus nombreux qui se presse au Collège de France aux leçons du vendredi est un public d'honnêtes gens, plutôt qu'un public de professionnels. . . Il est indispensable que les grands actes de l'action, que les grandes oeuvres de la philosophie et de l'art, que les grands résultats de la science et de la philosophie atteignent des hommes de tous métiers et de toutes cultures.[37]

Péguy saw in scientific determinism a threat not only to traditional and French spiritual values, but also he also saw the potential threat of the domination of individual liberty by the all-powerful totalitarian State, personified perhaps by the Sorbonne. He was thus taking the teachings and warnings of Bergsonian philosophy into a broader dimension than the purely philosophical and into the social and political arena. Of Péguy's position in relation to the perhaps menacing power of the Sorbonne, Jean Roussel wrote in 1952:

> L'expérience que nous avons acquise aujourd'hui permet de voir que la fameuse querelle de la Sorbonne dépassait les limites de l'Université: un drame commence qui atteindra toute son ampleur et toute sa virulence avec les régimes totalitaires. Péguy était seulement un peu en avance. Dénonçant une odieuse tyrannie, il était le seul, à voir que les droits de la personne humaine, les principes mêmes de la République étaient en jeu, . . . le débat qu'ouvre Péguy dépasse la personnalité des *ducs de Sorbonne.*[38]

Not only did Péguy publicize and support Bergson's philosophy, but he did that which Bergson, possibly because of his reserved nature, could not or would not do, that is take to the public forum the argument and struggle of the intuitive and spiritual against materialism. But Péguy, a Catholic *croyant et pratiquant*, also raised the conflict to the religious level, again something that Bergson, himself, would not and probably could not do. The details of this conflict are less important than the prominence and publicity that it gave to Bergson's doctrines.

The Popularity of Bergson's Philosophy in the France of the 1900's

Between 1900 and 1914, Bergson was one of the most popular philosophers in the world, not only were his books widely read and translated into many languages but he became an international celebrity. Furthermore, in France there was a popular Bergsonian vogue, and attendance at his five o'clock lectures on Fridays became all the rage in society. In April 1902, Charles Péguy gave the following graphic description of a typical Bergsonian lecture:

> Quand j'assiste régulièrement le vendredi au cours de M. Bergson au Collège de France, à quatre heures trois quarts, je suis frappé de ceci: Dans la grande salle à peu près pleine, sur les cent cinquante assistants et plus, . . . il y a de tout le monde: je vois des hommes, des vieillards, des dames, des jeunes filles, beaucoup des jeunes gens, des Français, des Russes, des étrangers, des mathématiciens, des naturalistes, j'y vois des étudiants es lettres, des étudiants es sciences, des étudiants en médecine, j'y vois des ingénieurs, des économistes, des juristes, des laïques et des clercs, que Téry ne manquerait pas de nommer des curés, j'y vois des poètes, des artistes, . . . j'y vois Émile Boivin qui prend des notes pour quelqu'un de province; on y descend des *cahiers*, de *Pages libres*, de *Jean-Pierre*, des *Journaux pour tous*; on y vient de la Sorbonne et, je pense de l'École normale; j'y vois des bourgeois notoires, des socialistes, des anarchistes: j'y vois de tout, excepté des universitaires.[39] [Péguy's italics]

The popularity of Bergson's lectures were not short-lived, for several years after Péguy's interesting description, Bergson discussed his lectures in an interview with Jacques Morland. In the subsequent fascinating article entitled, "Une heure chez M. Bergson," published in *L'opinion* of August 19th 1911, Morland writes:

> Si la jeunesse d'aujourd'hui prend goût à la philosophie, on peut bien dire que c'est grâce à M. Bergson. Les leçons de ce maître attirent au Collège de France une foule attentive. C'est qu'il apporte à ses auditeurs quelque chose de mieux encore que des idées: une méthode neuve, original par laquelle

beaucoup d'esprits ont été séduits . . . Par sa façon d'exposer sa philosophie, en suggérant ce qu'il a à dire plutôt qu'en le disant, il charme les esprits délicats qui aiment les nuances. Quelques amateurs vont à son cours comme à un beau concert. M. Bergson, lui-même, compare volontiers la philosophie et la musique.[40]

Three years later, attendance at Bergson's lectures was recorded in sketches and photographs which appeared in the popular illustrated paper, *Excelsior* of February 14, 1914.[41] According to Philippe Soulez[42] there are records of students demanding that only those holding student cards be admitted, as well as of elderly female socialites complaining that although they arrived early after a long journey they were still unable to find a place in the amphitheater. Suggestions were made for changing the venue of Bergson's lectures to a location with more space, and even to the Grand Amphithéâtre of the Sorbonne and indeed (according to one proposal) to the Opera. Contemporary photographs show late arrivals standing outside and looking in the windows. At the announcement of Bergson's election to the Académie Française in 1914 the podium was covered with flowers and Bergson, on his arrival, was heard to remark: "Mais . . . je ne suis pas une danseuse!" The latter occasion is recorded in a drawing which appeared in a contemporary magazine (possibly *Excelsior*), the caption of which states:

LE PROFESSEUR BERGSON VA COMMENCER SON COURS
. . . philosophie de M. Henri Bergson à la . . . et très suivi par les femmes de la [plus haute société] parisienne. C'est le cours à la mode . . . Nos mondaines envoient leurs valets [retenir] à l'avance leur place dans l'amphithéâtre . . . Les quelques minutes, qui précèdent l'entrée du professeur, sont remplies des plus frivoles conversations qui s'échange [avec un subtil] bruissement des manteaux que . . . dirait du prélude d'un opéra . . . [Lors]que le maître en s'inclinant annonce qu'il va commencer sa leçon un silence religieux . . . se fait dans la vaste salle. Les mondaines ravies dégustent la parole élégante du professeur, applaudissent avec une discrétion bienséante ses périodes harmonieusement cadencées parfois l'une d'elle tirant de son petit sac un carnet précieux, s'applique à consigner une note rapide et le cours s'achève dans . . . la fièvre des félicitations et dans l'empressement d'invitation à dîner.[43]

In addition, there were apparently 'mystical pilgrimages' to Bergson's summer home in Switzerland, where locks of his hair from the local barber's were saved and treated as holy relics. As late as 1913 some two thousand students turned out for one of his visiting lectures in New York's City College.[44] Thus at this period of Bergson's fame, it was not only students or teachers of philosophy who attended his lectures, but fashionable ladies and their escorts came much as they might attend a concert or the opera, not necessarily because of any great knowledge or interest in the subject matter but rather to see (and be seen) and hear the celebrated, eminent and charismatic professor. It would appear likely, that on returning to their salons these socialites delighted their guests and themselves by recounting the occasion and something of the philosopher's remarks. It would appear equally probable that socialites such as Marcel Proust learned second hand of some of Bergson's ideas and philosophy in this manner. Furthermore, it is not unlikely that errors crept into the account of the philosophers remarks, and that what one overheard in the salons was not accurate Bergsonism. That these conversations might have been a source of Proust's, possibly somewhat incorrect knowledge of Bergsonism, seems very plausible since he incorporates such an event in the text of À la recherche.

Bergson and the Norwegian Philosopher

A possible insight into the indirect or hearsay influence of Bergson on Proust is given by Proust himself in Sodome et Gomorrhe, when the Proustian narrator, after a diner at La Raspelière reflects on sleep, dreams and the effect of hypnotics on sleep and memory, and invokes the names of Bergson, Boutroux and a 'Norwegian philosopher':

> . . . je fus surpris d'apprendre par le philsophe norvégien, qui le tenait de M. Boutroux, "son éminent collègue—pardon, son confrère," ce que M. Bergson pensait des altérations particulières de la mémoire dues aux hypnotiques. "Bien entendu," aurait dit M. Bergson à M. Boutroux, à en croire le philosophe norvégien, "les hypnotiques pris de temps en temps à doses modérées, n'ont pas d'influence sur cette solide mémoire de notre vie de tous les jours. . . Je ne sais si cette conversation entre M. Bergson et M. Boutroux est exacte. Le philosophe norvégien, pourtant si profond et si claire, si passionnément attentif, a pu mal comprendre. (III 373)

This passage is important and enlightening for a number of reasons. First, it would appear to be a modified autobiographical rendition of an event that occurred on September 30th 1920, at the occasion of a meeting of the committee adjudicating the prix Blumenthal. The committee consisted of Bergson, Proust, Boutroux together with Barrès, Boylesve, Gide and Valéry. At this meeting Proust succeeded in having the prize awarded to his friend Jacques Rivière as mentioned in Chapter I. According to Edmond Jaloux,[45] during the meeting Bergson and Proust discussed, at some length, insomnia and the effects of hypnotics on sleep and memory as described in *Sodome et Gomorrhe*. The second point of importance is that in the text of *À la recherche* the narrator does not refer to a direct conversation with Bergson, but of a hearsay conversation between Bergson and Boutroux, reported to the narrator by a third party 'le philosophe norvégien.'[46] Surely, this give us insight as to the possible origins some of Proust's knowledge of Bergson's ideas, namely that of conversations and second-hand reports by others, rather than the direct interaction, personal or textual, between Proust and Bergson. In addition, Proust is clearly aware that inaccuracies can creep into such hearsay conversations.

But Proust gives us even further insight as to the possible origins of similarities and inaccuracies, for in the letter to Georges de Lauris written ten years before the prix Blumenthal incident, Proust clearly states that he does not need to read any more of Bergson's writings, for with the little he has already read, he can clearly extrapolate to the remainder of Bergson's philosophy and thought:

> Je suis content que vous ayez lu du Bergson et que vous l'ayez aimé. C'est comme si nous avions été ensemble sur une altitude. Je ne connais pas *l'Évolution créatrice* (et à cause du grand prix que j'attache à votre opinion, je vais la lire immédiatement). Mais j'ai assez lu de Bergson, et la parabole de sa pensée étant déjà assez décrivable après une seule génération pour que quelque *Évolution créatrice* qui ait suivi, je ne puisse quand vous dites Bergson, savoir ce que vous voulez dire. . . .[47]

It would seem highly probable that, without reading or studying Bergson's books more than mentioned by Megay, and without personally attending his lectures, Proust could have acquired a working knowledge, probably not completely correct, of Bergson's philosophy, through conversations and hearsay with the prominent socialites who were present at Bergson's lectures and who Proust subsequently met at social gatherings. In addition, as he suggests to Georges de Lauris, the highly intelligent Proust could have extrapolated what he considered to be Bergonism from what he had already read or overheard, and incorporated, possibly inadvertently, some of these ideas into his novel.

Related to this, perhaps indictect acquisition of ideas, is the notion of *idées-mères* put forward by Thibaudet who, under the rubric of "En quête d'idées-mères," writes:

> La production des idées-mères, sous forme éloquente et littéraire est la fonction centrale de la littérature française depuis Descartes et Port-Royal. Elle lui

donne ses cadres, dessine son relief, s'offre d'abord pour en rendre témoignage.
La génération précédente [précédente à 1885–1905] avait fourni à la France
et à l'Europe, avec Berson, l'idée-mère d'une philosophie dynamique . . .[48]

Perhaps some of Bergson's *idées mères*, acquired through hearsay or
intelligent extrapolation, were seeds of thought that, falling on the
fertile soil of Marcel Proust's mind, evolved, developed and flourished,
like the enchanted grain *Sesame,* into the uniquely original species
that is *À la recherche du temps perdu.*

Conclusion

Bergson and Proust were, in part, the product of their age and part of
the rising movement against the scientific determinism that pervaded
late 19th century France. Both were highly gifted, highly original and
their texts are very different yet, as outlined in the preceding chapters,
contain many common elements. The source of these common ideas
and concepts, imbedded with dissimilar styles in very different texts,
poses an interesting enigma.

In view of the variety of elements where there is similarity, it seems
unlikely that this resemblance and parallelism can be attributed to a
single cause, but more likely to a mixture of reasons. I think we can
eliminate from the discussion, two of the possibilities enumerated at
the beginning of this chapter, namely that of a direct, conscious and
intentional incorporation by Proust of Bergson's philosophy from a
reading of the latter's texts as well as that of the common influence of
John Ruskin.

It would seem not unlikely that some of the major common de-
nominators between the two writers, namely the principal themes of
time, memory, thought and some aspects of self resulted, in part,
from the sort of second-hand or hearsay acquisition of information,
often incomplete and inaccurate, discussed above and recounted in
the 'Norwegian philosopher' episode of *Sodome et Gomorrhe.* However, the similarity between the two authors runs deeper than merely
the major themes of time and memory, for there are many other more
subtle common elements which we have detected and discussed in
this study. These include the dominance of the analogic or qualitative
over the digital and quantitative; the superiority of intuition and *impressions* over logic and intellect; the common elements in the function of art; the quest for *l'essence des choses* or the qualitative essence of reality; the Bergsonian *deux aspects du Moi,* which becomes
transformed into the superficial and profound voices of the narrator

illustrated in the passage of *François le Champi* and *la belle laitière*; as well as the Bergsonian concepts of the actual self mirrored as the virtual self in memory which takes the form of the continual reflection of narrator and hero that pervades the entire Proustian text. In addition there are the even more subtle similarities such as the notions of the endogenous text and that of the uncertainty or indeterminacy principle, as well as the common imagery used to describe the flow of time and discussed in Chapter 6. It would seem that all these latter somewhat more complex and obscure resemblances are unlikely to have arisen from hearsay acquisition. Perhaps then, these occurred by the sort of indirect influence to which André Gide and Marcel Raymond refer, the parallel yet independent convergence of thoughts and ideas that pervaded France and Europe of that period and that influenced in like manner, the arts, science, philosophy and literature.

Addendum—Chronology of the life and works of Bergson and Proust

Henri Bergson 1859–1941
Marcel Proust 1871–1922

Date	Henri BERGSON [49] [50] [51]	Marcel PROUST[52]
1859	Born in Paris, October 18th. Father, Polish; mother, English (from Doncaster).	
1868–78	Student at lycée Condorcet (then lycée Fontanes). Parents living in London where he goes for holidays.	
1878	Enters École Normale Supérieure	
1871		Born in Paris, July 10th
1881	Teacher at lycée d'Angers	
1882		Enters lycée Condorcet
1883–88	Teaches at Clermont-Ferrand	
1888	Teaches at lycée Louis-le-Grand and Henri IV	Class of philosophy, his teacher is Alphonse Darlu
1889	Doctorate thesis which is published as *Essai sur les données immédiates de la conscience*.	Bachelier ès lettres
1889		Military service for one year.
1891		Student in the Sorbonne & Faculté de Droit.
1892	January, marries Louise Neuberger, cousin of Proust.	*Garçon d'honneur* at the wedding of Bergson & Louise Neuberger
1892		Invites Fernand Gregh to dine with him and Bergson[53]
1895		Licence ès lettres (philosophie).
1896	*Matière et mémoire*	*Jean Santeuil* (1895–99)
1898–	Maître de conférence	

1900	at École Normale	
1899	*Le rire* published as three articles in *Revue de Paris*.	Starts reading John Ruskin, and translating the *Bible of Amiens*.
1900	*Le rire* published as a book. Professor at Collège de France. Chair of Greek and Latin philosophy	Meets Marie Nordlinger who helps with Ruksin translation. Death of Ruskin.
1904	Chair of modern philosophy at Collège de France	Publication of translation of *Bible of Amiens*.
1904	(May 28th) Presents to the *Académie des Science Morales et Politiques* a report on Ruskin's *Bible of Amiens* translated and prefaced by Proust [54]	
1905		*Sur la lecture* published in magazine *Renaissance latine*. Later to appear as preface to Ruskin's *Sesame and Lilies*.
1906		Publication of *Sésame et les lys*.
1907	*L'évolution créatrice*	
1909		Starts writing *Combray*. Writes that he intends to read *L'évolution créatrice*.
1909–1910		Makes notes concerning *Matière et Mémoire* in his *Cahier*
1912		Finishes first part of *Les intermittences du coeur*. Le Figaro publishes portions of *Combray*.
1913		Publication of *Du côté de chez Swann*. Interview with *Le Temps*.
1914	Elected to the Académie Française. Enters in 1918.	

1919	*L'énergie sprituelle.*	Publication of *À l'ombre des jeunes filles en fleurs.* Awarded prix Goncourt
1920		Publication of *Le côté de Guermantes I*
1920	Bergson and Proust members of the committee adjudicating the Prix Blumenthal.	At committee meeting they discuss their respective remedies for insomnia.
1921		*Le côté de Guermantes II-Sodome et Gomorrhe I* published.
1922	*Durée et simultanéité.* Discussion with Einstein at Société Française de Philosophie.	*Le Temps retrouvé.* November 18th. Death of Marcel Proust.
1928	Nobel prize in literature.	
1932	*Les deux sources de la morale et de la religion.*	
1934	*La pensée et le mouvant.*(collection of previously published articles)	
1941	January 3rd. Death of Henri Bergson.	

Notes

1   André Gide, *Journal 1889–1939* (Paris: Gallimard, Pléiade, 1939) 782–783.

2   Marcel Proust à G. De Lauris in G. De Lauris, *A un ami, correspondance inédite*, 1903–1922, année 1910, document LXIV, (Amiot-Dumont, Paris, 1949) 205. Quoted in Bergson, ML, 1610.

3   Floris Delattre, *Ruskin et Bergson: de l'intuition esthétique à l'intuition métaphysique* (Oxford: Oxford UP, 1947) 1.

4   Albert Thibaudet, *Histoire de la littérature française de 1789 à nos jours*, (Paris: Stock, 1936) 524.

5   Marcel Proust, *Choix de lettres*, ed. Philip Kolb (Paris: Plon, 1965) 287.

6   Joyce N. Megay, *Bergson et Proust: Essai de mise au point de la question de l'influence de Bergson sur Proust* (Paris: J. Vrin, 1976) 22.

7   Jean Autret, *L'influence de Ruskin sur la vie, les idées et l'oeuvre de Marcel Proust* (Genève: Droz, 1955).

8   Marcel Proust, *Contre Sainte-Beuve: précédé de pastiches et mélanges*. (Paris: Gallimard, Bibliothèque de la Pléide, 1971) 69, 105, 436–506.

9   Initially published in *La Renaissance latine* on June 15th, 1905 and later included in modified form as "Journées de lecture" in *Pastiches et mélanges*, 1919. See Note 2 of IV, 411.

10 Marcel Proust, "Préface du traducteur: Sur la lecture," *Sésame et les lys* by John Ruskin, (Paris: Mercure de France, 1906) 7.

11 See also IV 1121

12 John Ruksin, *Sesame and Lilies*, (London: George Allen, 1913) 1–2.

13 Ruskin 142.

14 Marcel Proust, *Choix de lettres,* ed. Philip Kolb (Paris: Plon, 1965) 74.

15 Proust, *lettres* 134.

16 Proust, *lettres* 134.

17 Autret 161.

18 Delattre 5.

19 Delattre 5.

20 Philippe Soulez, *Bergson: biographie* (Paris: Flammarion, 1997) 129.

21 Delattre 9.

22 Marcel Raymond, 'Bergson et la poesie' *Henri Bergson: Essais et témoignages*, ed. Albert Béguin and Pierre Thévenaz (Neuchatel: La Baconnière, 1943) 286.

23 Philippe Soulez, *Bergson: biographie* (Paris: Flammarion, 1997) 111.

24 André Gide, *Journal 1889–1939* (Paris: Gallimard, Pléiade, 1939) 782–783.

25 Umberto Eco, *L'oeuvre ouverte* trans. Chantal Roux de Bézieux (Paris: Seuil, 1965) 28.

26 Michel Serres, *Éloge de la philosophie en langue française* (Paris: Fayard, 1995) 212–213.

27 Serres 215.

28 Charles F Stuckey, *Claude Monet* (Chicago: Art Institute of Chicago, 1995).

29 Stuckey 9.

30 Catherine Lampert, *Rodin* (London: Arts Council of Great Britain, 1986).

31 Propos de Rodin. Quoted by Jean Paulhan, *Les fleurs de Tarbes ou la terreur dans les lettres* (Paris: Gallimard, 1990) 121.

32 Charles Baudelaire, "Les fleurs du mal," *Oeuvres complètes* (Paris: Seuil, 1968) 65.

33 Emile Durkheim, *Pragmatisme et sociologie* (Paris: Vrin, 1955).

34 R. C. Grogin, *The Bergsonian Controversy in France 1910–1914.* (Calgary: U. of Calgary P, 1988).

35 Emmanuel Mounier, 'Péguy, médiateur de Bergson'. *Henri Bergson: Essais et témoignages*, ed. Albert Béguin and Pierre Thévenaz (Neuchatel: La Baconnière, 1943) 317.

36 Mounier, 314.

37 Charles Péguy, *Oeuvres en prose: 1898–1908* (Paris: Gallimard, 1959) 1483.

38 Jean Roussel, *Charles Péguy* (Paris: Éditions Universitaires, 1953) 62.

39 Péguy 483.

40 Jacques Morland, "Une heure chez M. Bergson" *L'opinion, journal de la semaine*, samedi 19 août, 1911, IV, 33, 241–242. Reproduced in ML 939.

41 Reproduced by Madeleine Barthélemy-Madaule, *Bergson* (Paris: Seuil, 1967) 21.

42 Soulez 110.

43 Soulez Illustrations. (Unreadable portions in the caption are indicated by . . . Words in [ ] are my interpretation of missing portions.

44   Grogin, ix.

45   Edmond Jaloux, *Avec Marcel Proust* (Paris: La Palatine, 1953) 18–19. Quoted in note 1, p 370 of *À la recherche* III 1557, and by Megay, 19.

46   The 'Norwegian philosopher' was in all probability a Swedish philosopher, Algot Henrik Leonard Ruhe (1867–1944). Ruhe translated some of Bergson's work into Swedish and wrote a biography on Bergson in English. In addition, Ruhe wrote an article on Proust which appeared in the Swedish journal *Var Tid,* in 1917. In a letter to Jacques Rivière, Proust explains that it was Bergson who introduced him to Ruhe. Thus the 'Norwegian philosopher' was clearly a source of second-hand Bergsonism for Proust. See III 1524 & 1557.

47   Marcel Proust à G. De Lauris in G. De Lauris, *A un ami, correspondance inédite*, 1903–1922, année 1910, document LXIV, (Amiot-Dumont, Paris, 1949) 205. Quoted in Bergson, ML, 1610.

48   Thibaudet. See note 4.

49   Madeleine Barthélemy-Madaule, *Bergson* (Paris: Seuil, 1967) 184–187.

50   Michel Dansel, *Les Nobel français de littérature* (Paris: André Bonne, 1967) 105–120.

51   Philippe Soulez, *Bergson: biographie* (Paris: Flammarion, 1997).

52   Jean-Yves Tadié, "Chronologie," *À la recherche du temps perdu* by Marcel Proust, Paris: Gallimard, Bibliothèque de la Pléiade, 1987) I, cix–cxliii.

53   Joyce N. Megay, "Proust et Bergson en 1909," *Bulletin de la société des amis de Marcel Proust et des amis de Combray* 25 (1975): 89–96.

54   ML, 629. See also: Megay 96.

Bibliography

This bibliography is divided into three sections:

1. The primary works of Henri Bergson and of Marcel Proust.
2. Studies of the works of Bergson and Proust.
3. Texts relevant to issues of science, literature and language.

1. Primary Works

Bergson, Henri. *Essai sur les données immédiates de la consciences.* 1889. Paris: Quadrige /PUF, 1991.

———. *Matière et mémoire.* 1896. Paris: Quadrige / PUF, 1990.

———. *Le rire.* 1900. Paris: Quadrige / PUF, 1995.

———. *L'évolution créatrice.* 1907. Paris: Quadrige / PUF, 1991.

———. *L'énergie sprituelle.* 1919. Paris: Quadrige / PUF, 1993.

———. *Durée et simultanéité.* 1922. Paris: Quadrige / PUF, 1992.

———. *Les deux sources de la morale et de la religion.* 1932. Paris: Quadrige / PUF, 1995.

———. *La pensée et le mouvant.* 1934. Paris: Quadrige / PUF, 1993.

———. *Écrits et paroles.* Rose-Marie Mossé-Bastide, ed. Paris: PUF 1957-59.

———. *Oeuvres.* André Robinet and Henri Gouhier, eds. Paris: PUF, 1959.

————. *Mélanges*. Textes publiés et annotés par André Robinet. Paris: PUF, 1972.

Proust, Marcel. *À la recherche du temps perdu*. Édition publié sous la direction de Pierre Clarac et André Ferré. 3 vol. Paris: Gallimard, Bibliothèque de la Pléiade, 1954.

————. *À la recherche du temps perdu*. Édition publié sous la direction de Jean-Yves Tadié. 4 vol. Paris: Gallimard, Bibliothèque de la Pléiade, 1987–89.

————. *Sur la lecture*. Préface du traducteur; John Ruskin, *Sésame et les Lys*. Paris: Mercure de France, 1906.

————. *Les plaisirs et les jours*. 1896. Paris: Gallimard, 1992.

————. *Pastiches et mélanges*. Paris: Gallimard. 1919.

————. *Contre Sainte-Beuve: suivi de nouveaux mélanges*. Paris: Gallimard, 1954.

————. *Contre Sainte-Beuve: précédé de pastiches et mélanges et suivi de essais et articles*. Paris: Gallimard, Bibliothèque de la Pléiade, 1971.

————. *Choix de lettres*. Ed. Philip Kolb. Paris: Plon, 1965.

————. *Textes retrouvés*. Eds. Philip Kolb and Larkin B. Price. Urbana: U of Illinois P, 1968.

————. *Bricquebec: prototype d'À l'ombre des jeunes filles en fleurs*. Ed. Richard Bales. Oxford: Clarendon, 1989.

2. Studies of the Works of Bergson and Proust

Adolphe, Lydie. *La dialectique des images chez Bergson*. Paris: PUF, 1951.

Agathon. (Pseudonyme of Alfred de Tarde) *L'esprit de la nouvelle Sorbonne*. Paris: Mercure de France, 1911.

Antliff, Mark. *Inventing Bergson: Cultural Politics and the Parisian Avant-Garde*. Princeton: Princeton UP, 1993.

Aubert, Nathalie. "Marcel Proust: de la pratique traduisante à la métaphore." *French Forum* 23 (1998): 217–33.

Autret, Jean. *L'influence de Ruskin sur la vie, les idées et l'oeuvre de Marcel Proust.* Genève: Droz, 1955.

Barthélemy-Madaule, Madeleine. *Bergson et Teilhard de Chardin.* Paris: Seuil, 1963.

———. *Bergson adversaire de Kant.* Paris: PUF, 1966.

———. *Bergson.* Paris: Seuil, 1967.

Béguin, Albert, and Pierre Thévenaz, eds. *Henri Bergson: essais et témoignages.* Neuchatel: Baconnière, 1943.

Bonnet, Henri. "Jean Ricardou et la métaphore proustienne," *Bulletin de la Société des Amis de Marcel Proust et des Amis de Combray.* 1976, *26* 286–294.

Brée, Germaine. *Du temps perdu au temps retrouvé.* Paris: Les Belles Lettres, 1969.

———. and Carlos Lynes Jr., Introduction. *Combray.* By Marcel Proust. New York: Appleton-Century-Crofts, 1952.

Brincourt, André and Jean Brincourt. *Les oeuvres et les lumières: À la recherche de l'esthétique à travers Bergson, Proust, Malraux.* Paris: La Table Ronde, 1955.

Capek, Milic. *Bergson and Modern Physics.* Dordrecht-Holland: Reidel, 1971.

Cattaui, Georges, & Philip Kolb, eds. *Entretiens sur Marcel Proust.* Paris: Mouton, 1966.

Champigny, Robert. "Proust, Bergson and Other Philosophers." *Proust: A Collection of Critical Essays.* Ed. René Girard. Englewood Cliffs: Prentice-Hall, 1962.

Chefdor, Monique. Ed. *In Search of Marcel Proust.* New York: Anderson, Ritchie and Simon, 1973.

Dansel, Michel. "Henri Bergson." *Les Nobel français de littérature.* Paris: André Bonne, 1967.

Dantzig, Charles, ed. *Le grand livre de Proust.* Paris: Les Belles Lettres, 1996.

Delattre, Floris. *Ruskin et Bergson: de l'intuition esthétique à l'intuition métaphysique.* Oxford: Oxford UP, 1947.

————. *Bergson et Proust: accords et dissonances*. Paris: Albin Michel, 1948.

Deleuze, Gilles. *Le bergsonisme*. Paris: PUF, 1968.

————. *Proust et les signes*. Paris: PUF, 1993.

de Man, Paul. *Allegories of Reading: Figural Language in Rousseau, Nietsche, Rilke and Proust*. New Haven: Yale UP, 1979.

Demoncel, Jean-Claude. *Le symbole d'Hécate: philosphie deleuzienne et roman proustien*. Paris: Édition HYX, 1996.

Doubrovsky, Serge. *La place de la madeleine: écriture et fantasme chez Proust*. Paris: Mercure de France, 1974.

Erickson John D. "The Proust-Einstein Relation," *Marcel Proust, a Critical Panorama*. Ed. Larkin B Price. Urbana: U of Chicago P, 1973.

Genette, Gérard. *Figures III*. Paris: Seuil, 1972.

Girard, René, ed. *Proust: A Collection of Critical Essays*. Englewood Cliffs: Prentice-Hall, 1962.

Graham, Victor E. *Bibliographie des études sur Marcel Proust et son oeuvre*. Genève: Droz, 1976.

Grogin, R. C. *The Bergsonian Controversy in France 1910–1914.*Calgary: U. of Calgary P, 1988.

Gunter, P.A.Y. *Henri Bergson: A Bibliography*. 2nd ed. Bowling Green, Philosophy Documentation Centre, 1986.

Henry, Anne. *Marcel Proust: théories pour une esthétique*. Paris: Klincksieck, 1981.

————. *Proust romancier: Le tombeau égyptien*. Paris: Flammarion, 1983.

————. *Proust*. Paris: Balland, 1986.

Hughes, Edward J. *Marcel Proust: A Study in the Quality of Awareness*. Cambridge: Cambridge UP, 1983.

Jackson, Elizabeth R. *L'évolution de la mémoire involontaire dans l'oeuvre de Marcel Proust*. Paris: Nizet, 1966.

Kolb, Philip. *La correspondance de Marcel Proust: chronologie et commentaire critique.* Urbana: U of Illinois P. 1949.

———. "The birth of Elstir and Vinteuil." *Marcel Proust: A Critical Panorama.* Ed. Larkin B Price. Urbana: U of Illinois P, 1973.

Kristeva, Julia. *Proust and the Sense of Time.* Trans. Stephen Bann. New York: Columbia UP, 1993.

Mauriac, François. *Du coté de chez Proust.* Paris: La Table Ronde, 1947.

Maurois, André. *De Proust à Camus.* Paris: Perrin, 1965.

———. *À la recherche de Marcel Proust.* Paris: Hachette, 1949.

Médina, José. "Charles Bally: De Bergson à Saussure." *Langages.* March 1977. 95–104.

Megay, Joyce N. "Proust et Bergson en 1909." *Bulletin de la Société des Amis de Marcel Proust et des Amis de Combray.* 25, 1975. 89–96.

———. *Bergson et Proust: Essai de mise au point de la question de l'influence de Bergson sur Proust.* Paris: J. Vrin, 1976.

Milly, Jean. *Proust et le style.* Genève: Slatkine reprints, 1991.

Moore, F.T.C., *Bergson: Thinking Backwards.* Cambridge: Cambridge UP, 1996.

Muller, Marcel. *Les voix narratives dans la recherche du temps perdu.* Genève: Droz, 1983.

———. *Préfiguration et structure romanesque dans À la recherche du temps perdu.* Lexington: French Forum, 1979.

———. "The Rhetoric of Pseudo-Nature: or Tropes and Dialectic in Proust's novel." *Style.* 22, (Fall): Fayetteville: U of Arkansas, 1988.

———. "Création et procréation ou allégorie et jalousie dans À la recherche du temps perdu." Proceedings of the Cerisy Colloquium of 1997

Painter, George D. *Marcel Proust: A Biography.* 2 vols. New York: Random House, 1978.

Papanicolaou, Andrew C. & Pete A.Y. Gunter, eds. *Bergson and Modern Thought: Towards a Unified Science*. London: Harwood, 1987.

Pierre-Quint, Léon. *Comment parut "Du côté de chez Swann"*. Paris: Kra, 1930.

———. "Bergson et Proust." *Henri Bergson: essais et témoignages*. Albert Béguin and Pierre Thévenaz, eds. Neuchatel: Baconnière, 1943. 328.

———. *Marcel Proust: Sa vie, son oeuvre*. Paris: Sagittaire, 1946.

Pilkington, A.E. *Bergson and his Influence: A Reassessment*. Cambridge: Cambridge UP, 1976.

Pimentel, Luz Aurora. *Metaphoric Narration: Paranarrative Dimension in À la Recherche du Temps Perdu*. Toronto: U of Toronto P. 1990

Poulet, Georges. *Études sur le temps humain*. Edinburgh: Edinburgh UP, 1949.

———. *L'espace proustien*. Paris: Gallimard, 1982.

Roussel, Jean. *Charles Péguy*. Paris: Éditions Universitaires, 1953.

Sergeant, Philippe. *Bergson, matière à penser*. Paris: EC Éditions, 1996.

Shattuck, Roger. *Proust*. Glasgow: William Collins, 1984.

Soulez, Philippe. *Bergson politique*. Paris: PUF, 1989.

———. *Bergson: biographie*. Paris: Flammarion, 1997.

Thibaudet, Albert. *Le bergsonisme*. 2 vols. Paris: Gallimard, 1923.

———. *Histoire de la littérature française de 1789 à nos jours*. Paris: Stock, 1936.

Turquet-Milnes, Gladys. *From Pascal to Proust*. London: Butler and Tanner, 1926.

Vieillard-Baron, Jean-Louis. *Bergson*. Paris: PUF, 1993.

Watson, Beatrice. "Le bergsonisme de Proust." MA Diss. Chicago: U of Chicago, 1927.

3. Science, Literature and Language

Arrivé, Michel. "Signifiant saussurien et signifiant lacanien." *Langages*, March, 1985.

Atkins, P.W. *The Second Law*. New York: Scientific American Books, 1984.

Badré, Frédéric. *Paulhan le juste*. Paris: Grasset, 1996.

Barbour, Julian B. *The Discovery of Dynamics*. Cambridge: Cambridge UP, 1989. Vol 1 *Absolute or Relative Motion*.

Barthes, Roland. *Le degré zéro de l'écriture*. Paris: Seuil, 1953.

———. "Science versus Literature." *Introduction to Structuralism*. Ed. Michael Lane.New York: Basic Books, 1970.

———. *The Pleasure of the Text*. Trans. Richard Miller. New York: Hill & Wang, 1975.

Baudelaire, Charles. *Oeuvres complètes*. Paris: Seuil, 1968.

Berlin, Isaiah. *Against the Current*. Ed. H. Hardy. New York: Viking, 1980.

Bernard, Claude. *Introduction à l'étude de la médecine expérimentale*. Paris: Delagrave, 1921.

Blanchot, Maurice. *Comment la littérature est-elle possible?* Paris: José Corti, 1942.

Bloom, Harold. *The Anxiety of Influence: A Theory of Poetry*. 2nd ed. Oxford: Oxford UP, 1997.

Carruthers, Mary. *The Book of Memory: A Study of Memory in Medieval Culture*. Cambridge UP, 1990.

Chomsky, Noam. *Language and Thought*. Wakefield: Bell, 1995.

Claudel, Paul. *Oeuvres complètes*. Paris: Gallimard, 1965.

Dawkins, Richard. *River out of Eden: A Darwinian View of Life*. New York: Basic Books, 1995.

Descartes, René. *Discours de la méthode*. Paris: GF-Flammarion, 1966.

Durkheim, Emile. *Pragmatisme et sociologie*. Paris: Vrin, 1955.

De Saussure, Ferdinand. *Cours de linguistique générale*. 1916. Paris: Payot & Rivages, 1995.

Eco, Umberto. *L'oeuvre ouverte*. Trans. Chantal Roux de Bézieux. Paris: Seuil, 1965.

Eddington, Arthur S. *New Pathways in Science*. Cambridge: Cambridge UP, 1935.

——. *The Nature of the Physical World*. Cambridge: Cambridge UP, 1942.

——. *The Philosophy of Physical Science*. Cambridge: Cambridge UP, 1949.

Flammarion, Camille. *Astronomie populaire*. Paris: Flammarion, 1920.

France, Anatole. *Oeuvres complètes illustrées de Anatole France*. Paris: Calmann-Lévy, 1949.

Gide, André. *Journal 1889–1939*. Paris: Gallimard, Bibliothèque de la Pléiade, 1939.

Gilson, Bernard. *Vers un développement de la philsophie dialectique*. Paris: Vrin, 1995.

Gilson, Étienne. *La philosophie au moyen âge*. Paris: Payot, 1947.

Gleick, James. *Chaos: Making a New Science*. New York: Viking, 1987.

Gregory, Richard L. Ed. *The Oxford Companion to the Mind*. Oxford: Oxford UP, 1987.

Guern, M. le, *Sémantique de la métaphore et de la métonymie*. Paris: Larousse, 1978.

Heidegger, Martin. *Being and Time*. Trans. Joan Stambaugh. Albany: State U of NY, 1996.

Hellige, Joseph B. *Hemispheric Asymmetry: What's Right and What's Left*. Cambridge: Harvard UP, 1993.

Hollier, David, ed. *A New History of French Literature*. Cambridge: Harvard UP, 1989.

Hordé T., and C. Tanet. "Métaphore et métonymie." *Dictionnaire historique de la langue française.* Ed. Alain Rey. Paris: Le Robert, 1992.

Howard, David, and Brian Lewis Butterworth. "Neurolinguistics." *The Oxford Companion to the Mind.* Ed. Richard L Gregory. Oxford: Oxford UP, 1987.

Humboldt, Wilhelm von. *On Language.* Trans. Peter Heath. Cambridge UP, 1988.

Jacob, François. *La logique du vivant.* Paris: Gallimard, 1970.

———. *The Possible and the Actual.* Seattle: U. Washington P. 1982.

Jakobson, Roman. "Linguistics and Poetics." *Style in Language.* Ed. T.A. Sebeok. Cambridge: M.I.T. Press, 1960.

———. "Two Aspects of Language and Two Types of Aphasic Disturbances," *Fundamentals of Language.* Roman Jakobson and Morris Halle, eds. 'S-Gravenhage: Monton. 1956.

———. *Brain and language: Cerebral Hemispheres and Linguistic Structure in Mutual Light.* Columbus: Slavica, 1980.

Judrin, Roger. *La vocation transparente de Jean Paulhan.* Paris: Gallimard, 1961.

Kant, Immanuel. *Selections.* Ed. Theodore Meyer Greene. New York: Scribner's, 1929.

Keller, Helen. *The Story of my Life.* New York: Doubleday, 1954.

Lamartine, Alphonse de. *Méditations poétiques.* Paris: Hachette, 1915.

Landow, George P. *Hypertext: The Convergence of Contemporary Critical Theory and Technology.* Baltimore: Johns Hopkins UP, 1992.

Laslett, Peter. Ed. *The Physical Basis of Mind.* Oxford: Blackwell, 1950.

Lefebvre, M.-J. *Jean Paulhan: Une philosophie et une pratique de l'expression et de la réflexion.* Paris: Gallimard, 1949.

Matthews, Eric. *Twentieth-century French Philosophy.* Oxford UP, 1996.

McInerney, Peter K. *Time and Experience*. Philadelphia: Temple UP, 1991.

Monod, Jacques. *Le hasard et la nécessité*. Paris: Seuil, 1970.

Montaigne, Michel de. *Essais*. Vol. I. Paris: Gallimard, 1965.

————. *Essais*. Vol. II. Paris: Gallimard, 1965.

————. *Essais*. Vol. III. Paris: Gallimard, 1965.

Neisser, Ulric. *Cognition and Reality*. San Francisco: Freeman, 1976.

Ong, Walter J., *Orality and Literacy: The Technologizing of the Word*. New York: Routledge, 1982.

Ortony, Andrew. "Metaphor," *The Oxford Companion to the Mind*. Ed. Richard L. Gregory. Oxford: Oxford UP, 1987.

————. Ed. *Metaphor and Thought*. Cambridge: Cambridge UP, 1993.

Pascal, Blaise. *Oeuvres complètes*. Paris: Seuil, 1963.

Paulhan, Jean. *Les fleurs de Tarbes ou la terreur dans les lettres*. Paris: Gallimard, 1990.

Paulson, William. *The Noise of Culture: Literary Texts in a World of Information*. Ithaca: Cornell UP, 1988.

————. "Closing the circle: Science, Literature and the Passion of Matter." *New England Review and Bread Loaf Quarterly,* 12, 4, (Summer 1990)

————. "Writing that Matters." *SubStance* Special Issue on Michel Serres. Madison: U Wisconsin P, 1997.

Péguy, Charles. *Oeuvres en prose: 1898-1908*. Paris: Gallimard, Bibliothèque de la Pléiade, 1959.

Pinker, Steven. *The Language Instinct*. New York: William Morrow, 1994.

————. *How the Mind Works*. New York: Norton, 1997.

Poincaré, Henri. *Science et méthode*. Paris: Flammarion, 1909.

Renan, Ernest. *Souvenir d'enfance et de jeunesse*. Paris: Calmann-Lévy, 1937.

Rimbaud, Arthur. *Oeuvres*. Paris: Mercure, 1952.

Rousset, Jean. *L'intérieur et l'extérieur*. Paris: José Corti, 1968.

Ruskin, John. *Sesame and Lilies*. London: George Allen, 1913.

Russell, Bertrand. *A History of Western Philosophy*. New York: Simon & Schuster, 1945.

Sokal, Alan, and Jean Bricmont. *Impostures intellectuelles*. Paris: Odile Jacob, 1997.

Saussure, Ferdinand de. *Cours de linguistique générale*. Édition critique préparée par Tullio de Mauro. Paris: Payot & Rivages, 1995.

Schacter, Daniel L. *Searching for Memory*. New York: Basic Books, 1996.

Schrödinger, Erwin. *Science and Humanism: Physics in our Time*. Cambridge: Cambridge UP, 1951.

Serres, Michel. *Hermès IV: La distribution*. Paris: Minuit, 1977.

———. *Le parasite*. Paris: Grasset, 1980.

———. *Le tiers-instruit*. Paris: François Bourin, 1991.

———. *Éclaircissements*. Paris: Flammarion, 1994.

———. *Éloge de la philosophie en langue française*. Paris: Fayard, 1995.

Sklar, Lawrence. *Philosophy and Spacetime Physics*. Berkley, U of California P, 1985.

———. *Physics and Chance: Philosophical Issues in the Foundations of Statistical Mechanics*. Cambridge: Cambridge UP, 1995.

Snow, C.P. *The Two Cultures*. 1959. Cambridge: Cambridge UP, 1993.

Tulving E., & W. Donaldson, eds. *Organization of Memory*. New York: Academic Press, 1972.

Wilden, Anthony. *The Rules are no Game*. London & New York: Routledge & Kegan Paul, 1987.

———. *System and Structure*. London: Tavistock, 1972.

Author Index

Only the first of a series of names may be noted. Does not include Bergson, Proust or the Bibliography

Thematic Index

Only the first of a series of citations may be noted

A

Abacus 1, 40
Abacus and Rainbow 40
Alliance de mots 77
Ambiguity 159, 162
Amiens, Bible of 222
Analogic 33–39
Analyse & intuition 47
Anxiety of Influence 4
Art & esthetics 189–218
Art and memory 196

B

Bal de têtes 86, 177
Bible of Amiens 6
Binaries 39
Blumenthal, Prix 13, 235
Bon sens 50

C

Carnot cycle 16, 26
Carquethuit 70, 228
Chance and necessity 39
Cinematography 101
Clausius 16
Continuous & discontinuous 39
Contre Sainte-Beuve 12
Création de soi par soi 85

D

Déchiffrer 62
Demon, Bergson's 214
Demon, Maxwell's 218
Determinism 19
Deux aspects du Moi 129–133, 200
Deux esprits de Pascal 36
Dialectic 52, 53
Digital & analogic 33, 203
Discontinuous 39
DNA 35
Dogma 20
Double helix 35
Doubling of self in memory 134–136
Dualism 54

E

École Normale 21, 45, 174
Élan vital 48
Elstir 70, 73
Endogenous text 141
Entropy 16, 17
Epiphany 121
Esprit de géométrie et esprit de finesse 17
Essences des choses 60, 137

F

François le Champi 83, 123

Studies in the Humanities

Edited by Guy Mermier

The Studies in the Humanities series welcomes manuscripts discussing various aspects of the humanities. The series' emphasis is on medieval and Renaissance literatures with a focus on Western civilizations and cultures. Submissions dealing with linguistics, history, politics, or sociology within the same time frame and geographical bounds are also encouraged. Manuscripts may be submitted in English, French, or Italian. The preferred style manual is the MLA Handbook (1995).

For additional information about this series or for the submission of manuscripts, please contact:

Peter Lang Publishing, Inc.
Acquisitions Department
516 N. Charles St., 2nd Floor
Baltimore, MD 21201